# Psychoanalysis and Psychology

# Psychoanalysis and Psychology

## Minding the Gap

**Stephen Frosh**

NEW YORK UNIVERSITY PRESS
Washington Square
New York

Published in the U.S.A. in 1989 by
NEW YORK UNIVERSITY PRESS
Washington Square
New York, NY 10003

Printed in the People's Republic of China

Library of Congress Cataloging-in-Publication Data

Frosh, Stephen.
    Psychoanalysis and psychology.

    Bibliography: p.
    Includes index.
    1. Psychoanalysis.   2. Psychology.   I. Title.
BF173.F9   1989        150.19'5        88–34497
ISBN  0–8147–2595–3
ISBN  0–8147–2596–1  (pbk.)

**To Daniel**
(born with this book)

# Contents

# Author's Note and Acknowledgements

This book arises out of the tension, which I hope is a creative one, between my theoretical interests in psychoanalysis and my work as a clinical and academic psychologist. I have been influenced by some recent attempts to use psychoanalytic concepts to reformulate psychology, and particularly by the book *Changing the Subject* by Julian Henriques, Wendy Hollway, Cathy Urwin, Couze Venn and Valerie Walkerdine (Methuen, 1984). I would like to thank Maria Black, Linda Buckingham, Glyn Humphreys, Lynette Moodley and Valerie Walkerdine for reading and commenting on drafts of various chapters of the book.

Parts of Chapter 5 were originally presented as a talk on 'Psychoanalysis and Racism' to the *Psychoanalysis and the Public Sphere* conference organised by Free Association Books and North East London Polytechnic in London in October 1987.

*Stephen Frosh*

# Introduction

## Psychoanalysis, psychology and science

There is a long history of opposition between psychology, both in its academic and (to a lesser extent) its clinical forms, and psychoanalysis. This has some of its roots in the automatic antagonism between two disciplines that are contesting the same field – in this case, explanations of human behaviour. But it also reflects a polarity in the philosophical bases and empirical procedures characteristic of the two enterprises. Psychologists have adopted a model for their discipline which is founded on the example of the natural sciences. Emphasis is placed on the careful collection of observational data, the generation of hypotheses that involve operational concepts and measurable predictions, and the design and implementation of experimental procedures for use with human 'subjects' that emulate the arrangements governing laboratory investigations of non-human phenomena. Theorising is related to testable hypotheses; experiments are approved to the extent that they employ appropriately sampled and numerous populations of study, objective assessment procedures and clearly defined interventions with specific effects, with all extraneous influences 'controlled' Although it is recognised that there is a place for other modes of investigation, such as naturalistic observations and single case experimental designs, these are regarded either as precursors of proper experimental work, or as second-best substitutes when full experimental control is impossible.

On the face of it, the psychoanalytic procedure could hardly be further from this idealised view of experimental psychology. Psychoanalysis has its origins and main realm of action in the consulting room. Its data, with the exception of some direct observation procedures with children, is collected in a highly 'reactive' way, in the context of a dialogue between a patient and

1

an analyst who, usually, is employed to help her or him resolve some distress. Theories are generated from these interactions, but are adapted to be congruent with statements made by the founding-father of psychoanalysis, Sigmund Freud – although the exact formulation of the theory will depend on the analytic school to which the analyst owes allegiance, and quite possibly on the affiliations of the analyst's own analyst. What determines the acceptability of a theory is its persuasive power, which in turn appears to be a function of its relationship with previous theories, its logical consistency and its usefulness in providing interpretations of material presented by patients. That is, whereas psychologists characteristically aim to establish the veridicality of a theory through empirical testing and quantitative documentation of results, psychoanalysts do so through clinical practice and attempts to use it to 'make sense' of otherwise indecipherable phenomena.

It is perhaps not surprising, from the description just given, that much of the debate between psychologists and psychoanalysts has centred around the 'scientific' status of the two disciplines. The discussions this has produced are stimulating and often highly entertaining, but they rarely succeed in persuading any psychologist or psychoanalyst to reform their practice – perhaps because the issue of scientificity is not really the central issue. To the extent that the question of 'scientific' status matters, one can make the following brief points. First, psychology has emulated the model of the natural sciences as far as it can, but the openness of many psychologists to informed guesses, theorising based on intuitions about their own behaviour and that of others, and model building of an abstract kind reveals that they do not necessarily feel constrained to keep all their statements on an operational level. It may be the case that such creative flexibility is the hallmark of all good science, but accommodating this perception requires a rather wider notion of 'scientific procedure' than has commonly been employed by psychologists. Secondly, psychologists have often made a distinction between the empirical rigour that is possible when investigating phenomena that can be demonstrated under laboratory conditions – for instance, certain perceptual processes – and those more naturalistic and 'applied' events which occur casually, in a variable and uncontrolled way. Again, as far as is possible the latter are investigated with the aid of the hypothetico-deductive procedures described above, but there is widespread awareness that a more imaginative and less reliable method may have at times to be employed if one is to obtain more than the 'elegant trivialities' that social psychology is often accused of producing.

The issue of science and psychoanalysis is even more interesting. There is no doubt that Freud himself was wedded to the view of psychoanalysis as a science, an attempt to supply explanations of phenomena which would reveal their source in natural causes that can be identified reliably across whole populations. To a considerable extent, this remains the outlook of many psychoanalysts, although there has also been a great deal of interest in the 'hermeneutic' approach that regards psychoanalysis as primarily a mode of interpretative activity, making sense of the communications of patient and analyst. As Rustin (1987) notes, hermeneutic theorists

> have presented psychoanalysis as a hermeneutic discipline concerned with the elucidation of meanings, rather than with the determination of causes. Whilst this undoubtedly accounts better than empiricist polemic for some aspects of psychoanalytic procedure, it provides its justification only at a considerable cost to psychoanalysis' original claims to be a form of scientific knowledge: psychoanalysts from Freud onwards have claimed to be providing theories of mental topography which characterise consistently (if not universally) occurring relations of cause and effect within postulated structures of the mind. (p. 109)

Psychologists have conventionally rejected these claims that psychoanalysis is a scientific discipline, because of the reactivity of speculation and measures listed earlier, as well as the necessarily non-observable status of key concepts such as the unconscious. But there is now a library of suitable responses to this rejection from which analysts, previously defensive and to some extent willing to give up their scientific credentials, can choose. For example, Farrell (1981) is one of many researchers to argue that psychology's traditional view of science is too restrictive and would exclude much of the activity of the natural sciences if applied to them. He suggests that a narrow use of the term 'scientific' to include only theories composed of falsifiable parts excludes some approaches to knowledge which may nevertheless be rational and which consequently warrant the lable 'science'. Will (1986) has mounted a spirited defence of the status of psychoanalysis as a social science on the grounds that the causal internal structures proposed by psychoanalysts are paralleled by similar uses of hypothetical constructs in science and, particularly, other social sciences. In a similar vein, Rustin (1987), while troubled by the plurality of competing theories that seem sometimes to gain currency without any reference to evidence, nevertheless argues that the practice of psychoanalysts, particularly as regards training, is completely congruent with scientific activity.

> Psychoanalysis undoubtedly has a real object for scientific study and has organised itself in such a way as to produce rational and consensual means of generating knowledge. The evidence of scrupulous attention to reliable method in analytic training and for the advance of analytic knowledge in the face of perceived anomalies and therapeutic failures seems to me to exist for inspection. (p. 129)

An additional point concerns the hypothetico-deductive structure of the analytic encounter itself, despite its reactivity. An analyst has a theory in her or his mind, derived from previous training and experience. The patient's words are listened to with care, a hypothesis is formed (derived from the interplay between the theory and the words), and eventually the analyst makes an experimental intervention – an interpretation. In the light of the results of this experiment (the patient's response), the hypothesis is discarded or refined, and further interpretations are made. There are a number of difficulties with this analogy, mostly produced by the reactivity described above. For instance, the extent to which the analyst's 'experimental' interpretation actually causes its own confirmation through its suggestive power is unknown, and the criteria by means of which the 'results' (patient's response) are evaluated cannot be specified in any objective way. This reveals again the general limitation that bedevils the argument that psychoanalysis is a science. It is not that analysts do not believe in the desirability or possibility of objectivity; indeed, a considerable amount of effort is devoted towards encouraging clarity of perception and thought in trainee analysts and in enabling them to identify and therefore overcome their own subjective biases. But the scientific intent and structure of the psychoanalytic endeavour is consistently undermined by the difficulty of producing validation criteria which are generalisable and replicable outside the encounter of two specific individuals in one particular consulting room. The procedures and arguments of psychoanalysis may well be rational, and it is part of the purpose of this book to show how instructive a light they throw on psychological phenomena; but the variability of interpretation that is made possible by the uncertainty of its validation processes limits the extent to which it can be regarded as a formal 'science'.

**Of subjects and subjectivity**

It was suggested before that the debate on the scientific status of psychology and, particularly, psychoanalysis is not central to the real issues that lie between the two disciplines. This is because it actually indicates a deeper division, one with which this book is much concerned. This is the division between alternative views of the psychological 'subject' – the central human element of investigation. For psychologists, the 'subjects' of their discipline are more properly objects, to be studied in the same way as non-human and, if possible, inanimate materials. Researchers aim to reduce the reactivity of their experiments by reducing the impact of their own 'subjective' expectations on its results, and also by reducing the effects of the speculations and hypotheses generated by people acting as 'subjects'. The purpose of a psychological description is to offer, in terms which are as objective as possible, an account of the mental or interpersonal processes which are operating in a person, at the level of those processes rather than at the level of the subjective intent of the person concerned. There is thus an avoidance of 'subjectivity' in the sense of the internal experience of the individual, and also of considerations of how each human becomes, and is organised as, such an experiencing 'subject'.

In contrast to this approach, psychoanalysts, characteristically working within a clinical context, prioritise the subjectivity of the person they are studying. Like psychologists, they might aim to provide an objective description of the forces operating on the person, a description which the person would not have been able to give. However, the constituents of this description would be different; they would involve intentions, wishes, desires – subjective states which are given causal status in psychoanalytic accounts. This different orientation produces a completely different kind of theory. Whereas the objective gaze of the psychologist aims to identify the processes that make psychological phenomena possible, the psychoanalyst attempts to make the actions and emotions of the subject intelligible through the provision of a causal explanation that is *at the level of the subject* – that is expressive of the intentions and wishes of the person concerned, of, one might say, the subject's desire. The tension between psychology and psychoanalysis is not, therefore, just one of method; it also represents a struggle over the position of subjectivity in the scheme of things, and over the nature of the human subject – whether it is explicable in terms of the processes that describe its action, or only in terms of the structures of meaning and intention that make the direction of its movement intelligible.

It is this tension that governs the trajectory of this book. The argument can, in outline, be stated simply. Psychoanalysts have much to learn from psychologists in terms of clarity of ideas, acknowledgement of the complexity and power of cognitive processes, and methodological stringency. Psychologists, however, have more to learn from psychoanalysts. This is because, despite all its failings, psychoanalysis asks questions about human functioning which lie outside the scope of traditional academic psychology, but which ought to be central to it. Psychology restricts itself to a description of those processes that make certain psychological actions possible – the translation of information into one form or another, certain responses to socialisation and maturation pressures, the use of language to express thoughts. As will be discussed in more detail in Chapter 1, this is a 'syntactic' approach to mental activity, articulating the grammar that produces its particular form. Psychoanalysis, despite its frequent wildness of theory and occasional wildness of practice, shows its strength in its willingness to ask 'semantic' questions of great provocativeness. It asks, in other words, for the meaning of actions, their significance and intention, and the subjective position they hold within the life of the person concerned. In doing so, psychoanalysis demonstrates the inadequacy of the questions asked by psychology, if one is concerned to develop a discipline that genuinely engages with the *experiences* as well as the competencies of human subjects.

**The book**

This is not a clinically oriented book. Rather, it attempts to use psychoanalytic concepts as they arise in various areas to develop an evaluation and critique of conventional psychological theory and to demonstrate the possibilities for an enriched approach. As noted earlier, many aspects of psychoanalysis are open to criticism. However, the main agenda is to display the gains which can be achieved when the account of subjectivity offered by psychoanalysis is used creatively in spheres in which psychology has restricted itself to dealing with psychological processes. The particular areas chosen are those in which both disciplines have provided well-articulated theories, and in which the complicating issue of the role of social events also operates. The movement is from apparently 'internal' events – models of thought – through developmental theories, to two areas where the question of social influences on behaviour and on subjectivity can be clearly observed.

The book begins with an examination of the constructs used by psychologists and psychoanalysts when theorising basic mental processes. *Chapter 1* describes the kind of explanations of mental activity employed in each of the two disciplines, paying particular attention to the question of the usefulness of 'reductionist' perspectives. The paradigm case for psychology is that of cognitive models of mental functioning, with recent discussions on artificial intelligence exemplifying some of the most important issues.

It is suggested that psychology has produced powerful models of mental processes, but few concepts for dealing with the content of these processes, leaving questions of intentionality and meaning unanswered. Psychoanalysts, too, have produced models of mental functions, but they have been more commonly engaged in identifying the basic meaning-blocks out of which consciousness and the unconscious are constructed. A number of criticisms of the models produced by psychoanalysts can be made, for example in terms of their methodological weaknesses and also of the concreteness of many of the images of thinking produced, particularly in some Kleinian work. Psychoanalysis, however, does at least address the

issue of subjective meanings, even though, like psychology, it is
weak in relating this to social experiences.

The issue of social influences is taken further in *Chapter 2*, which
is concerned with developmental theory. A methodological critique
of psychoanalytic approaches to the study of children is offered,
but it is also suggested that the clinical knowledge which analysts
derive of their child patients is of substantial value. Psychoanalysis
offers some criteria by which to evaluate psychological theories,
particularly in regard to the place given to emotional life and –
more generally – the degree of recognition given to the construction
of subjectivity during the developmental period. With these criteria
in mind, Piagetian theory is examined, followed by an analysis of
attachment and socialisation theory. The chapter concludes with
a brief account of recent attempts to amalgamate the empirical
procedures of developmental psychology with the concerns of
psychoanalysis.

*Chapter 3* maintains a developmental stance in its examination
of what has become a central area of interest in psychology and
psychoanalysis – language. Some psychological and psychoanalytic
theories of language are outlined in terms of their ability to provide
answers to a range of questions on language development. It is
suggested that this is one area where there is some degree
of compatibility, or rather complementarity, between the two
approaches. Psychology provides some interesting accounts of the
cognitive processes necessary for language acquisition, and of the
stages through which this process passes. In addition, some
psychological theories supply insights on the communicational
context which surrounds language development. Psychoanalysis,
which is relatively weak on many of these questions, is strong in
its exposition of the emotional significance of language use, and
the power of language to have a formative role in the development
of consciousness. Furthermore, Lacanian psychoanalysis at least,
despite some vagaries of linguistic theorising, provides important
new ways into an examination of the ideological role of language –
of how language can carry sociality into the core of human
subjectivity.

*Chapter 4* presents an account of the response of psychology
and psychoanalysis to the reconsideration of gender assumptions
provoked by feminism. Here, the inadequacy of psychological
theory is very striking. Psychologists have confined themselves to

describing differences between male and female behaviour, and to developing theories of social role acquisition. The most promising strand of recent theorising derives from the work of cognitive social psychologists, who view gender as a central dimension used in the definition of the self. However, not only does this remain a poorly worked out and vague approach; it also continues to employ traditional images of gender alongside a very superficial model of change. Crucially, psychological theories continue to assume the existence of the gendered subject – that is, the individual already constituted as masculine or feminine – rather than investigating the mechanisms whereby gender becomes experienced as the central subjective division. Psychoanalysts, notoriously conformist in many of their gender assumptions, have also produced some challenging insights into the origins of gender differences – or 'sexual difference'. What is focused on here is the approach, shared by Freud and Lacan, of arguing that sexual difference arises through a specific set of experiences surrounding castration anxiety, rather than being somehow ordained anatomically. In this way, and despite the limitations of its androcentrism, psychoanalysis is able to theorise sexual difference both as a constructing axis of human subjectivity, and as a socially given dimension.

Finally, *Chapter 5* is an attempt to read a social phenomenon, racism, through psychological and psychoanalytic eyes. Psychology has traditionally been unable to pursue this path, offering instead a reductionist account focusing on prejudice as an individual (albeit socially influenced) cognitive aberration. Psychoanalysts have shared no less in reductionist and also in racist patterns of theory. Nevertheless, it is suggested that psychoanalysis holds the seeds of a more radical and socially sophisticated analysis of racism. This arises out of its portrayal of certain subjective states as linked to social phenomena. In this chapter, the argument is developed that while racism is an attribute of the social world, it is possible to use psychoanalytic ideas to describe its perpetuation and experiential power among individuals. Some important psychoanalytically-informed analyses of racism are described; these suggest that the psychology of racists may be understood in part as a defensive reaction to the conditions of modernity, and may be linked to a rejection of multiplicity that itself is a function of a terror of personal dissolution. The general point at issue here is that psychoanalysis, through its exploration of the formation and structure of subjectivity, allows for links between social and individual phenomena at a level which is not available to psychology. This, indeed, is one of the primary arguments of the book.

A word should be said here about the theories described. In the cases of both psychology and psychoanalysis a series of selections have been made in an attempt to reveal the major assumptions of the approaches, rather than to provide a complete overview of research. In psychology, this has resulted in an emphasis on cognitive theory, although space is also given to socialisation accounts. In psychoanalysis, it is the more challenging elements in Freudian, Kleinian and Lacanian thought that are repeatedly returned to, on the grounds that it is these schools – and particularly the latter two – that provide the most cogent challenge to the trajectory taken by psychology. Thus, this book is not a survey of all possible positions on the various topics, but an attempt to engage critically with the assumptions of psychology through use of some of the most provocative concepts of psychoanalysis.

# 1   Models of the Mind

## Explaining mental phenomena

The concept of 'mind' is a complicated one for both psychologists
and psychoanalysts. Among psychologists, there remains a good
deal of uncertainty concerning the status of mental phenomena,
and of the 'mind' itself, as objects of scientific investigation.
Although the most influential early modern text defined psychology
as the 'science of mental life' (James, 1890), most later accounts,
operating under the influence of behaviourism, reformulated it as
'the science of behaviour'. The difference between the two phrases
symbolises a dichotomy which has characterised psychology for
the past hundred years. Farr (1987) notes that, 'in the course of
its, still brief, history psychology has been *either* the science of
mind *or* the science of behaviour. It has never been *both* at one
and the same time' (p. 3). In contemporary psychology, it is once
again the 'science of mind' tendency that is dominant, through the
impact of what has come to be known as the 'cognitive revolution'
of the past twenty years.

In a few areas, particularly some branches of clinical psychology,
psychology remains a purely behaviourist science, avoiding discussion of mental events on the grounds either that they are inaccessible to operational means of study or that they are epiphenomena,
produced as responses to stimuli or as the consequences of
behavioural acts. Alternatively, some physiological psychologists
remain unhappy with the concept of the 'mind' precisely because
it is mentalistic – they hold a suspicion that, somehow, discussing
the mind allows a spiritual or mystical dimension to enter into
what ought to be a materialist science. 'The brain' is the only
legitimate discourse for them.

Notwithstanding these instances of anti-mentalism, however, if
one surveys the range of current psychological investigations as a

11

whole, from neuropsychology to social and personality psychology, there is a striking dominance of cognitive approaches – of studies of how 'information' (perceptions of various kinds) is processed to bring about changes in the state of the individual. In part, this turn to cognitive psychology has been a response to the aridity of behaviourist ideas, particularly in terms of their failure to provide theories or methods of study to deal with cognitive functions such as perception, thought and – perhaps most significantly – language. In addition, the immense advances in computer technology in recent years have enabled what were previously only speculative or indirectly accessible mental functions to be operationalised in the form of computer models, thus making them amenable to quantitative as well as qualitative analysis. This has made the mind respectable again as an object of scientific study, although, as will be discussed, it is a particular view of the mind – something which has procedures that can be modelled by computer programs – that is accepted by cognitivists.

Psychoanalysts are, generally speaking, much happier than psychologists with the notion of 'the mind'. The problem in their approach, however, is that they mean several different things by 'mind', some of them incorporating mystical elements (as in Jung's version of the nature of the self) and others far removed either from ordinary conceptualisations or from those used by psychologists. Different schools of psychoanalysis have developed completely different pictures of the structure of the mind and the processes that are supposed to characterise it; in no case is it clear what the relationship of these structures and processes is to the brain, and frequently it is impossible to decide upon ways of evaluating the validity of any one model in comparison with any other. In addition, whereas the 'mind' visualised by psychologists is constituted by cognitive maps, perceptual, linguistic and memory processes and the like, that theorised by psychoanalysts contains a collection of 'ideas', impulses and desires and (if one is to read them literally) motivating representations of people and parts of people – particularly breasts and penises. Thus, it seems as though when psychologists and psychoanalysts study the mind, they are studying rather different things.

Perhaps a helpful way to embark on a comparison of the underlying concerns of the two disciplines is to consider what it is they are attempting to do when they develop models of mental functioning. Johnson-Laird (1983) lays down the guantlet for psychology in the following way:

> to understand a phenomenon is to have a working model of it, albeit a model that may contain simulated components. (p. 4)

This formulation succinctly expresses the philosophy behind cognitive psychology. For example, the question of how memory 'works' is answered by the construction of a (theoretical) working 'model' of memory. This aims to describe the operations which must be carried out on information if it is to be learnt, stored and retrieved in a way consistent with what is known about what happens to material that humans actually learn and remember. Memory research therefore consists of three linked processes: descriptions of what happens when people remember and forget things (largely in the form of accounts of how experimental procedures of various kinds influence memory performance); construction of abstract models which summarise these descriptions and present hypotheses concerning the type of operations that the system must be capable of (e.g. 'information that is to be stored over a long period of time is converted into a semantic form organised in hierarchical units; there must be some kind of converter in the system that can do this'); and experimental testing of the accuracy of these models either through investigations of the performance of human 'subjects' or through computer simulations examining what would happen to information if it was to be processed in the way that the models suggest. The end result of this process is a more sophisticated model which provides a fuller description of what happens to information as it passes through the system and of the rules governing the transformations that the information undergoes (e.g. 'verbal material is changed from an acoustic to a semantic store; this must happen by a comparison of the heard words with other known words in something that we will call a "logogen"').

Cognitive psychology has produced a number of extremely powerful and sophisticated models of the kind outlined above; they are powerful in the sense that they link together a large number of experimental and observational findings in informative ways and in that they make non-obvious predictions which are actually borne out when tested experimentally (e.g. the performance of normal people in experimental laboratories and the

behaviour of brain damaged patients both contribute to the model
of reading constructed by Coltheart, 1985). They have also been
applied productively in a number of areas, from those which are
very closely related to the original experimental situations (e.g.
radar tracking, monitoring of airline controls, reading) to social
psychological situations that might seem to be only metaphorically
'information processing' (e.g. judgement of other people's personalities).

It is revealing, however, to consider slightly more schematically
what it is that this form of psychology attempts to do – what it is
that Johnson-Laird means when he refers to 'understanding'
in the quotation given above. Cognitive psychology takes a
phenomenon and attempts to reproduce it; what kind of 'understanding' is generated here? Essentially, it is the descriptive
understanding that answers the question, 'What does this system
look like and how does it work?' However important this question
is, it remains a limited one; it describes the syntax of the system –
the rules by which it operates – but it makes no comment on its
semantics, the meanings that the system generates or incorporates.
In this sense, it asks the same questions about people as one might
ask about a car moving along a road: it is interesting and
informative to know how the various mechanical elements in the
car interact to make the motion possible; it is equally interesting
to know what operations the driver has to engage in to activate
these mechanics. This much a 'syntactic' psychology of the car
might provide. But one might also want to know where the car
was going and why – what the meaning of the journey was.

The explanations of mental phenomena provided by cognitive
psychology are thus of the 'how' rather than the 'why' form. There
are various comments psychologists might make on this. One
concerns the possibility that 'why' questions are properly the
province of other areas of psychology – for instance, the area of
'motivational' studies. However, despite the fact that 'motivation'
is a traditional category in most psychology syllabuses, it generally
takes the impersonal form of biological reductionism (e.g. 'drive'
theory, sociobiology, psychophysiology) or it uses concepts such
as the desire for personal validation (cf. Harré, 1979) which tend
to assume the existence of pre-given and universal human purposes.
'Motivation' then becomes the issue of how these purposes are
expressed behaviourally, rather than an explanation of their origins

and significance. More generally, it will be seen from the various topics encountered in this book that in many significant areas psychology fails to address the semantic question, instead limiting itself to the kind of description of mental processes which is characteristic of cognitive psychology.

There is a more interesting retort to the criticism that the kind of understanding represented in Johnson-Laird's formulation is unduly limited. This is the suggestion that one does not need a separate 'semantic' approach, but that meanings are themselves immanent in the system described by the cognitive model. In other words, it can be argued that there is no 'cause' for the system in the motivational sense; there are only mental functions which have meanings as an automatic consequence of their activity. This is in most respects the argument of theorists of artificial intelligence, an area of work which is central to cognitive psychology, and that raises important issues for the whole question of what constitutes an explanation of a psychological phenomenon. But before describing these issues, it is worth considering the explanatory framework adopted by psychoanalysts, as they deal explicitly (some might say exclusively) with the semantics of experience.

### The semantics of experience

Freud's insistence on the status of psychoanalysis as a science is well known, and can be attested to throughout his work, from the early *Project for a Scientific Psychology* to late works such as the *New Introductory Lectures of 1933*, in which the following statement appears:

> Psychoanalysis, in my opinion, is incapable of creating a Weltanschauung of its own. It does not need one; it is a part of science and can adhere to the scientific Weltanschauung. (p. 181)

For Freud, this means that psychoanalysis operates according to the principles of scientific investigation: careful observation of phenomena under controlled conditions (the consulting room, for psychoanalysts), objective recording, clear presentation of hypotheses and the development and alteration of theories on the basis of empirical findings. (Whether psychoanalysis adheres to these principles in practice is, of course, a famous centre for psychology-psychoanalysis antagonism – but see Rustin (1987) for the argument that psychoanalysis' practice is *more* scientific than may appear from description of its theories.) But the notion of a scientific Weltanschauung to which psychoanalysis subscribes also means something else, perhaps more important, to Freud. This is that mental phenomena follow the materialist, causal laws of all other matter – that there are deterministic principles that can be used to *explain* psychological phenomena. It is this word, 'explain', which is crucial for an understanding of the psychoanalytic enterprise, a word which goes further than the cognitivist use of the term 'understand', discussed above. For psychoanalysts, to gain a full grasp of a mental event is not simply to describe and model it, although answers to the procedural question of 'how' something occurs are certainly interesting. 'Explanation' goes further: it involves uncovering what it is that something signifies – what underlying meaning it has.

Two aspects of this explanatory model are worthy of discussion at this point. The concept of 'psychic determinism' looms large in Freud's theoretical framework, and is seen by him as an indispensable element in the scientific approach. What is meant by this is that all psychological events, however random and accidental they may appear to be on the surface, actually are the products of underlying intentions. Everything, in other words, has a cause: 'To believe in determinism is to believe basically that everything is subject to interpretation' (Mannoni, 1971, p. 82). At the heart of the psychoanalytic procedure is an assumption that there is no 'chance' in psychic life, that absolutely everything can be taken to indicate and reveal the set of underlying, unconscious desires that direct the individual's experience. Even the smallest act, the slightest gap or slip in consciousness, can be followed through to this hidden, determining core. Interpretation in psychoanalysis is not casual or relativistic; it aims to reveal the *true meaning* and *origin* of an event, its real determining principle.

> One point . . . of psychoanalysis is to bring home to people not only that certain things that they do are interpretable in specific ways, but also that they really intend them in that spirit even if they are not aware of so doing. (Hamlyn, 1971, p. 184)

As Erdelyi (1985) notes, Freud's espousal of the notion of the unconscious is intimately connected with his belief in determinism; it is because psychic events are not random, but are all firmly caused by some underlying principle, that the concept of the unconscious is necessary. For Freud, this is a scientific principle carried over from the determinism assumed by the physical sciences of his day. Just as material events are always produced by a determining cause, so psychological events have an underlying psychological origin. More specifically, all actions are motivated by a set of intentions, and it is the discovery of these motivating intentions that satisfies the requirements of an explanation. As Erdelyi also notes, the displacement of scientific determinism by more probabilistic models of causation has largely passed psychoanalysis by, creating confusions and dissensions particularly around the matter of psychoanalysis' 'scientific' status. The issue here is the problem of ascertaining clear causes, whether conscious or unconscious, for phenomena which may not be random or meaningless, but which may nevertheless not be produced through discrete intentions or wishes. Freud's idea that actions may be 'overdetermined' by a number of different unconscious intentions is an unsatisfactory solution, as it still relies on the identification of discrete causes. It is partly in recognition of this set of problems that some latter-day psychoanalytic theorists have adopted a more 'hermeneutic' approach which attempts to move away from the focus on causes towards an interpretative understanding of how meanings are generated in psychoanalytic practice. Although this approach has problems of its own, particularly that its neglect of causes threatens to reduce psychoanalysis to phenomenology (see Rustin, 1987), it does have the virtue of emphasising how a psychological 'intention' may not always be intended in a simple sense. Rather, the meanings produced in the unconscious may themselves arise from conflicting and multiple forces – a realisation which has in some hands made psychoanalysis congruent with more recent structuralist thought (e.g. MacCabe, 1981).

The second aspect of the explanatory model to be commented on here is implicit in the first. In designating an intention as the centre of a psychological explanation, psychoanalysis is drawing a semantic element into its procedures. Freud himself expresses this succinctly when describing what he means by his use of the word 'sense': 'We mean nothing other by it than the intention it serves and its position in a psychical continuity. In most of our researches we can replace "sense" by "intention" or "purpose"' (Freud, 1917, p. 66). What is semantic about this is that it does not just deal with the processes that make expression of such a sense possible; it also demands that in every single case the question of what that sense is, is addressed. This is a radically different procedure from the cognitive psychological position that there is no underlying 'meaning' driving the system of psychological functions; it is also, as Brown (1959) points out in his discussion of neurotic symptoms, dreams and errors, very different from the behaviourist approach to uncovering causes.

> [If] it were possible to explain these phenomena on behaviouristic principles, as the result of superficial associations of ideas, then they would have a cause but no meaning. Meaningfulness means expression of a purpose or an intention. The crux of Freud's discovery is that neurotic symptoms, as well as the dreams and errors of everyday life, do have meaning and that the meaning of meaning has to be radically revised because they have meaning. (pp. 3–4)

No psychological explanation is complete without a reference to the meaning of the phenomenon being explained, and for psychoanalysts that 'meaning' always signifies an underlying purpose or, in more fashionable language, desire.

The psychoanalytic model has been presented at this point as a reminder that it is possible to ask 'why' questions in psychology and to uncover plausible answers to such questions. It is perhaps harder to suggest ways of modelling the semantic content of what occurs – but as will be seen later, this can be used either as a criticism of psychoanalysis or as a refutation of the claims of artificial intelligence. It is also very difficult to develop operational tests of psychoanalytic hypotheses: how is one to know for sure that the correct explanation of an act has been alighted upon, or, indeed, whether that act really was determined by an intention, rather than just being an accident? Cioffi (1970) is representative of a position amongst psychologists and philosophers that doubts psychoanalysis' claims concerning psychic determinism: 'We did not interpret dreams, symptoms, errors, etc. because it was discovered that they were meaningful, but we insisted that they were meaningful in order that we might interpret them' (p. 498).

The purpose of psychoanalysis, in this view, is not scientific at all; rather, it serves the religious end of providing a meaning to life, when actually much that occurs is random, unintended, purposeless – that is, meaningless. This is close to the traditional Skinnerian position that no true causes are to be found inside the person (Skinner, 1971), a position which most cognitive psychologists, with their interests in rule-governed behaviour and information processing, would contest. However, the general debate over whether meanings are coherent elements for psychological study remains an important one, present both in philosophical debates over consciousness and in the 'ghost in the machine' discussions of current cognitive psychologists – the issue, for instance, of whether there is any core experiencing mental element or 'self', or whether psychological meanings arise as a consequence of psychological processes. Psychoanalysis, simply by asking its 'why' question, takes up a position opposed to the general psychological tendency to prioritise problems of function over those of meaning. It suggests that the psychological focus on the operation of rules and part-processes leads to neglect of the crucial causal factors that lie behind mental activity, factors which must be portrayed in the language of intentions and desires. The legitimacy of this argument – of whether function can be explained by some 'higher-order' element such as intention – is partly the subject of the many debates on reductionism in psychology.

## Reductionism

One element shared by some branches of both psychology and psychoanalysis is a tendency towards biological reductionism. Freud was unabashed in his admiration for biology and his view that the prospects for a genuinely causal account of human psychology lie in an exploration of physiological and biochemical processes.

> The deficiencies in our description would probably vanish if we were already in a position to replace the psychological terms by physiological or chemical ones . . . Biology is truly a land of unlimited possibilities. (Freud, 1920, p. 334)

In many areas of psychoanalysis, notably the American 'ego-psychology' school, metapsychology (the description of basic mental processes) consists of a series of hypothesised *biological* entities, specifically interactions between 'drives' of various kinds. This is not just a matter of considering the meanings which become attached to physiological events – for example, to the anatomical differences between the sexes. It is a quite literal reference to underlying biological states, forms of psychic 'energy' that, in being distributed around the mental apparatus, cause certain psychological events. Perhaps the most extreme advocate of this position was, ironically, the one-time political revolutionary Wilhelm Reich, for whom biology became the absolute determinant of all action, with the repression of natural, heterosexual desire leading literally to a damming-up and distortion of sexual energy and the formation of neurotic character structures.

> My contention is that every individual who has managed to preserve a bit of naturalness knows that there is only one thing wrong with neurotic patients: the lack of *full and repeated sexual satisfaction.* (Reich in Mitchell, 1974, p. 131)

Even in some schools of psychoanalysis that emphasise the role of social relations in development, there is still an assumption that the final cause of mental functioning is biological. Kleinian psychoanalysis, for instance, has developed an elaborate portrayal of the mental life of infants, in which it is proposed that unconscious phantasies operate from birth in the context of relationships with social 'objects'; however, at the root of these phantasies are biological drives or 'instincts', notably those of life and death, Klein (1957) is very clear on the innateness of the conflict between love and hate; in the end, all psychological processes are seen as being constructed on the basis of these in-built energic drives.

In mainstream psychology, reductionist approaches which seek to explain psychological phenomena by reference to 'underlying' biological states are extremely influential. Marr (1982) describes this position cogently, while claiming that he himself has moved away from it:

> Truth, I also believed, was basically neural, and the central aim of all research was a thorough functional analysis of the Central Nervous System. (p. 14)

Other positions are more moderate, resisting the strong statement that it is at the biological level that all psychological causes reside; nevertheless, they still envision the project of psychology as an attempt to identify how the (pre-assumed) link between levels operates:

> The task of psychology is to explain human perception, learning, cognition, and so forth in terms that ultimately will unite psychological theory to physiology in one way or another. (Dennett, 1979, p. 58)

As will be argued below, while links between psychology and physiology are interesting, a non-reductionist view would be that the 'task' of psychology is to provide explanations of psychological phenomena at a *psychological* level. It is more appropriately the task of physiology to achieve the goal outlined in the quotation from Dennett above.

Reductionist approaches are dominant in several areas, for instance in the study of 'psychopathology', where the research interests of psychologists as well as psychiatrists are massed in the direction of uncovering the presumed biochemical abnormalities that produce states such as schizophrenia and depression. More generally, reductionism operates forcefully in many psychologists' implicit and explicit models of how mental events occur, even if the actual level at which those psychologists are working is psychological. In cognitive psychology, for instance, while many models of mental functioning are developed along the lines described earlier, with little or no reference to the physical operations of the brain, there is often visible an assumption not only that the models have to be consistent with the realities of brain structure and function, but that it is in uncovering the way in which the brain produces cognitions that a true explanation of mentation will be found. Mehler *et al.* (1984), for instance, describe what they refer to as 'a trend in the study of language that identifies the understanding of linguistic processes exclusively with the localisation of those processes in the brain' (p. 85). They comment,

> Generally, the areas which have suffered most from believing that any phenomenon under investigation may be explained simply by pointing to its locus are: studies of lateralisation in

normal subjects; studies of the effects of brain lesions; and hemispheric specialisation during language development. (p. 89)

It is not the question of whether studies at the physiological level are important in their own right that is at issue here; it is rather the belief shared by many psychologists working in a variety of areas that the identification of physiological processes constitutes an explanation of a psychological event. This belief suggests that no 'mental' level needs to be considered; it is the physiological processes of the brain that are the real causal entities. Psychology, in principle at least, reduces to neuroanatomy and brain chemistry.

It is important to recognise the achievements of reductionist psychology. Those advances which have been made in identifying the biological structures and processes that make psychological events possible lie completely within the reductionist mode; particularly in cases of organic dysfunction, this information is of vital importance. A major strength of the subdiscipline of neuropsychology lies in its ability to create models of mental functioning from observations of brain activity and dysfunction – and this need not be done at the expense of recognition of the accompanying humanity and subjectivity of the people being studied (see Humphreys and Riddoch, 1987; Sacks, 1985). The work of the Soviet neuropsychologist, Luria, is the classic expression of the employment of a reductionist mode of investigation alongside a deep sensitivity to the meanings and effects of neurological impairment on the individuals concerned (e.g. Luria, 1969; 1973). Indeed, the works just quoted present a richer and more compelling vision of human integrity than many aggressively anti-biologistic, sociologically sophisticated tracts. In psychoanalysis, whilst many psychoanalysts and critics of psychoanalysis dissent from Freud's biologistic concepts, few would deny that he was able to use them in parallel with a highly sophisticated appreciation of the complexities of human subjectivity.

There has been a considerable oppositional movement to biologism within both psychoanalysis and psychology, a movement that has had varying amounts of success. In psychoanalysis, the argument has tended to be a humanistic one, that the biological concepts employed by Freud and by some of his followers are inappropriate for the construction of a truly personal psychology. Guntrip (1973) catches the flavour of this position in words with which many psychologists would agree: biology is an inappropriate source discipline for psychology because it is only

> a study of the *machinery* of personal life, not of its *essential quality*, to use Freud's own term, a study of the mechanisms of behaviour and not of the meaningful personal experience that is the essence of the personal self. (p. 49)

What Guntrip is appealing to here is a commonly felt disquiet at the way an approach that is concerned with meanings and intentions appears to rest on an impersonal, mechanical base. Freud's position makes intentions and desires only intermediary causes, representations of physiological processes that are operating underneath. Guntrip's suggestion, developed fully in the object relations school of psychoanalysis to which he belonged, is that whilst one must have a functioning physiological base for psychology to be possible, this base does not provide any insights into the nature of the psychological world. Psychological understandings have to be couched, therefore, in psychological terms, for example in terms of good and bad object relations, of the uses of defences, or of desires for certain kinds of human relationships. Even sex and aggression, the twin pantheons of psychoanalytic biologism, are re-interpreted as responses to psychosocial events; sexuality, while having biological components, is taken up into the service of a psychological search for intimate personal relations; aggression is a response to the frustration of this search. Biology provides what is needed for psychology to be possible, but its phenomena are at the wrong level for it to be able to explain psychological events.

It is this notion of the appropriate level at which an explanation has to be couched that has become crucial in the debate on reductionism and that has been clarified most helpfully by cognitive psychologists. Marr (1982), for instance, makes a point that could have come straight out of the debate within psychoanalysis: 'the key observation is that neurophysiology and psychophysics have as their business to *describe* the behaviour of cells or of subjects but not to *explain* such behaviour' (p. 15). He then goes on to argue that a full understanding of any system cannot be built up purely from knowledge of the elementary components of that system, but also requires information on the interactions of these elements and the systemic properties they produce.

If one hopes to achieve a full understanding of a system as complicated as a nervous system . . . then one must be prepared to contemplate different kinds of explanation at different levels of description that are linked, at least in principle, into a cohesive whole. (Marr, 1982, p. 20)

Mehler *et al.* (1984), focusing on studies of word recognition and speech perception, make similar points in arguing that 'cogent accounts of the psychological processes involved require the establishment of purely psychological constructs, which are to be judged in terms of their explanatory usefulness rather than their compatibility with formal descriptions, on the one hand, and neurophysiological data on the other' (p. 83). Although neurophysiology may influence psychological theories if it produces psychologically relevant data, in principle, Mehler *et al.* claim, psychological and neurophysiological levels of explanation are distinct – their objectives differ and consequently their appropriate theoretical constructs differ. In the context of language research, the goal of a psychological explanation 'can be taken as describing the real-time sequence of decisions and information exchanges that figure in the production and processing of langue', whereas neurophysiological accounts aim to specify the 'physical structure and processes that mediate language use' (p. 86). Because of the different objectives of explanations at different levels, it may not be possible to translate concepts from one level to another; any 'attempted mapping between levels can only be successful to the extent that it respects the integrity of such constructs at each level' (p. 103).

The argument here is not just that biology cannot currently, in our present state of knowledge, provide the necessary information to generate complete explanations of psychological states (an argument that many psychophysiologists might accept, for instance in discussions on depression or personality). It is, rather, that biological reductionism is an *inappropriate* philosophy for psychology, because it provides information at the wrong level, and because it omits considerations of certain crucial areas of human functioning. Take the first of these issues, the argument that information is provided at the wrong level. One might want to ask a straightforward question about a person's behaviour: 'Why did Jack hit Jill?' The answer to such a question could be, 'Because the neurones in Jack's CNS fired in such-and-such a way, leading to the movement of his arm so that it came into contact with Jill's face'. Or it could be, 'Because he was filled with rage and wanted to hurt her'. Neither of these are complete explanations, but it is readily apparent that it is the second of them that is closer to an answer to the question 'Why did Jack hit Jill?' This is because such questions refer to intentions and psychological states, they are not queries about the physiological processes that make such states possible. It is also the case that the information present in the second explanation may not even be implicit in the first; that is, it may not be the case that one can move from the physiological to the psychological level.

For instance, take an elaboration of the question in response to the second answer, that goes: 'Yes, but why did he *hit* her?' The new answer might refer to psychodynamic and social processes: 'Because, like most men, he has no way of expressing rage except through violence, and he unconsciously believes that women are there to be hit.' This is a more complete explanation, because, taken together with the previous answer, it presents both an immediate cause for Jack's behaviour and a contextual explanation (the link between men's feelings, violence and patriarchy) that gives guidance as to why Jack behaved in that way and no other. All this must in some way operate neurochemically, for sure, but there is no way of describing the brain system that could provide the sort of meaningful information that is present in the psychological account. Putnam (1973) presents this idea in an abstract form as follows: 'from the fact that the behaviour of a system can be *deduced* from its description as a system of elementary particles it does not follow that it can be *explained* from that description' (p. 131). Many courses of action are possible in terms of brain processes; why and how any one is chosen above any other is a psychological question.

In the example given above, reference was made to social phenomena as a way of completing the explanation of Jack's behaviour. It is precisely here that much of the debate over the implications of reductionist and non-reductionist positions within psychology have resided. As demonstrated by Rose *et al.* (1984), it is empirically the case that there is a link between adherence to biological reductionism and reactionary politics. For example, the race and IQ battle has precisely been between those who see

differences in intelligence as being due to biological differences
and those who argue that it is sociopolitical forces that are primarily
operative; sociobiology, which attempts to explain human social
behaviour in evolutionary terms, frequently serves as a justification
for the social status quo, or even for outright oppression (see, for
instance, Wilson, 1979). While there is no strict logical connection,
there is a powerful tendency for reductionism to lead to the notion
that the only appropriate causal entities are individualistic and/or
biological, so social events are irrelevant or, perhaps, are explicable
as the products of the behaviour of numbers of individuals. An
example here would be a description of football violence in
terms of the aggressive personalities of football supporters; these
personalities might then be seen as a product of certain biological
tendencies. As happens in the case of sociobiology, the middle
stage of this logic can also be omitted: for instance, ostensibly
non-individualistic accounts of social events, such as portrayals of
crowd phenomena in terms of territoriality and display, can
themselves be reductionist if they employ biological notions in an
explanatory mode.

The point is that there is no notion that social structures may
be relevant explanations of individual behaviour, or that ideological
forces such as patriarchy or racism may have autonomous existence
independent of particular individuals, and therefore may be
potential components of psychological explanations. As will be
seen in later chapters of this book, such social realisations have
begun to creep into psychoanalysis; psychology, perhaps because
of the legacy of reductionism and also because of the desire of
influential psychologists to be viewed as 'natural' rather than
'social' scientists, often seems still to be labouring in the dark.

Critics of reductionism frequently include adherents of the idea
that 'the mind is a machine' in their strictures. One of the things
that is ironic about this is that psychologists who are wedded to
the notion of computer modelling – to artificial intelligence (AI),
that is – number amongst them some of the foremost critics of
biological reductionism. In a way, this has to be the case: if one
believes that it is possible to reproduce human processes in a
computer, then one cannot believe that these processes are
determined by the biology of the brain. Instead, AI theoreticians
have to believe that it is something about the *functional* organisation of the brain, the way mental processes are arranged, that is

central to psychological understanding. Using a standard analogy that takes the computer program and the machine as being in the same relationship as the mind and the brain, Johnson-Laird (1983) opposes biologism as follows:

[The] mind can be studied independently from the brain. Psychology (the study of the programs) can be pursued independently from neurophysiology (the study of the machine and the machine code). The neurophysiological substrate must provide a physical basis for the processes of the mind, but granted that the substrate offers the computational power of recursive functions, its physical nature places no constraints on the patterns of thought. (p. 9)

Models of the mind, therefore, need to be concerned with the rules and operations embedded in psychological programs or 'software', and not with the hardware – whether it be a particular computer or the human brain. Boden (1987) is even more explicit in her rejection of reductionist models in favour of a 'humanist' enterprise which, she argues, is supported rather than subverted by research in artificial intelligence. Not only is the AI emphasis on representation at odds with behaviourism, but

contrary to popular opinion, artificial intelligence researchers do *not* interpret their work as supporting the reductionist view, that psychological explanations are in principle dispensable since everything mental is 'really' just something happening in the brain. On the contrary, they choose to describe and explain their programs in mentalistic terms . . . because they find it more natural and illuminating to do so than to refer merely to 'behaviouristic' input–output correlations or to 'physiological' details of machine engineering. (pp. 400–1)

The stance that AI takes up with respect to reductionism is an intriguing one. On the one hand, it rejects biologism; on the other, it argues that there is nothing special about human processes that would make it impossible in principle to model them on a non-human machine – it is, therefore, an unlikely blueprint for a 'personal psychology' of the kind envisaged by many psychoanalysts, or for an account of people that prioritises social factors.

Most importantly, this dual stance of AI is linked to an account of consciousness and of meanings that goes to the heart of the debate about what constitutes a psychological explanation.

## Artificial minds

Artificial intelligence (AI) has many origins, but it is perhaps Craik (1943) who, amongst early theorists, most clearly stated its core assumption.

> My hypothesis, then, is that thought models, or parallels, reality – that its essential feature is not 'the mind', 'the self', 'sense-data', nor propositions but symbolism, and that this symbolism is largely of the same kind as that which is familiar to us in mechanical devices which aid thought and calculation. (In Johnson-Laird, 1983, p. 3)

It is, of course, not symbolism in the psychoanalytic sense that Craik is referring to, but in the computational sense: abstract representations of entities, expressible essentially in numerical terms. In this view, thought can be understood as the manipulation of these abstract symbols, a series of operations that combine and recombine them according to specifiable rules. This idea is central to AI; in fact, it is what makes the claims of AI theorists possible. For if thought is in essence a process of the manipulation of symbols, then it can also be coded in a computational form – and hence can, in principle at least, be simulated on a computer. It is this that also produces the analogy between thought and computer software: just as a computer program consists of a set of rules for the manipulation of symbols and can be implemented in any machine with the ability to understand these rules, so mental processes are a set of similar rules, which are in fact implemented in large numbers of brains having different physical characteristics. The machine or the brain are what make 'instantiation' of the program possible, but they are not the program itself; without the software, the brain/machine is just an empty box. Mental events are computational events; in the strongest versions of AI, programs in operation are not just simulations of thought, they *are* thought.

One distinctive characteristic of AI is its empirical nature.

Dennett (1979) refers to AI programs as thought experiments, asking the question 'How could any system (with features A,B,C . . .) possibly accomplish X?' (p. 59). Instead of developing general cognitive theories, AI workers undertake to simulate the performance of humans on specific tasks, for example the perception of visual stimulus arrays or the processing of natural language. The argument is, in its weakest form, that if the simulation is successful, then there may be a relationship between the rules that are embedded in the computer program and the operations that are actually undertaken by human 'information processors'. If the task is sufficiently general, the constraints placed upon the computer sufficiently human-like, and the performance of the machine sufficiently accurate, the claims increase in their strength until they become fully-fledged models of human functioning.

It is at this stage that the claims of 'strong AI' come into play, in which the analogy between computer software and human thought hardens into something that resembles an identity. Johnson-Laird (1983), for example, derives from his 'functionalist' position (that what is important in psychology is the functional organisation of the brain rather than the mechanics of brain processes) the more general argument that any theory of the mind must produce accounts of mental processes which can be rewritten as computer programs. It is only in this way, he suggests, that mental phenomena can ever be articulated in operational terms, avoiding 'magical' ingredients such as 'intuition' (p. 6). Conversely, the doctrine of functionalism makes all thought a computational process, and hence computers are actually thinking when they engage in computations that result in the mimicking of human performance.

> If functionalism is correct it follows not only that scientific theories of mentality can be simulated by computer programs, but also that in principle mentality can be embodied within an appropriately programmed computer: computers can think because thinking is a computational process. (Johnson-Laird, 1983, p. 10)

While other authors, such as Marr (1982) and Boden (1987), have been careful not to confuse heuristic programs for simulating thought with theories of thought itself, there is a powerful tradition within AI that claims exactly that identity. The seminal notion of a 'Turing Machine', named after Alan Turing, captures (and partly originated) precisely this idea. Stated formally, a Turing Machine is 'a hypothetical device that takes for granted the notions of writing a symbol on a memory tape, reading a symbol from it, shifting the tape one square to the left or right, and changing the machine from one internal state to another as a function of the symbol read on the tape and the current state of the machine' (Johnson-Laird, 1983, p. 6). More loosely, a Turing Machine is a digital computer, operating on the basis of coded instructions that determine how symbols will be manipulated. The famous 'Turing test' (Turing, 1950) embodies an argument that is still put forward to support the putative identity between machine and human intelligence. Put simply, the test is as follows: if a machine can be made to respond to a specific input in exactly the same way as a human being would, then just as we would say that the human is 'thinking', so must we say that the machine is 'thinking'. In other words, if one can exactly simulate the output of human thought-processes on a machine, then the machine quite literally thinks.

The Turing test has been a popular model for AI workers, as well as for cognitive psychologists in general. In large part, this is probably because it is attractively operational. Whereas most traditional discussions of thought refer to hypothesised internal states that can be reported upon by individuals but that cannot be directly measured, the Turing test adopts the philosophical position that it is only what one can directly observe that can be an object of scientific knowledge. This 'positivist' stance is also the one favoured by most psychologists: creating a respectable psychological science is seen as depending upon the development of objective means of reliably measuring and categorising behavioural states. Internal events are not of that order; rather, they are never more than hypothetical entities, their existence deduced from the observable behaviour of the person concerned. Thought has precisely these characteristics: we can never know directly what is happening 'in the mind' of another person; all we have to go on is their behaviour, including the statements that they make. We presume thought because we observe the inputs and outputs of another person's mind. Under such conditions, we have no more right to say that a person is thinking than to say that a computer is thinking; put the other way, if the behaviour of a person leads us to impute to her or him the quality 'thinking', then the identical behaviour of a computer should lead to exactly the same imputation.

The limitation of the Turing test, and of the general approach that it exemplifies, is that it suggests that similar sets of behaviour are produced by similar causes. Hence, if one can accurately simulate a human input–output relationship on a machine, then one can propose that the machine thinks, and that it does so *in the same way* as does the human. This suggestion conflates two separate steps. First, suggesting that a machine 'thinks' is perfectly acceptable if one simply defines thinking as an operation that converts information of one form into another. But the suggestion that the kind of thinking that goes on in a computer is the same as that engaged in by humans may or may not be tenable; it certainly cannot be assumed to be true simply by an identity of outputs. Two things may behave in exactly the same way under all constructable circumstances and yet have different internal organisations and modes of operation. Ironically, the first part of Turing's (1950) paper, in which his test is described, demonstrates this.

The Turing test is supposed to be a variant of what Turing calls the 'imitation game', in which a man and a woman, put in separate rooms, are interrogated through a teletype by a third person whose job it is to find out which is which. If, say, the man can answer questions in a way that makes it impossible to distinguish him from the woman, then there will be no way of telling the two apart under these conditions. But the man will, in actuality, still be a man and the woman a woman, even if the interrogator muddles them up. Or take the famous variant of Turing's test in which two AI scientists go into two rooms, separated by a wall with a small hole at its base. One of the scientists puts his foot through the hole, and the other alternately stamps on it or drops a stone on it. The first scientist cannot tell the difference, he just knows that both make his toes hurt. Does that mean that the falling stone is the same as the stamping foot? To repeat, just because the behaviour of two things looks (and feels) similar, it does not mean that the things themselves are the same.

All this means that one cannot assume identity of 'software' from similarity of effects. But AI is often much more subtle than to make that assumption in any simplistic way. Rey (1986) makes the relevant distinction between the functionalism of AI and the naivety of behaviourism.

> Strong AI is patently a version of what have come to be called 'functionalist' theories of mind, which in general distinguish themselves from mere 'behavioural' theories by appealing not only to inputs and outputs, but also to a system's *internal* states in the ascription of mental terms. If a system's inputs and outputs are not mediated by the *right sorts* of internal states – in the case of strong AI, the *right sort* of program – then the system will not be regarded as satisfying some mental predicate, no matter how much its behaviour may resemble the behaviour of a system that does. (pp. 170–1)

This argument, alongside those of theorists who posit the import-ance of intentional descriptions (at least as analogies) in explanations of machine behaviour (e.g. Boden, 1987), show that AI theorists have themselves moved beyond adherence to the Turing test as their trademark, developing more sophisticated notions of what their programming ingenuities reveal. If the behaviour of a machine indicates that it is 'thinking', one is still left with the question of what type of thinking this is; that is, is it the 'right sort of program' to be taken as analogous or identical to the 'programs' in the human mind? Obviously, this poses the huge problem of what the 'right sort of program' might be, a problem that is extremely difficult to answer in any general or *a priori* way. From the cognitive perspective, as long as one retains a functionalist focus, the right sort of program will be one that not only mimics the output of mental activity but does so through the use of rules which are of the same kind as those that actually govern human information processing – if these can be defined non-tautologically. Psychoanalysis, however, because of its emphasis on semantics – on the priority of meaning over function – suggests that AI may never grasp the full nature of psychic activity. As will be described in more detail later, the 'right sort of program' from a psychoana-lytic point of view would have to include not just a series of rules for achieving a particular goal, which is the distinct strength of artificial intelligence (as of computer programming in general), but also a mechanism for generating these goals in the first place. What psychoanalysis suggests is distinctive about human thought is that unconscious meaning processes direct the activities of consciousness and determine the kind of 'information processing' that goes on. These meaning processes may not be of the variety that can be modelled cognitively, precisely because they are semantic in nature and cannot be understood functionally. Thus, by adopting a functionalist perspective, cognitive psychologists may be limiting their ability to explain central aspects of mental life.

Before developing the psychoanalytic perspective more fully, there is an important debate that has surfaced within academic psychology over this very issue of whether, whatever it looks like or does, a computer program can ever *in principle* be the right sort of program to model human thought. In particular, the argument that artificial intelligence is qualitatively different from human intelligence has been advanced by John Searle.

**The Chinese room**

In a series of publications, Searle has mounted a critique of what he terms 'strong AI', which he designates as the 'claim that the appropriately programmed computer literally has cognitive states and that the programs thereby explain human cognition' (1980, p. 417). This critique has a number of linked elements that can be specified as: (1) the central component of human cognition is intentionality, which means that cognitions are directed towards things, that they are always *about* something; (2) intentionality is a product of the brain, it is 'a natural biological phenomenon, caused by processes in the brain and realised in the structure of the brain' (1984, p. 87); (3) computer programs can *never*, in principle, reproduce human thought processes, because they lack intentionality, because the operations that are directed by programs are always purely formal and computational. 'In the linguistic jargon, [computer programs] have only a syntax but no semantics. Such intentionality as computers appear to have is solely in the minds of those who program them and those who use them, those who send in the input and those who interpret the output' (1980, p. 422). The effect of this critique, taken as a whole, is to suggest that AI is limited to the creation of clever machines that can do a lot of difficult things, but without revealing anything of importance about the processes occurring in the human mind.

It is worth unpacking the various elements in Searle's argument. First, his suggestion that the core item of interest in human cognition is intentionality parallels the 'semantic' position of psychoanalysis, that what is important in explanations of human psychology is to uncover the meaning that an act or experience has, its 'why?' components. Prioritising intentionality leads to a demand for a purposive account of thought which emphasises mental contents above their form and above the computational processes that operate upon them, an account which is restricted to the manipulation of formal symbols. Against the behaviouristic objection that all we can know are observable states, Searle simply asserts that intentionality is a fact of human existence, and that to neglect it is to omit the central component of human psychology: 'Just as it was bad science to treat systems that lack Intentionality as if they had it, so it is equally bad science to treat systems that have intrinsic Intentionality as if they lacked it' (1984, p. 99).

As was described earlier, this is a powerful argument against the completeness of any psychological theory that does not explicitly deal with meanings. But it is also one which cognitivists have often attempted to rebut, most importantly with claims that what we experience as 'understanding' or meaning is an intrinsic property of a formal system of computational processes, not something magically separate and unique. As will be seen below, some of the strongest replies to Searle have been couched in roughly this form.

Searle's emphasis on the specific biological properties of human brains is a very interesting one, apparently reductionist and yet avoiding the simple inadequacies of straightforwardly reductionist theories. He is as strongly opposed to mystical notions of where personal meanings and other intentional states come from as are any of the AI workers – in fact, it is *they* whom he accuses of mind–body dualism because of their belief that thoughts are the instantiation of computer programs in *any* hardware, that, therefore, 'minds' (or at least mental phenomena) are separable from brains. For Searle, brains cause minds: 'Intrinsic Intentional phenomena are caused by neurophysiological processes going on in the brain and they occur in and are realised in the structure of the brain' (1984, p. 90). Intentionality, however, is not produced by the firing of a special 'meaning' neurone which causes it in a simple one-to-one sense; rather, intentionality and, indeed, everything that we call 'mind' is a facet of brain functioning, produced as part of what the brain does. There is no need to explain the mental separately from the physical; it *is* the physical, it is just what happens when the brain is working. The brain moves muscles, processes information, produces sensations, develops representations, encodes experiences and creates intentions. Intentionality is just the way people are made. Minds, therefore, are parts of brains: 'Whatever else intentionality is, it is a biological phenomenon, and it is as likely to be causally dependent on the specific biochemistry of its origins as lactation, photosynthesis, or any other biological phenomena' (1980, p. 424). To reproduce minds, one has to reproduce brains, or at least something with the same causal properties as the brain; that is, one has to study the hardware as well as the software, in order to develop the right kind of intention-producing machine. AI, if it is aimed at providing information on human mental processes, is studying the wrong things.

'Could a machine think?' On the argument advanced here *only* a machine could think, and only very special kinds of machines, namely brains and machines with internal causal powers equivalent to those of brains. And that is why strong AI has little to tell us about thinking, since it is not about machines but about programs, and no program by itself is sufficient for thinking. (Searle, 1980, p. 417)

The final element in Searle's argument, that computer programs by their very nature lack intentionality, goes to the heart of his attempted refutation of the Turing test and of the claims of AI in general. The position he takes is that computer programs contain purely formal operations, computations on empty elements, whereas intentional states are characterised precisely by the fact that they are not just formal, but that they have content. Searle's argument in this respect is captured in his 'Chinese room experiment' which, when first aired in *The Behavioral and Brain Sciences*, was provocative enough to generate 28 different responses from a whole alphabet of Searle's opponents. The essence of this thought-experiment is as follows.

Suppose a non-Chinese-speaker is locked in a room with a large number of uninterpretable Chinese symbols and a rule book. Suppose that more Chinese symbols are fed in from outside the room, and that the rule book tells the person which of the symbols already present should be pushed out of the room in response to which symbols coming in. The kind of rule might be, 'When a squiggle-squiggle symbol comes in, push a squiggle-squoggle symbol out'. Suppose that the incoming symbols are called (by people outside the room) 'questions' and the outgoing symbols are called 'answers', and suppose that the rule book is so complete, and the person so adept at following the rules, that the answers are indistinguishable from those of native Chinese speakers. From the point of view of the people outside the room, it looks as though the person inside is understanding Chinese; after all, the answers are exactly those that would be given by someone who really does understand Chinese. (This is, of course, exactly the Turing test.) From the point of view of the person inside the room, however, Chinese is as mysterious as ever it was; more strongly, there is no way that it could ever be learnt by this means. Searle makes his argument more vivid by inviting comparisons with the situation in which the English-speaking person in the room pushes out English answers to English questions: these answers might turn out to be exactly the same as those produced in Chinese, but the processes involved would be very different. In the English case, the person understands what the questions and answers mean; in the Chinese case, she or he simply follows instructions about what to do with meaningless patterns.

The Chinese room experiment is used by Searle to illustrate his argument that if something is no more than a set of computational operations over purely formal elements (i.e. rules for combining contentless symbols), it can never reproduce the semantic component of human functioning – in this instance, the way people understand what something means. To understand Chinese, one needs more than a set of symbols and a rule book for combining them; one needs a way of linking these symbols with real objects, events, experiences or ideas – things which give them meaning. It is precisely these links, Searle is suggesting, that are missing in computer programs.

As long as the program is defined in terms of computational operations on purely formally defined elements, what the example suggests is that these by themselves have no interesting connection with understanding . . . whatever purely formal principles you put into the computer, they will not be sufficient for understanding, since a human will be able to follow the formal principles without understanding anything. (1980, p. 418)

Once again, this is making the distinction between a 'syntactic' approach to psychology, which is concerned with the rules governing mental actions, and a 'semantic' approach emphasising the content of those actions and their significance.

Searle's polemic has stimulated a large number of responses from AI workers and others. Many of these dispute what is suggested to be Searle's insistence that minds can only reside in brains; however, as Searle actually claims that minds are produced by any machines which have the same causal properties as brains, this is not quite the point. The most interesting responses are those that pick up on the issue of whether something which is essentially computational (i.e. a computer program) can ever develop a semantic dimension or, in Searle's terms, can ever possess intentionality. There are two ideas here that are most productive; the first is that Searle is looking at the wrong level in his search for intentionality; the second asserts that computer programs simulate minds when their formal properties become linked to semantic ones.

The first response to Searle is one that he considers himself in his 1980 paper, under the heading of the 'Systems Reply' to the Chinese room experiment. In that context, the reply refers to the argument that it is not the person in the room who 'understands' Chinese, but the conjunction of the person plus the rule book and the symbols. Searle demonstrates rather easily that this is an insufficient response: even if the person learnt all the rules for combining the symbols, she or he would still not understand Chinese, as the symbols would remain meaningless. But there is a more subtle version of the systems reply, which is alluded to by Dennett (1980) who, in his rejoinder to Searle, takes up the quest for consciousness which can be found in Searle's paper. Dennett suggests that Searle's

concern with the *internal* properties of control systems is a misconceived attempt to capture the interior *point of view* of a conscious agent. He does not see how any mere computer, chopping away at a formal program, could harbour such a point of view. But that is because he is looking *too deep*. It is just as mysterious if we peer into the synapse-filled jungles of the brain and wonder where consciousness is hiding. It is not at that level of description that a proper subject of consciousness will be found. (p. 430)

Consciousness is not produced by any single box in the mind; rather, it is produced out of the functioning of the whole system: it is a higher-order event that, it is true, is not located in a computer program, but it is not located anywhere else either. Searle's confusion is to mistake the project of AI by mistaking the functions of the brain. The 'purpose' of brain activity is not to produce intentionality, but to control information processing: 'what a brain is *for* is governing the right, appropriate, intelligent input–output relations, where these are deemed to be, in the end, relations between sensory inputs and behavioural outputs of some sort' (Dennett, 1980, p. 429). Intentionality, and consciousness in general, occurs in the course of brain activity of this kind. Ironically, this is rather like Searle's own notion that one does not have to explain mental functioning at all: the 'mind' is simply produced as a facet of the operations of the brain, as part of its systemic activity.

The argument that Searle is approaching AI at the wrong level is one that is connected with what Marr (1982) identifies as a long-standing confusion amongst advocates and critics of AI. This is the confusion between representations or 'algorithms', which attempt to simulate the behaviour of a human system, and what Marr calls computational *theory*, phrased to tackle questions such as 'What is the goal of the computation, why is it appropriate, and what is the logic of the strategy by which it can be carried out?' (p. 25). This looks very much like a semantic question which cannot be answered by the simulation itself, but only by reference to directing ideas linking the operations of the information processing system with something outside it – some rules, goals or intentions. If this division is accepted, then Searle's critique, it is argued, is misguided: it attacks AI for making claims that sophisticated AI workers would not make. Specifically, this response to Searle accepts his argument that functionalist approaches which concern themselves only with simulations can never produce a 'semantic' model, but goes on to assert that questions of meaning are nevertheless viable questions within the AI project.

So, for instance, Fodor (1980) agrees with Searle that intentionality derives from the semantic, rather than the functional, properties of mental representations, but refutes his notion that it is only machines with a certain kind of construction (i.e. brains) that can produce meanings. Fodor suggests that 'the idea that what counts is how the organism is connected to the world seems far more plausible' (p. 431). AI in its functionalist guise is concerned with the manipulation of symbols; a semantic dimension is added when one considers the (difficult) further question of how symbols develop semantic properties. Pylyshyn (1980) makes a similar point, more forcefully:

> Searle does not even consider the possibility that a purely formal computational model might constitute an essential part of an adequate theory, where the latter also contained an account of the system's transducers and an account of how the symbols came to acquire the role that they have in the functioning of the system. (p. 443)

A complete theory, in Pylyshyn's view, is one which provides a description of the system and its operations, but which also gives a causal account of why that system operates in the way it does – of what the system means.

> A cognitive theory claims that the system behaves in a certain way *because* certain expressions represent certain things (that is, have a certain *semantic* interpretation). (p. 443)

Functionalist AI plus a semantic account of what determines the meanings of the symbols and the purposes their combination serves, would produce a complete theory.

It is instructive to consider where this debate has led. In the earlier discussion on the nature of 'explanation' in psychology, the cognitive position was given by Johnson-Laird's (1983) idea that understanding a phenomenon is a matter of constructing a working model of it. Artificial intelligence research, which has produced a number of very powerful machines and intriguing working models of precisely the kind that Johnson-Laird is referring to, is a paradigm for all attempted explanations of that kind. Yet, even amongst some enthusiasts for the general project of AI, there is a recognition that such explanations may leave something significant out of the equation. To some extent, these workers postulate that it is the current state of AI research which is lacking, and that more sophisticated programs will overcome the problems of complex representation that make AI only a rough approximation to a psychology of consciousness. However, the more serious accusation levelled at AI work is a philosophical one, that AI is in principle an inappropriate model for human thought because it reduces the notion of 'meaning' to the question of how information becomes converted from one form to another. Specifically, the functionalist philosophy that underpins AI and that assumes that the workings of the mind are intrinsically computational (Johnson-Laird, 1983, p. 11), appears inadequate on its own to deal with questions of meaning, intention and consciousness.

Whether or not functionalism can provide *part of* the explanation of mental processes is another issue. Research in artificial intelligence has produced a number of new perceptions and conceptualisations which have enriched discussions of mental processes in very important ways. These gains have as much to do with clarifications of the limitations of the functionalist philosophy as with the programs that have been created. The programs have generated an array of hypotheses concerning the rules governing the transformation of information from one form to another, greatly improving the sophistication of psychological understanding of complex information processing procedures. However, because the AI concern is with operations enacted upon formal symbols, it has become important to clarify the relationships between mental processes and mental contents.

Although a number of different responses to critiques such as that of Searle have been proposed, there is one group of arguments that have had a clarifying impact on theories of consciousness and that also present a defence of the AI project. Paradoxically, these arguments begin with a recognition that AI, and the cognitive metaphor upon which it is based, is too limited a model of human mental function if it restricts itself to formal processes. Searle's argument that this approach reduces psychology to a study of syntax is a powerful and persuasive one; at best, the functionalist approach assumes that meanings are produced automatically by the system of formal operations, without theorising what those meanings are. However, acceptance of this aspect of Searle's argument does not necessarily involve acceptance of the position that AI can never, *in principle*, deal with questions of meaning. For some theorists, AI has demonstrated the immanence of meaning in the representational system, so displaying the possibility of location of semantic properties of mind in a material, non-mystical context. Thus, in Boden's (1987) humanistic reading AI reveals,

> in a scientifically acceptable manner, how it is possible for psychological beings to be grounded in a material world and yet be properly distinguished from 'mere matter'. Far from showing that human beings are 'nothing but machines', it confirms our insistence that we are essentially subjective creatures living through our own mental construction of reality. (p. 473)

In this reading, subjectivity is constituted by intentionality, with this intentionality being grounded in internal representational systems that are similar in kind to those modelled by computer programs. Thus, what AI demonstrates is not the exact content of human consciousness, but the necessary conditions for the existence of a consciousness with content: 'the crucial notion in understanding how subjectivity can be grounded in objective causal mechanisms is the concept of an internal model or representation' (Boden, 1987, p. 428) – something common to computers and to human beings, even if the content of these representations may differ.

This last point, concerning the constitution of mental contents, is obviously a crucial one. What is the 'meaning of meaning'? Boden herself asserts the analogical standing of computer models, in effect arguing that they do not clarify the human situation further than to show how subjectivity is possible.

> Although I have defended the practice of positing analogies between minds and machines, I have agreed that the categories of subjectivity, meaning, and purpose as currently understood can be attributed to artifacts only in a secondary sense, their justification ultimately deriving from the skill and interests of the artificer. (p. 425)

It is the human programmer who establishes the meaning of the program. However, the arguments proposed by Fodor (1980) and Pylyshyn (1980) in their responses to Searle are more specific about what it is that adds the semantic dimension to the formalism of AI. It is, for both these theorists in different ways, the links between representations and the outside world that give the representations meaning; that is, thought is about something and that something has to do with the material reality which thought symbolises. In order to model subjectivity, then, AI has to go further than functionalism; it also has to specify the significance that becomes attached to formal symbols – the way in which their inner reverberations are connected to real events and experiences in the world. This suggests that a divide will always exist between the thoughts of computers and people. Whatever similarities may exist in mental processes, mental contents will always be different because of the difference in the experiences to which computers and people are exposed; this difference is not simply one of complexity, but also of the kinds of meanings that are possible.

Thus, the issue is not one of denying the possibility of a semantic component in AI: if concepts are associated with one another and related to material events in the real world, then this means they have meaning, however limited it may be in specific cases. It is rather to ask the question, what kind of meanings are characteristic of human beings? It is here that AI does reach its limits, because the development of personal meanings – the construction of subjectivity – occurs within a human biological and social context which is not shared by computers. In other words, the 'meaning of meaning' is derived from experience; for humans this entails experience of biology, of personal relations, and of social structures. Whilst all these experiences contain 'information' in the AI sense, they are not just information; they are also productive of consciousness – they are the source of its structure and content. It is for this reason and in this way that psychoanalysis adds something to the cognitive metaphor, because it deals directly with what is specific about human subjectivity, with the human meaning of meaning.

A final point should be made here. Although AI theorists have in some cases argued that meaning resides in the relationship between representations and the outside world, in practice the functionalist concern with modelling formal processes results in a picture of the mind as something which is abstract and self-contained. This picture is an asocial one: mental processes are simply operations, the mechanics of the mind. Any influence of the social world on consciousness will always be embedded in mental contents, untheorised by functionalist AI. The effect of cognitivist theories portraying the mind as a set of computational operations on formal elements is, therefore, to produce a psychology which is separated from social processes, a psychology that suggests that it is possible to 'explain' the functioning of individuals without any reference to the actual world in which they are embedded. This is one reason why critics of reductionism often digress to attack AI as well: for however little it may be concerned with biology, AI, by eschewing meanings and purposes in its account of the mind, produces a picture of the individual as autonomous and non-social in her or his construction, and of psychology as a discipline that can operate in a social void.

## Mental contents

The contrast presented in this chapter has been between a functionalist cognitive psychology that concentrates on modelling psychological processes, and a psychoanalysis concerned with the identification and explanation of mental contents. In the previous section it was argued that the most productive area of current cognitive psychological research, artificial intelligence, demonstrates particularly clearly both the promise and limitations of the functionalist endeavour. On the one hand, AI has produced some powerful examples of the kind of cognitive rules that may be operative in human information processing, and has substantially altered conceptualisations of mental processes. On the other hand, critics of AI have argued that its functionalist stance results in a neglect of mental contents and of questions of meaning, a neglect that makes AI and, by extension, cognitive psychology, inadequate as a full model of human psychology. The problem this raises is: if there is a semantic dimension that underpins psychological processes – if meaning may be productive of function – then what kind of psychological meanings may be relevant? In other words, what are the mental contents that distinguish humans from machines? The remainder of this chapter is concerned with some possible answers to this question to be found within psychoanalytic theory.

Understanding the content of psychological events is the central task of psychoanalysis. As mentioned earlier in this chapter, the concern of psychoanalysis with explanations in terms of purpose and meaning makes it a motivational approach, dealing with the question of 'why' a person acts in a specified way – of what end the information processing serves. The problem that psychoanalysis has always wrestled with, and of which many psychologists have been aware, is that it is often very difficult to establish what these purposes and meanings are. Simply asking the person concerned (what can be called the 'phenomenological' method) produces a certain amount of information, but it is limited both in comprehensiveness and in validity. Individuals, even if they do not deliberately lie about the reasons for their actions, are often unaware of them and are probably frequently mistaken when they do guess at causes, as psychologists (e.g. Nisbett and Wilson, 1977) as well as psychoanalysts have shown. In the face of this difficulty, psychologists have tended to vacate the arena, resorting either to a causal behaviourism (behaviours are controlled by contingencies external to the person, with internal 'motives' actually being posthoc rationalisations – see Nisbett and Wilson, 1977) or to a weaker form of positivism taking observable phenomena as the only legitimate data for scientific investigation. The common result of this latter strategy is a failure to deal with internal meanings at all.

The response of psychoanalysis to the limitations of the phenomenological method is also its defining characteristic: the assumption that within each person there is a causal sphere of activity which is inaccessible to ordinary awareness and conscious control. The deterministic stance of psychoanalysis asserts that all psychic events have meaning, but these meanings are commonly unavailable to the person to whom they belong.

> Since the purpose of these purposive expressions is generally unknown to the person whose purpose they express, Freud is driven to embrace the paradox that there are in a human being purposes of which he knows nothing, involuntary purposes, or, in more technical Freudian language, 'unconscious ideas'. (Brown, 1959, p. 4)

The Freudian unconscious is presented as an explanatory concept: it is where the meanings that direct experience – the desires and purposes that *are* the semantic component of mental life – reside. Or rather, as the 'unconscious' is not itself a place, it is the state that causal ideas have within the mind. According to Freud, ideas are either conscious, preconscious or unconscious. If they are conscious, they are present in awareness; if they are preconscious, they are available to consciousness should the need for them arise. But if they are unconscious, then they are repressed – unattainable by the person concerned except under special circumstances, such as dreaming or being psychoanalysed. Conscious ideas can be, and frequently are, causal: a person may have a clear aim and may do something in order to achieve it. But where explanations in terms of conscious ideas fail, unconscious ones are relevant; and this occurs in a large number of instances because the fact of an idea being unconscious increases its power. According to Freud, unconscious ideas 'proliferate in the dark': precisely because there is no conscious control over them, unconscious desires continuously make themselves felt by pressing for fulfilment. Frequently, all that the conscious ego can do is to make the best of these urges, to try (through the operation of the defence mechanisms, which are themselves largely unconscious) to convert them into something tolerable and socially acceptable. Hence Freud's famous image of the relationship between the ego, the core of everyday conscious-ness and realistic activity, and the id, the centre of unconscious desire.

> The ego's relation to the id might be compared with that of a rider to his horse. The horse supplies the locomotive energy, while the rider has the privilege of deciding on the goal and of guiding the powerful animal's movement. But only too often there arises between the ego and the id the not precisely ideal situation of the rider being obliged to guide the horse along the path by which it itself wants to go. (Freud, 1933, pp. 109–10)

The notion that some mental processes are unconscious in a simple descriptive sense is a familiar one from areas outside of psychoanalysis (although the influence of psychoanalysis has been so great as to make completely uninfiltrated areas hard to come by). Cognitive theorists have been open to the idea that it is possible to make a distinction between the products of mental activity (which are available to consciousness) and the processes which bring them about (which are not). Johnson-Laird (1983) is once again a good guide here.

> The demarcation between what is accessible and what is inaccessible to consciousness is related to the difference between knowing *that* something is the case and knowing *how* to do something. (p. 466)

We may know that we think something, and even be able to offer some suggestions as to why we are thinking it, but we are unable to give a direct account of how it is that the thoughts arise. The reason for this is that the structures that govern the combination of mental elements are self-contained, only passing the results of their activity on to the operating system as a whole. To use an analogy employed earlier, this is like saying that one can quite happily drive a car without having any knowledge of the mechanical processes that translate one's actions into the car's actual movements. Once again, however, this is not a semantic distinction: it still says nothing about where one is going. Psychoanalysis makes greater claims for the role of the unconscious in mental life: it is seen not as a box in which the mechanics of the mind are hidden, but as a source from which meanings emanate. In this respect, it is a profoundly different concept from any cognitive 'unconscious'; it is, in fact, presented as an answer to questions that cognitive theories do not generally ask.

The Freudian unconscious is a hypothetical construct, a type of organism which is beginning to enjoy some renewed popularity within psychology. What this means is that it has no directly observable existence; rather, it is presented as a necessary concept that makes sense of material which actually is observable. The unconscious is knowable only through its effects – through the discontinuities that it inflicts on consciousness.

> [We] call a psychical process unconscious whose existence we are obliged to assume – for some such reason as we infer it from its effects – but of which we know nothing . . . In order to explain a slip of the tongue, for instance, we find ourselves obliged to assume that the intention to make a particular remark

was present in the subject. We infer it with certainty from the interference with the remark which had occurred, but the intention did not put itself through and was thus unconscious. (Freud, 1933, p. 102)

The existence of unconscious ideas is assumed because without this construct there is no way of making sense of psychic phenomena – and it is assumed that all psychic phenomena do have a sense. Thus, although the unconscious is a basic assumption in psychoanalysis, it actually depends for its rationale on a belief in psychic determinism, of the kind discussed earlier. *If* it is accepted that no psychological events are random, but that all have causes, then (given that people can very often give no, or only an incomplete, account of the reasons for their thoughts or actions) the existence of a causal unconscious follows. This is why, in the context of a determinist philosophy, the existence of unconscious causes is a necessary idea. All this assumes that the causes of psychological phenomena are *internal* rather than, for instance, being the operations of external social factors – an assumption for which Timpanaro (1976) criticises Freud and which is one source of psychoanalysis' tendency to undervalue the power of social forces.

A further characteristic of unconscious mental elements is that they are psychological entities rather than, for instance, physiological ones. Explanatory notions in psychoanalysis, there- fore, always have psychological components even when (as in Freud's own theories) they make reference to anatomical or physiological states – a perspective that contrasts with many psychological approaches, in which processes are described in psychological terms, but their origins are reductionistically assumed to be biological (e.g. biological explanations of gender differences). Freud himself was rather guarded on this point, partly due to his devotion to biological phenomena as the only genuine final causes. But in his explicit formulations on the unconscious, he maintained a view of it as a psychological realm. For one thing, it obeys a neat version of the Turing test: the evidence that one uses for postulating the existence of unconscious ideas is of the same form as that which one might use for the imputation of ordinary consciousness to other people in everyday life:

Consciousness makes each of us aware only of his own states of mind; that other people, too, possess a consciousness is an inference which we draw by analogy from their observable utterances and actions, in order to make this behaviour of theirs intelligible to us . . . Psychoanalysis demands nothing more than that we should apply this process of inference to ourselves also. (Freud, 1915, pp. 170–1)

If conscious states are psychological, then there is no reason to suppose that unconscious ones are not – just as AI theorists might call the information-processing activity of a computer 'thought' if it looks exactly like the activity of a human. In addition, suggesting that unconscious ideas are not psychological raises insuperable questions about when events become 'mental': if conscious ideas are psychological, then the elements that make them up and the structures from which they arise may also lay claim to that label. This is despite the fact that unconscious ideas obey different, freer, rules from those which are familiar from observation of consciousness: in particular, they are supposed not to labour under constraints due to embargoes on contradiction, awareness of negation, or the existence of time. Ideas may take many forms, have many kinds of contents, be combined in many different ways, and still be regarded as psychological entities; it is precisely the project of psychoanalysis to explore these variations in content and form that are endemic to the human mind.

## The meaning of meaning

Throughout this chapter, the way that psychoanalysis places causal significance on unconscious desires or purposes has been emphasised. In the quotation given previously, for instance, Freud infers from the slip of a person's tongue that there is some hidden 'intention' which is operating unconsciously. The search for meanings, for the material that fixes the content of psychological entities, thus begins to resolve into a search for underlying intentions. This highlights an important difference between the sorts of explanation that are tenable in psychological theories as opposed to the natural scientific ones which psychologists have traditionally looked to for guidance. Workers in the natural sciences conventionally avoid the use of teleological concepts, in which the cause of an event is given in terms of aims and goals. Such explanations in the context of inanimate entities are seen as having anti-materialist or vitalist tendencies. Teleological explanations of the form 'X did Y because she wanted to achieve such-and-such a thing' are, however, perfectly acceptable in everyday attempts at understanding the actions of people.

In contemporary psychology, with the exception of hard-line behaviourists and psychophysiologists (not, it must be admitted, a particularly small group), there is also considerable use of references to goals and plans as explanations of behaviours, with Miller, Galanter and Pribram's (1960) classic text continuing to be highly influential in this regard. Cognitivists and AI theorists as well as psychoanalysts are aware that among the many important ways in which humans differ from inanimate objects is the way in which their behaviour can be generated in accordance with desires and aims; that is, behaviour may be regulated according to goal-directed plans. Any psychological theory that attempts to encompass human activity must therefore employ concepts that can account for such purposes and their power. This is, of course, a corollary of Searle's (1984) comment that it is bad science to treat systems which have intentionality as if they lacked it.

The types of explanation with which psychoanalysis is concerned, then, are teleological ones, dealing with purposive mental contents: desires, wishes and intentions. In this respect, psychoanalysis as a discipline goes further than does psychology, postulating the existence of powerful internal causes which may be the unconscious generators of the plans and goals whose presence is accepted, but largely left untheorised, by psychologists. However, there is a range of psychoanalytic descriptions of what the content of these internal causes are, and from what basic elements they arise. The breadth of this range can be seen as vitiating psychoanalytic claims to knowledge of mental contents; on the other hand, it also reflects the way that the 'semantic question' is crucial for both the theory and practice of psychoanalysis.

This semantic question can be stated simply as, 'What are the meanings to which psychoanalytic explanations refer?' Freud's own view is a distinctly biological one: at the root of all mental activity are sex and aggression, manifestations of the Life and Death drives that are the central elements of Freud's later metapsychology. It is to the satisfaction of the demands made by

these drives, through their psychic representations, that human
behaviour is dedicated. The 'purpose of life', opines Freud (1930),
'is simply the programme of the pleasure principle' (p. 263); human
activity is powered by the energy of the drives as they strive for
release, the goal being to return the system to 'rest' by releasing
this energy and satisfying the drives. Because the direct realisation
in consciousness of the demands of the drives is impossible in a
social world, they become converted by the operations of the ego
and its defence mechanisms (themselves unconscious) into a wide
variety of forms, some of them acceptable (dreams, art, intellectual
activity), some of them less so (slips of tongue and pen, neuroses).
But the drives themselves, being unconscious, are eternally pushing
for fulfilment, desires without end, agitating to be heard and
satisfied. So, for Freud, an explanation of a psychological event is
one that in the end refers back to an unconscious sexual or
aggressive desire, these being the derivatives of in-built psycho-
biological structures. The meaning of symbols, the content of
mental elements, is therefore always at heart a sexual or (less
commonly) a destructive urge.

Post-Freudian theorists have proposed numerous alternative
versions of the basic semantic elements of the mind, two of which
are of particular historical and critical significance. One major
critique of Freud's biologism comes from the object relations
school of psychoanalysis, which argues that far from sex and
aggression being the motivating forces of the personality, they
are themselves produced by a deeper, social drive towards the
formation of fulfilling, intimate personal relationships (e.g.
Guntrip, 1973). Object relations theory derives its name precisely
from this founding idea: that the operation of the psyche is driven
by a desire to enter into relationships with other people or (initially)
parts of people, these being generically termed 'objects'. There
are no pre-given mental structures, according to this approach; all
there is is the infant's naturally relationship-oriented activity. The
mind itself does not exist from the start of life, but appears as a
substitute formation when the external world proves not to be
able always to perfectly meet the child's needs, leaving a space in
which desire can be created. External objects, in both their
gratifying and their frustrating form, then become represented in
an internalised way as a means of controlling the rejections
experienced in the world, and of substituting phantasised rewards

for the more elusive real ones. These internalised objects come to serve as mental structures: taken together with the desire for good object relationships they provide the bedrock on which psychological accounts can rest. Reference to a person's object relational structure, which comes to signify the internal model that she or he has of the relational world, reveals the patterns of defence, inhibition and expectation that are characteristic of that person. The *meaning* of a person's desire, however, is always at root a search for the perfect relationship.

For Kleinians, the sources of meaning are a combination of Freudian drives and of object relationships. This feat is achieved by their unique view of drives as always directed towards objects; that is, the biological 'instincts' of life and (particularly) death are inborn but, in contrast to Freud's view of the essential 'blindness' of the drives (the arbitrariness of their objects), they contain within them a direction, a goal in the form of an object of a particular kind. As in the Freudian approach, drives push towards their satisfaction, so motivation becomes a matter of establishing which major drive is asserting itself and to what degree. Usually, in Klein's theory, the dominant drive is the destructive one, operating either directly (e.g. through envy) or through the defences ranged against it (e.g. reparation). But because Klein assumes that each drive has its inherent object, the building-blocks of the psyche are more complex than is true either for Freudians or for object relations theorists. Thus, Klein hypothesises the existence of a mental life from birth, in the form of phantasy, which is the conversion of the biological drives into a psychic mode, and which also includes the coding of the desired objects. Although there is some variation in Klein's description of where these objects come from (see Greenberg and Mitchell, 1983), the dominant theory seems to be that they are inborn, as much part of the infant's biological heritage as are the drives themselves. So the 'part-objects' of early life, the breasts and penises which are reportedly the stuff of the infant's mental space, are also basic kernels of meaning. They are related to by the infant as if they were tangible, as if their internal existence had exactly the same status as objects in the external world; the earliest thoughts, from which mental life arises, are thus already infiltrated by pockets of pre-given significance. Bion, perhaps the most literally-minded exponent of the Kleinian position, conveys the feel of these early meanings in his description of what he calls 'β-elements'. β-elements represent

> the earliest matrix from which thoughts can be supposed to
> arise. It partakes of the quality of inanimate object and psychic
> object without any form of distinction between the two. Thoughts
> are things, things are thoughts, and they have personality. (Bion,
> 1963, p. 22)

In particular, according to Bion, the kind of things thoughts are
are *bodily* things; the infant's psychic life is coded in terms of her
or his experience of the body, which means it is coded primarily
in terms of feeding. Thus, the Kleinian and Bionic literature is
replete with references to incorporation, engorgement, revulsion,
evacuation. These are mental events, but in early life and in
unconscious residuals of that time they are experienced literally,
providing the templates from which all later meanings emerge.

Despite these (and other) variations and developments in
psychoanalytic conceptualisations of the basic elements of the
mind, the project of psychoanalysis in this field remains constant.
The search for the meaning of a person's experience leads
back historically to early life, and 'down' topographically to the
identification of unconscious, internally-held elements that fix the
significance of mental events. This argument represents a two-fold
critique of psychological models. First, psychoanalysts argue the
necessity of a diachronic approach to explanation: it is only
through a historical account of how meanings accrue that current
functioning can be fully understood. An organism without history –
a computer simulation, for instance – is one with only minimal
meaning. All three psychoanalytic accounts mentioned above
agree on this and on the way the meanings to be identified are
derived in some way from the interplay between biological being
and social experience – again unparalleled by the abstract models
of the cognitivists. Secondly, the synchronic analysis given by
psychoanalysts is very different from that of psychologists. Whereas
the latter restrict themselves to mapping the systemic properties
of mental activity, psychoanalysts relentlessly pursue its causal
origins. The various psychoanalytic theories all suggest that identification of the patterns of desire that underlie and govern psychic
events is the essential component of any understanding of the
activity of a person's mental 'system'. Without this, one has

description without explanation and process without cause.

The outline of primeval mental elements given above is only a partial representation of the psychoanalytic position; alongside these elements are mental processes which act on them in a structuring way. These processes are psychoanalysis' equivalent of 'software', operating on material to combine, convert and order it. Again, there have been developments in psychoanalytic concept-ualisations of the processes that characterise mental life. Freud's major distinction in this area is between 'primary' and 'secondary' processes. Interestingly, an apparently similar distinction between primary and secondary thought processes has long been respectable within cognitive psychology (e.g. Neisser, 1967). This distinction is rather different from the Freudian one, however, as it parallels the 'process–product' differentiation described earlier as defining cognitive notions of the unconscious. At most, cognitivists employ a primary–secondary process scheme to describe the difference between thought which is unordered, unmonitored by conscious-ness, irrational and often creative (primary process), and thought which is logical, well-formed, ordered and conscious (secondary process). The value of this scheme is that it allows creative and irrational aspects of mental life to be incorporated into the cognitive model. However, because of its refusal of the notion of the dynamic unconscious, primary processes remain incompletely theorised in the cognitive approach – again, described rather than explained. This makes it far less radical in its interpretation of primary processes than is psychoanalysis.

In Freud's account, primary processes are the language of the unconscious: unfettered expressions of the pleasure principle, carriers of desire, lying outside the rules of logic, allowing contradictions, associations and 'parallel processing' to occur in an unrestricted way. These processes are 'primary' in two senses: they are present in the earliest, primitive patterns of thought that characterise infant life, and they continue as the sources of the more ordered secondary processes which mark the activities of consciousness. These secondary processes are what are usually referred to as thoughts (as opposed to fantasies): they arise to make ordinary functioning in the social and material world possible, to order and integrate the chaotic rumblings of the unconscious into a manageable form. The work that is done in mental life, then, is as follows: unconscious desire produces representations in the form of primary processes, which are then converted by the operations of the ego's defence mechanisms into more manageable states, including more ordered modes of thought. Underneath, however, lies the continuing subversiveness of primary activity. Put slightly differently, this model also suggests that what psychologists investigate as 'cognitive functioning' tend to be the products of secondary processing, which is built on the experience of failure and substitution that is necessary because primary processes are unsustainable in a social world. Cognitive processes are not, therefore, basic ones; they are derivatives of unconscious desire, compromises produced by the painful realities of life.

Along with the perceptual apparatus that makes reality-testing possible, the 'operators' in the Freudian model that convert primary into secondary processes are the defence mechanisms of the ego, making mental life more manageable by synthesising and defusing it. In Klein's work, this idea is made more central: here, the fundamental mental processes *are* defence mechanisms, namely those of projection and introjection. The existence of primeval defences is made possible, in Klein's account, by the existence at birth of an inchoate and fragile ego which has the capacity to use some crude defences, particularly projective defences, to cope with the anxiety produced by the Death drive. Simply, Klein (e.g. 1957) proposes that the infant is born in danger of being overwhelmed by anxiety; to cope with this, the destructive feelings that give rise to this anxiety are, in phantasy, pushed out (projected) on to the mother (the 'object' or, initially, collection of part-objects). This procedure, with the protective splitting of good from bad feelings that goes along with it, makes the anxiety more manageable, especially if the outside object is a calm and supportive one. The infant can then, through its relationship with the mother, re-absorb (introject) the previously projected emotions, now made more manageable and coded as new internal objects. In particular, the lessening of anxiety through the mediation of the external object means that it can gradually be experienced as less threatening, so that the split good and bad feelings can be progressively integrated – an occurrence that marks the highly significant shift from what Klein calls the 'paranoid-schizoid position' to the 'depressive' position. Bion (1963) portrays this projection–introjection process in a vivid and characteristically concrete way.

Reframing the model to represent the feelings of the infant we have the following version: the infant, filled with painful lumps of faeces, guilt, fear of impending death, chunks of greed, meanness and urine, evacuates these bad objects into the breast that is not there. As it does so the good object turns the no-breast (mouth) into a breast, the faeces and urine into milk, the fears of impending death and anxiety into vitality and confidence, the greed and meanness into feelings of love and generosity, and the infant sucks its bad property, now translated into goodness, back again. (p. 31)

What Bion brings out here is the combination of internal and external processes that operates to produce the mental structure of the infant. Although, in accordance with the general Kleinian position, the urgency behind mental activity is pictured as deriving from instinctual drive processes – the destructive urge and the anxiety to which it gives rise – the social world in which the child is embedded has a crucial mediating function which in its turn is causal of the condition of the child's internal world. The mother, in her role as external object and hence as the infant's primary social environment, is charged with the task of containing the child's bad feelings (the 'bad property' of Bion's vision – faeces, guilt, etc.) and translating them into new, more tolerable mental contents. Meaning thus becomes fixed through an interaction of the pre-given internal world with the external world (the good object's response). One of the roles of the external world, not mentioned in this quotation from Bion, is that it serves a reality function: for example, it enables the infant to test out the extent to which its destructive rages really are dangerous. It is from this test that Kleinians believe ordinary thought develops: 'the origin of thought lies in testing phantasy against reality; that is, . . . thought is not only contrasted with phantasy, but based on it and derived from it' (Segal, 1964, p. 45).

Bion (1963) makes an additional significant point by reference to a more ordered mode of action (called $\alpha$-function, which has parallels with Freudian secondary processes) that is carried out on $\beta$-elements to produce thoughts: 'from the point of view of meaning, thinking depends on the successful introjection of the good breast that is originally responsible for the performance of $\alpha$-function' (pp. 31–2). Sociality thus enters into the child literally with the mother's milk: it is in the handling of these early interactions that the degree of containment possible in the world is experienced (determining the level and kind of defences that the child has to employ), and that the messages of sociality – the axes around which development becomes organised – are incorporated into the structure of the psyche. In this way, the view of Kleinians that projection and introjection are basic processes in mental life opens the way for a theory of the mind that is genuinely dialectical, in which the conflicts of the inner world are interwoven with the contradictions of the external one (see also Frosh, 1987).

The strength of these psychoanalytic accounts lies in their interweaving of meaning and process, content and rules for operating on content. Meaning, in the form of unconscious intention or desire, is primary, causing the activity of the mental system. However, process, particularly as envisaged in the Kleinian theory of projection and introjection, feeds back on these desires, carrying the messages of the environment and social world back into the individual's psyche, thus creating new meanings. The critique that this approach offers to psychology resides not only in its assertion of the centrality of the semantic dimension, reiterated throughout this chapter, but in its conceptualisation of mental processes as themselves bound up with the reproduction of subjective meanings. Information processing as conceived by cognitive psychology and illustrated in AI work, consists of formal operations on empty elements; the equivalent in psychoanalysis is a matter of content-enhancing actions on semantically-imbued particles. The criticism of psychology embodied in this difference is that, for all its formal power, it is superficial in its interrogation of mental life.

Psychoanalysis does not, however, stand as a fully formed discipline, even in this area. There are numerous criticisms that can be, and have been, made of the psychoanalytic account of meanings and of mental mechanisms. Many of these are concerned with the nature of psychoanalytic evidence, a topic that is a perennial favourite of anti-psychoanalytic psychologists (cf. Eysenck, 1985). Amongst all the attempts to test psychoanalytic theory in the laboratory, there is a substantive point at issue here. The unconscious, psychoanalysts propose, is knowable only through its effects, never directly. But these effects in consciousness – actions, thoughts, dreams – are themselves distorted by the activities of the unconscious: that is, they are produced as evidence for the existence of the thing that is taken to explain them. Archard (1984) spells out this tautology in the evidential status of the unconscious:

> it is not just that Freud's inference of the unconscious is indirect; it is that the experience or behaviour from which we infer the unconscious thought is taken to be none other than the latter's disguised representation of itself to consciousness. (p. 32)

In the absence of any direct alternative path to the unconscious, there is no way in which the theories concerning it – theories of existence, content and process – can ever be validated. This is, presumably, part of the reason why there are so many variant theories of the unconscious within psychoanalysis: there are few, if any, ways of reliably choosing between them. The theory of the unconscious, then, is precisely a theory; more rigorously, it can be thought of as a set of hypotheses providing guidance for practice and research, and supplying a narrative integrity for material which would otherwise be random and meaningless. Bion (1963) articulates well the limitations of psychoanalysis' approach from the point of view of conventional science, when he suggests that its 'description of empirical data is unsatisfactory as it is manifestly what is described in conversational English as a "theory" about what took place rather than a factual account of it' (p. 1). Such 'theories' can only be termed more or less persuasive, never verifiable, as there is no critical test which can tell them apart. Many psychoanalysts, on the other hand, would oppose this conclusion with the suggestion that in practice there are ways of checking out the validity of a statement about unconscious desires. Specifically, in the context of psychoanalytic therapy, the impact of an interpretation on the patient, her or his emotional and behavioural response, is a good test of the degree to which it is accurate (see Rustin, 1987). However, as outlined earlier, there are substantial problems with this view, both because of the subjectivity of the measurement criteria (for instance, the analyst's reading of the patient's emotional state or the degree of rapport between them) and the way the narrative stance of psychoanalysis can become part of the patient's story about her- or himself. In suspicious hands, this can be converted into the following:

> the inquisitorial technique of analysis itself – in which the 'good' patient is one who ultimately lets his resistances be overcome, and so to speak signs the confession which the analyst has pre-ordained and suggested to him – allows the moralism it has chased out of the door to come back in through the windows. (Timpanaro, 1976, p. 200)

This may or may not be a fair view; the point is that there is no way within the intellectual structures of psychoanalysis that it can ever be convincingly refuted. Under these conditions, psychoanalysts perhaps have something to learn from the more restrictive view of evidence used by many psychologists.

There are two further points of criticism that are relevant here. The psychoanalytic understanding of the nature of mental contents, particularly in its Kleinian form, is heavily inclined to treat them as things, literally 'objects' rather than as processes with a certain kind of content. This kind of thinking, as Hamilton (1984) points out, if seen in a patient would be regarded as a primitive, perhaps even 'psychotic' stance towards reality: 'When a psychoanalyst talks of "internal objects", "incorporation", "projection", "identification", "superegos", etc., he falls prey to the very thinking which he recognises in his patients as germane to their problems' (p. 246). In particular, psychoanalysis stands in danger of viewing thoughts as possessions, 'property' in Bion's terms, inscribed totally within the individual. It thus loses any vision of the social contribution to mental events, or of the significance of mental processes that cognitivists have so well established. Hamilton, integrating insights from contemporary developmental psychology and object relations theory, conveys this point well in her criticisms of Bion's work.

> The construction of meaning out of a mass of communicational signals is a very different action to that of feeding. The related infant, oriented towards communication, is engaged in the search for meaning, for pattern and predictability, from the moment that he is born. Slowly he builds up a picture out of the infinite number of signals or differences which are triggered by his own sensory and cognitive apparatus. (1984, p. 249)

The larger point here is a criticism of the tendency within Freudian and Kleinian psychoanalysis to see cognitive operations – 'knowledge' – as solely a response to the unfilfilled demands of the unconscious, rather than as a basic element of psychological functioning. Whereas psychologists prioritise intellectual over affective material to such an extent that they produce an aseptic image of a mental life without passion or content, psychoanalysts tend to downgrade cognition until, as will be described in the next two chapters, they are in danger of being left with no detailed theory of thinking at all.

Hamilton argues that knowledge cannot be explained in terms of what she calls the 'tragic vision' of Freudian and Kleinian psychoanalysis, as a response to absence, frustration and pain. Instead, she suggests, the search for meaning should be regarded as a fundamental semantic element in itself: it is simply in the nature of being human, no substitute for any other form of gratification, that we should strive to make sense of things. In line with Piagetian and other cognitive approaches, this suggests that knowing can itself be a drive, one which is directed towards relationships, to communication – to making sense of a social world. This means that it has to be theorised in its own right, and not simply as a substitute for 'deeper' fulfilments.

To be fair, both Klein and Bion acknowledge the strength of the infant's desire to understand experience. In Klein's case this 'epistemophilic impulse' (Klein, 1928) is a desire to explore the inside of the mother's body and is derived from anal-sadistic wishes to 'appropriate the contents of the womb' (p. 72), and the anxiety to which these wishes give rise. For Bion, the urge to know is more positive; however, it still has to deal with loss at every point. Waddell (1988) provides a summary contrast of the two positions:

> From his work with adults in the consulting room, Bion construed an infantile desire to reach after an experience that makes sense, that is true. There is a difference here from Klein's view, encapsulated in the respective ways of conceptualising the epistemophilic instinct. Klein thought of it as the infant's drive, fuelled by anxiety, to satisfy its curiosity, its desire, to know about the inside of the mother's body, dominated by sadism. Bion links the infant's desire for truth and his use of projective identification as a means of communication. As a consequence

maternal reverie makes available to the baby food for thought. The baby is drinking in qualities of mind, not static qualities, but one is subject both to moment by moment shifts and oscillations and, particularly in the case of the mother of a newborn, to periods of depression, of anxiety, of gaps in involvement. (Waddell, 1988, p. 327)

The impulse to know is thus still part of the 'tragic vision' mentioned by Hamilton. However, where Waddell's account does refute that of Hamilton is in its articulation of the relative fluidity of Bion's vision of what it is that the child incorporates – the literal fluidity of the mother's milk but also the metaphorical fluidity of thoughts and 'qualities of mind'. The intensity of the infant's early social encounters is, in these theories, built around anxiety and loss, but it also introduces the child to knowledge, meaning and truth.

The last point to make here reiterates a criticism made of the AI information-processing approach. Despite the potentiality for introducing a social dimension into its developmental theory, psychoanalysis tends to account for actions and experiences largely in terms of internal events, in the end resolving into basic unconscious desires. Its explanatory notions are always complex and sophisticated, yet rarely enough so to incorporate the power of social forces into its frame of reference. In fact, it may even be that psychoanalytic explanations are sometimes *too* complex, ignoring the impact of more immediate causes in the person's actual environment. Timpanaro (1976) provides a number of examples of how this tendency is evident in Freud's work on parapraxes; his more general argument is that psychoanalysis obscures the operations of material forces such as social class, in favour of a mythological idealism that is realisable only by appeal to underlying motives of a solely psychological kind.

We have seen this hypertrophy of psychologism corresponds on the one hand to a refusal to acknowledge the class division of society and the unhappiness it produces, and on the other to a dissociation of psychology from neurophysiology (and thus to an at least potential anti-materialism). We may now conclude that the sophisms and forced interpretations which we initially characterised as generically anti-scientific can themselves be said to form (if only indirectly) the 'ideological' limit of psychoanalysis. (p. 179)

When it accepts as an explanation only what goes on in the unconscious, psychoanalysis becomes as individualistic and asocial as cognitive theory. Both approaches then produce accounts of personal experience that are compartmentalised and isolationist, having no space for causal processes that extend further than one person's mind. In its account of how the mind is formed, psychoanalysis makes room for interpersonal events which are at least microsocial; but in its explanations of why a person is behaving in a particular way, or undergoing a particular experience, this social vision is all too often thrown away.

**Conclusion**

This chapter has been a long tour through the principles of explanation that underlie influential psychological and psycho-analytic models of the mind. Both approaches have something to offer, the former in its descriptions of the computational operations that combine mental elements to make cognition possible; the latter by uncovering the semantic elements that give these processes meaning. On the other hand, it has been argued that the cognitive neglect of 'why' questions limits the power of the theories it can generate, in particular leading to an over-simplification of issues surrounding consciousness and personal meanings. Psychoanalysis, whatever the arbitrariness of many of its proposals, at least asks important questions here: where do specifically human meanings come from, how do they arise, how do the symbols that are 'processed' as information become significant and what is it that they signify? These are questions that any complete theory of psychological functioning needs to address itself to, for without them a model can only deal with the empty play of clever procedures on abstract, content-less elements.

Finally, both approaches have substantial difficulties with the incorporation of social forces into their causal models. For AI theorists, sociality lies outside their immediate concerns; for psychoanalysts it seems to be regarded as either only marginally of interest, or as epiphenomenal – it is what one makes of society

that is seen as important, and this leads back again to the unconscious. Both these positions are ideologically limiting, because they
present portraits of the mind which suggest that mental phenomena
are completely separate from social ones, that individuals exist
in a kind of vacuum, which they gradually learn to fill. As the
discussions in subsequent chapters will attempt to make clear, this
is far from being the case: just as a complete theory of the mind
requires a dimension that deals with internal meanings, so it must
also find a place for the causal impacts made on every individual
by the social world.

# 2 The Internal History of the Child

Understanding children is a critical task for psychoanalysis, because of its assumption that the mental structures that direct a person's functioning are formed through the experiences of early childhood. Understanding these experiences and the manner in which they have an impact is, therefore, the only way to provide a complete explanation of the functioning of any individual, whether child or adult; it is also crucial for the therapeutic practice of psychoanalysis. More generally, psychoanalysis suggests that the history of a mental process is always preserved and has a continuing effect: childhood forms of things are not lost or transformed, but take their place as permanent building blocks in a final structure. As such, they exert a determining influence over behaviour throughout life, sometimes (as in regression) subverting conventional adult modes of action to reveal in an immediate way the existence of a 'child within'. Thus, comprehending childhood and the processes of change that take place over the childhood years is essential to understanding any mental process at all; the past is always present in the here and now.

In the case of psychology, the position is more complex, as many psychologists are not concerned with the origins of the phenomena which they are studying. To some extent, this means that psychology can function without a developmental theory; an account of a mental or behavioural process may need to be no more than a description of the immediate precursors or consequences of that process, or of its underlying machinery. Importantly, whereas psychoanalysts tend to believe that it is possible to discern the legacy of childhood in the adult, psychologists generally argue that adulthood in general and, specifically, mature psychological processes are transformed states, explicable

63

in their own terms rather than in terms of how they have come about. Development may be necessary for a process to reach its observed condition, but because development changes things, one cannot necessarily read the past in the present, nor explain current functioning in historical terms.

In this view, it is only because psychology claims to be a general discipline, encompassing all that is important about mental and behavioural life, that it needs for the sake of completeness to create a sub-speciality of developmental psychology. However, the work of developmentalists cannot be written off as peripheral to psychology. At a minimum, although psychology does not stand or fall as a product of the adequacy of its developmental theory (as psychoanalysis to a large extent does), all developmental psychologists are concerned with supplying a convincing charting of the journey from infancy to adult life. There is also an important body of thought within psychology which, like psychoanalysis, argues that understanding the way something comes about – for example, the way children learn language or form attachments – does increase understanding of the thing itself. This is seen particularly clearly in the work of Piaget, but is also present in much other work in areas such as socialisation and personality. In addition, the approaches of developmentalists often throw light on important issues in psychology in general. What developmental psychologists have to say about the nature of childhood is therefore significant for the discipline as a whole, either because it provides a commentary on the psychology of adulthood, or because it shares in and exemplifies tendencies that are present in all psychological investigations – or for both of these reasons.

In this chapter, the approach taken by developmental psychologists to some elements of development in early childhood is examined with the aid of concepts taken from psychoanalysis. This may seem an unusual way of proceeding, especially since it reverses the direction of influence characterising much recent work, in which the observational and empirical data of psychologists has been used to inform psychoanalytic theory (e.g. Lichtenberg, 1983). The approach adopted here, however, has more to do with the foci of study of psychology and psychoanalysis, in particular with their relatively non-overlapping interests – a curious phenomenon given both disciplines' claims to completeness. Neither psychology nor psychoanalysis provides a wholly rounded account of development, something which would require a full description both of the development of conscious activity (skills, thoughts, communication, behaviours, etc.) and subjectivity. On the whole, psychology has concentrated on the former, for instance providing insights into how children's cognitive abilities develop over time, or how they become 'socialised' to behave in ways that are recognised and approved of by their community. Psychoanalysis, on the other hand, has been concerned with the make-up of the child's phenomenal world – the internal structures that determine how reality is experienced and represented in the context of a gradually developing 'self'.

There have been many examples of interpenetration of the two disciplines, perhaps more than in any of the other areas discussed in this book (see, for example, Urwin's (1986) account of the influence of Freud on Piaget's early work). In particular, Freud's 'stage' theory of emotional development has been used by many psychologists either as a basis for their own theorising, or as a starting point for empirical studies. More recently, as mentioned above, some psychoanalysts have attempted to integrate their understanding of children's inner life with the observational methods and findings of developmental psychology; some of this work will be discussed towards the end of this chapter. But there are clear contradictions between the two approaches. On the one hand, the empirical stance of developmental psychology interrogates the methods of psychoanalysts. How can one read from what is observable to what is subjective and hidden – a problem which plagues psychoanalytic methodology in all fields, but even more cogently when the object of study is an infant who cannot clearly express his or her thoughts? In addition, the detailed attention that psychologists have paid to the complexities of cognitive development calls into question some of the grosser psychoanalytic assumptions concerning infants' capabilities. On the other hand, the insights of psychoanalysis into what is happening within a child subverts much of psychology in a number of ways. For instance, it offers a critique of psychology's neglect of emotional development; it is a characteristic of psychological theories that emotion is made secondary, following on from cognition or – at most – operating to speed up or slow down the effective operation of cognitive processes. For psychoanalysis, emotion is central, explaining and directing development. Only one of the disciplines can be right on this.

A second way in which psychoanalysis subverts developmental psychology is more general. Psychology characteristically takes as its starting point an image of the infant as a relatively coherent subject, in the sense of possessing psychological attributes and boundaries which identify her or him as an individual, with a self that exists from birth even if it is not fully formed. At the centre of this infant is a core of rationality which may be taken to define the child as human – an idea which is also present in other branches of psychological theory, in particular 'abnormal psychology', where loss of rationality is what defines psychopathology (see Banton *et al.*, 1985). Development is consequently viewed as a process by which an infant with a rational core but mistaken or confused ideas or ways of behaving (cognitive and socialisation theories respectively) gradually learns about the realities of the world, both physical and social, refining her or his consciousness and abilities on the way.

Psychoanalysis radically opposes this position. It is based on the premise that irrationality is central to human functioning, and that this irrationality is present in childhood and continues virtually unchanged throughout life. The attributes that psychologists take as their object of study are seen by psychoanalysts as relatively fragile achievements always struggling for survival in the face of unconscious desires. Even more fundamentally, psychoanalysis takes hold of the 'given' in psychology – the infant's core self – and analyses or de-constructs it, showing how it comes about and, in some theories (e.g. that of Lacan) how empty and fictitious it is. Thus, psychoanalysis not only questions psychology's findings and its choice of categories for study; it also offers a critique of the basis of psychology's vision of development. Psychoanalysis says: subjectivity develops from confused and amorphous beginnings to a confused and conflictful end; at no point can either rationality or selfhood be assumed.

This is the element in psychoanalysis that presents the most powerful challenge to developmental psychology. In what follows, the psychoanalytic vision is described in general terms to uncover its critical stance; socialisation and Piagetian theory is then examined in the light of these ideas, opening the way for a discussion of language development in Chapter 3.

## The psychoanalytic method

Psychoanalysis has developed a particular vision of how experiences in childhood are crucial for the rest of life, suggesting that they are formative of later psychic structures and that they remain present in these later structures in a relatively unaltered form. In this version of the child as 'father to the man' (in Freud's theory, 'mother to the woman' receives little space), it is through exploration of the desires and subjective formulations of childhood that an understanding of basic psychological processes can be developed. Hence the significance of Freud's (1905) *Three Essays on the Theory of Sexuality*: with the first outline of the possibility of infantile sexuality, Freud promulgated the law of infant determinism, that what happens to us early in life is what constructs our nature for all time. 'What happens to us', in this sense, is a mixture of two things: the activities of pre-given drives towards sex and (in the later version of the theory) aggression, and the impact of the relational world in which the child is embedded, the world of human objects and of the Oedipus complex.

Given the centrality of childhood experience for psychoanalytic theory, it is embarrassing to discover the turmoil in which psychoanalysts are still engaged over the issue of how the mind of the child is to be understood. The problem is both specific and general: specifically, that psychoanalysts disagree amongst themselves on the nature of the infant's subjective world; generally, that there can be no certain conclusions when there is no direct access to the contents of anybody's (adult or child) mind. This general difficulty has produced a number of fundamental disagreements, for instance concerning the nature of a child's mental contents (see Chapter 1), the speed and (to a lesser extent) the order with which developmental changes occur, and the degree to which pre-verbal children can be said to have a complex subjective life, particularly a complex fantasy life, at all.

The last of these related points has been a major area of dispute between Freudians and Kleinians since the 'Great Debates' of the 1940s; the position on infantile 'phantasies' still differentiates these two schools and also provides fertile ground for passionate idiosyncrasy amongst non-aligned analysts. The problem is one with which psychologists have taxed psychoanalysts for decades: how, methodologically, can one move from what one observes a child do (let alone, what one hears an adult *say* about her or his childhood) to what is actually happening inside the mind of the child – especially if this is hypothesised to be unconscious? Stern's (1985) comment, from a psychoanalyst wedded to the use of the observational techniques of developmental psychology, is a hostage to fortune relying on the benign neglect of predatory 'scientific' psychologists:

> Because we cannot know the subjective world that infants inhabit, we must invent it, so as to have a starting place for hypothesis-making. (p. 4)

It is, perhaps, the kind of 'invention' which psychoanalysts employ that the psychologist Schaffer (1984) has partially in mind in the following stricture. Welcoming the readiness of post-behaviourist developmentalists to take into account intrapsychic phenomena such as representations and intentions, he nevertheless laments,

> that the pendulum appears sometimes to be swinging to the opposite extreme – from a refusal to recognise anything but overt response patterns to the endowment of quite immature infants with highly sophisticated mental processes that would enable them to participate in the most intricate social exchanges on more or less equal terms. Thus infants from the early weeks on have been attributed with feelings of shared understanding, theories of mind, notions of intersubjectivity, communicative intentions and cooperative endeavours, with little attempt made to justify these concepts on the basis of unambiguous empirical observations. (p. vi)

To Schaffer, such attributions are 'flights of fantasy', obscuring the difficult task of providing a description of how these sophisticated abilities actually develop. Ironically, much the same thing would be said by Freudians attacking the Kleinian account of the existence of phantasy and projective defences in the new-born baby: that they are assuming too advanced a set of mental capacities in what is actually an inchoate and primitive being. But the problem is left unresolved by the polemic, whether it derives from Schaffer or from Freudians: how can one *ever* know ('on the basis of unambiguous empirical observations') what is occurring subjectively inside a child, or even inside oneself, given the activities of self-deceiving, unconscious processes?

Psychoanalysts have conventionally answered this question in a number of ways, of which two are relevant to this discussion. First, they have taken the stories of adult analysands, identified distorted or apparently immature patterns of relating and emotion, and linked these with postulated childhood experiences. In doing this, there is usually an assumption that what is being re-activated in analysis (worked through 'in the transference') is the childish feeling itself – for instance, love or hatred for a parent, or fantasies about birth, abandonment or castration. Feelings are literally being transferred from their childish context into the analytic encounter, where they are exposed, analysed and put in their proper place. In the course of this procedure, the analyst is given insights into the workings of the mind of the *child* as well as of the adult patient. This was Freud's approach: with the exception of the second-hand analysis of Little Hans and the observations of the 'fort-da game' reported in *Beyond the Pleasure Principle*, all his developmental theorising was derived from the recollections of adults. These recollections were not just active memories, but also appeared as the resurgence of patterns of fantasy, relating and emotion that Freud took to be characteristic of the childish mind.

There have been a number of consequences of this adult-centred approach to the study of childhood, many of them unfortunate. Peterfreund (1978), for example, identifies 'two fundamental conceptual fallacies, especially characteristic of psychoanalytic thought: the adultomorphism of infancy and the tendency to characterise early states of normal development in terms of hypotheses about later states of psychopathology' (p. 427). The former criticism, adultomorphism, has been applied particularly to the use of the term 'sexuality' to apply to young children's sensual experiences. For example, Jackson (1982), who devotes her book to an exploration of the development of sexuality throughout childhood, nevertheless regards the Freudian scheme as an over-extension of the term 'sex' taken from an adult perspective.

The mistake here is in classifying behaviour according to its external character rather than its subjective meaning. It is quite possible, using the former strategy, to lump together every kind

of sensual pleasure, but it is misleading to call them all sexual
. . . It is surely more logical, though, to view sex as one form
of pleasure rather than all pleasure as sexual. (pp. 72–3)

Leaving aside the unusual criticism of psychoanalysis as too
behaviouristic, this is a powerful argument: it is from the perspective of an adult view of the sexual meaning of sensual activity that
the naming of infantile 'sexuality' derives. This leads to a set of
assumptions about development which then become fixed as
the Freudian theory of psychosexual stages, without any direct
evidence of the subjective meanings that *children* place on their
experience. On the other hand, the strength of the Freudian
position is that it offers an account of continuities in development
which approaches such as Jackson's have difficulty in dealing with.
Looking back from adulthood, one has to ask where sexuality
comes from. Either it is completely inborn, perhaps programmed
to materialise at puberty in a pre-fabricated way, or it is constructed
in the course of development. The essentialist, heterosexist first
option is one rejected by most forms of psychoanalysis, including
traditional Freudianism; although a sexual drive is postulated,
sexuality as a complex of fantasy, desire and social behaviour is
something that only gradually takes shape. If this is so (as Jackson,
for one, seems to agree), then at what point do the originating
activities which grow into adult sexuality become 'sexual'
themselves – in adolescence, in the masturbatory play of childhood,
in the apparently pleasure-evoking sucking of the infant? What
Freud's characterisation of infantile sexuality very effectively
achieves is an account of sexuality which is continuous and that
links all its components without making any assumptions about its
eventual form. Conventional genital heterosexuality, for instance,
is not seen as the only model of sexuality, but as an outcome of a
number of factors, many of them conventionally 'perverse' in
themselves. Certainly the notion of sexuality is widened in the
process, but this at least has the effect of removing the most
pernicious ideological elements from discussions of what constitutes
'healthy' sexuality. Thus, although there is force in the criticism
that the experiences of children are being labelled in adult
terms when they may mean something different to the children
themselves, as a basis for a developmental theory the adultomorphism of the psychoanalytic approach is not without value.

The second 'conceptual fallacy' identified by Peterfreund is the tendency of psychoanalysts, absorbed in the unravelling of psychopathology in their adult patients, to describe the periods of childhood in terms of fixation points for adult dysfunction. Once again, the strength of this approach is that it supplies a continuous account of development: psychopathology is not something appearing *de novo* at a certain point in time, but it is potentiality within each one of us, first expressed during an appropriate period in childhood. Unfortunately, in practice what psychoanalysis has often produced is a normative reading of childhood in terms of a number of problematic issues which have to be dealt with at particular times in specifiable ways, if they are not to produce disturbances later on. This is normative because it easily slips into formulations that make only certain kinds of narrowly-defined experiences acceptable, a slippage that has fuelled the not inconsiderable psychoanalytic contribution to sexist and racist elements in the professional literature. It is one thing uncovering the childhood roots of adult difficulties, quite another to propose that certain events at a particular time will always produce pathology later. To the extent that this area has been investigated empirically, for instance by longitudinal studies, little support has been produced for the idea that the stages of childhood can best be thought of in terms borrowed from pathology.

It therefore seems likely that a relative predominance of proto-clinical issues in a particular age period is illusory and emerges from theoretical, methodological or clinical needs and biases in conjunction with cultural processes . . . There are no convincing grounds, from the observational point of view, for considering basic clinical issues as adequate overall definers of phases or stages of development. (Stern, 1985, p. 23)

The second relevant way in which psychoanalysts have attempted to develop a picture of the internal world of the child is through direct observation of children themselves, either in the context of 'infant observation' studies where the analyst (usually a trainee) attempts to make sense of detailed accounts of what young children do, or in the context of child analysis. In the former approach, the analyst records, in an unstructured way, everything that the child does during a certain period of time. These observations are

collected on a regular basis, including both periods in which the
child is alone and times when she or he is in interaction with
others – almost always, given the usual arrangements for infant
observation, the child's mother. The observer is expected to
endeavour to remain distant from what is going on, but it is
recognised that she or he will have emotional responses to the
child's actions; these responses are also to be recorded, as it is
thought that they may reveal something significant about the
emotional state of both observer and child.

There is no doubting that the conventional infant observation
programme, in which an observer watches the same child for a
number of months or years, is an extremely useful training
procedure, encouraging trainees to explore their feelings about
young children and to attempt to integrate what they are seeing
with psychoanalytic theories of child development and with adult
psychodynamic processes. It also offers a useful training ground
in 'counter-transference' in an extended sense. As noted above,
there is no direct way of gaining access to a young child's subjective
world; instead, one has to speculate on what internal states might
lie behind the expression of an externally observable behaviour.
One tool for this, which is used extensively in the analytic
encounter, is to explore the feelings that the child's behaviour
brings up in oneself, on the grounds that these feelings can
represent an unconscious communication of the child's subjective
state (see the discussions of counter-transference in Sandler, Dare
and Holder, 1973, and in Langs, 1976). It is this sort of emotional
understanding that differentiates the psychoanalytic approach to
observation from that espoused by developmental psychologists.

> It is a method with no claims to impartiality or objectivity.
> Rather the reverse, it is one rooted in subjectivity of a particular
> kind – with the capacity to look inward and outward simul-
> taneously . . . ; one that struggles to prevent observation being
> clouded and distorted through preconception. It is a method
> which requires the observer to be as minutely cognisant of his
> or her internal processes as of those of the subject of observation.
> (Waddell, 1988, pp. 313–14)

In place of psychology's emphasis on removing subjective influences on experimentation and observation, psychoanalysts (at least

those in the Kleinian tradition) augment their subjective responses as a way of attempting to calibrate the unfolding subjectivity of the child. This is no free and easy procedure, however; it requires an honest awareness of one's own state of mind and predilections for particular feelings, as well as a capacity to concentrate on both child and self at one and the same time. The unconscious of the observer is held to respond to the unconscious of the child in the same way as the unconscious of the analyst responds to that of the patient – a response which is difficult to observe and understand, but which can also, it is thought, be a more accurate record of subjective states than any other measure.

Whatever the considerable virtues of infant observations of this kind for the training of analysts, however, it is an approach fraught with immense difficulties if one is attempting to produce an 'objective' account of the child's subjectivity that could be accepted by all impartial observers. First, the unstructured nature of the observations is a recipe for unreliability of the simple psychometric kind: in believing that one is recording everything, one is always selecting, usually in accordance with pre-given, perhaps unconscious, biases. Without a structured format and rigorous training, observers may see what they want or expect to see. Secondly, the use of the observer's feelings as an observational technique is even worse from a psychometric point of view: even if the observer is honest about what she or he feels and when (by no means a foregone conclusion), there is no knowing what these feelings are caused by, let alone whether they are really registering what is occurring inside the child. At best, they are adult readings of children's emotions.

Finally, the unreliability of this way of studying the child is accentuated and illustrated by differences within the psychoanalytic movement over how children's behaviour should be interpreted; not surprisingly, analysts who have undergone a Kleinian training tend to see rather different things from those who have undergone a Freudian one. An interesting and rare documentary light on this is shown in the occasional published comparisons of different readings of infant behaviour (see, for example, 'Clinical Commentary VI', 1986); there are certainly overlaps in interpretation, but there are differences too, with both the overlaps and differences relating to agreement or disagreement on aspects of psychoanalytic theory.

Infant observations of the psychoanalytic kind, then, acutely reveal the central dilemma of this work. In order to move from the level of observations to that of theorising about a child's inner world, one has to interpret observational data as if one were in the child's shoes, that is, one has to interpret it subjectively. However many controls are placed around this procedure, by its very nature it introduces unreliability into the investigation, thus weakening the confidence with which one can derive conclusions from the data. No wonder, perhaps, that psychologists, obsessed with the scientificity of their work, have steered clear of investigations of subjectivity. In fact, awareness of the difficulties of observational procedures is one source of the contemporary interest amongst psychoanalysts in the more refined methodology of developmental psychology (see Lichtenberg, 1983); however, the problem of moving from the observational to the subjective level remains.

The other direct psychoanalytic source of information on children is that of child analysis. In this procedure, children are seen intensively for individual psychotherapy over a prolonged period of time; the main method of work is through a mixture of play, conversations and verbal interpretations, with the paraphernalia of psychoanalytic psychotherapy used with adults being mimicked as far as possible with the less verbal, less controllable child. Thus, the child's free play with toys is taken to have a similar status to that of verbal free association in adults; the analyst looks for strong emotions, idiosyncracies and irrationalities, as well as symbolic expressions of wishes and desires, and interprets them in the context of the transference – the special relationship formed between child and analyst, which is thought to reflect the child's relationships in the outside world. Once again, there are tremendous problems in evaluating the reliability and validity of any inferences which the analyst might make about the child's subjective experience. As with the infant observation procedure, there is no attempt at psychometric structuring of the observations. In addition, the involvement of the analyst in an intense relationship with the child, the use of interpretations (which might be construed by the unsympathetic as suggestions), and the therapeutic context, all make this 'observational procedure' extremely reactive, in the sense that it is likely to create the data which its theoretical premises predicts. At the very least, this kind of situation always leaves open the possibility that a child's behaviour may be accounted for by alternative explanations to those presented by the analyst. On the other hand, long-lasting and intense relationships of the kinds that form between child and analyst – especially if the analyst is an experienced one who has seen many children in the same context – may be the only possible basis upon which to make informed guesses about what a child might be feeling. It is, after all, what people generally do with one another in an unreliable but not always totally inaccurate way: we get to know each other, listen to or observe one another, and construct our relationships as if we have some knowledge of what the other is feeling, of what means 'yes' or indicates 'no'. Psychoanalysis is an unreliable method of developing theories of child development; there can be little doubt of that. But it is not necessarily invalid. It may be that the intensity of contact with children that the analytic situation prescribes, and the emotional literacy developed by good analysts through their training and experience, creates better conditions than those available to empirical psychologists for the construction of narratives that accurately describe children's inner lives.

## The psychoanalytic child

On child development, as on other topics in psychoanalysis, post-Freudian analysts vary considerably in the extent to which they maintain allegiance to Freud's original concepts, and in the bases for their own accounts. What is shared, however, is an interest in the unfolding subjectivity of the child, and a belief that it is this that provides the motor for development and determines its course. It is not just that inclusion of 'emotion' is necessary for a complete picture of child development, but that the child's affective experiences – in particular, those which dictate the organisation of unconscious phenomena – are the central features of her or his existence. Without consideration of these experiences, psychoanalysis suggests, there are no grounds for any theory of motivation or for explanations of the course that development takes. In this section, some of the main strands of psychoanalytic developmental thinking on the question of how subjectivity is formed are presented; the aim is to use this material to identify criteria by means of which the adequacy of developmental psychology's approach can be judged.

Freud's description of child development is couched in two distinct theoretical frameworks, one linked to the theory of drives and the other to a more 'object-relational' approach epitomised by the concept of the Oedipus complex (see Greenberg and Mitchell, 1983). The two frameworks intertwine, but have given rise to competing approaches in the post-Freudian literature, with Freudians and ego psychologists tending to employ the drive model while Kleinians and object relations theorists have emphasised the importance of the relational stance (see Frosh, 1987, chapters 4 and 5). For the purposes of this discussion, it is only necessary to describe the basic approaches characterising these different schools of thought, to provide a critical context for the discussion of developmental psychology.

In essence, the drive model locates the source of development in certain biological urges, notably those of the sexual instinct. The aim of these urges, or drives, is to achieve satisfaction through the release of energy; the history of the child is then one of organising and re-organising these drives around various parts of the body ('erotogenic zones' – oral, anal, phallic and genital) and through attachments to various 'auto-erotic' and, later, external objects, such as the infant's own thumb, the mother's breast or the mother herself. The basic drive, the child's gradual physical maturing, sensual experiences (generally occurring in the context of feeding or toiletting), and social relationships all intertwine to produce a series of re-organisations of sexuality until it eventually shapes into an adult form. In Freud's approach, the object-relational model coalesces with the drive theory at the point of the Oedipus complex, when the previously unbridled sexual impulses of the child are turned forcefully towards mother as primary love-object (in the case of the boy), only to encounter the threat and power of the father, who is the symbolic embodiment of the law forbidding incest. Thus, the impersonal and mainly narcissistic activity of the sexual drive takes its place in a social world, regulated and constructed by the realities of interpersonal relationships.

This drive and object-relational account of development concentrates on the organisation of sexuality as the child matures and encounters the demands of the social world. In itself, however, it does not describe how this process is experienced by the child – what the subjective marking of the developmental process is. Freud does not, in fact, focus particularly on this issue, preferring to concentrate more on the mechanics of the developmental procedure and its links with adult forms of sexuality, than on its experiential component. There are, nevertheless, some striking exceptions to this orientation, for example in the 1908 paper *On the Sexual Theories of Children*, which is a compelling account of children's struggles to comprehend sexuality. This paper, rather like later work by Piaget, investigates children's false readings of the world; unlike Piaget, the explanations given for these false readings are not just limitations on children's experiences and cognitive capacities, but more importantly are disturbing anxieties and desires. Thus, the boy's enjoyment of his penis and fear of castration leads him to attribute the possession of a penis to all people, male and female; this makes it impossible for him to discover the true way in which babies are born, leading on to the characteristic theory that 'The baby must be evacuated like a piece of excrement, like a stool' and to the idea that 'a man can give birth just as well as a woman' (p. 197). It is not just faulty cognitive constructs that can be seen in operation here, for these are to a considerable extent produced by the child's wishes and emotions.

The allocation of a causal role to the child's emotional life, and especially to unconscious emotions, is part of Freud's attempt to explain how from a chaotic mass of biological drives there arises a complex psychological being, with a sophisticated consciousness and an underworld of passion and desire. In many respects (and this is an idea formulated with most power by Klein), the driving force behind this achievement is that of anxiety. At least in Freud's later theory, it is assumed that the cause of repression and of other psychological defences is anxiety, which is in essence the experience of threat to the ego, the area of our ordinary consciousness and 'selfhood'. Anxiety of this kind derives from many events and sources: birth, separation from the mother, fear of castration, social anxiety, death (Freud, 1926, p. 297). It is also produced automatically by the exigencies of life in the social world, as the potentially destructive aspects of the sexual and aggressive drives are constrained by the operations of reality (see Frosh, 1987, chapter 2). The result of these losses and limitations is that the ego is formed as an amalgam of internalisations of lost objects, while the super-ego comes about in the aftermath of the Oedipus complex, as a massive introjection of the power of the father (Freud, 1923). Defence mechanisms operate unconsciously, but within the province of the ego, to provide protection against the clamourings of unconscious impulses; the individual's subjective space is organised and controlled by what it is possible and acceptable to desire. So behind everything – what one can allow oneself to think, know, fantasise and do – lie the operations of anxiety and of what is usually called emotion.

An important elaboration of the traditional Freudian account of development comes from Anna Freud, who in many ways is the most orthodox of post-Freudian psychoanalysts. She consistently maintains the significance of the balance between internal drives and external realities, leading her to focus on the unfolding of ego functions in relation to drive stages as a crucial development issue. It is this developing relationship between ego and id, she suggests, that has been relatively neglected in Freudian theory. Traditional psychoanalysis lays down the developmental sequences 'only with regard to particular, circumscribed parts of the child's personality' – the sequence of libidinal phases and the associations with each of these that is shown by various expressions of the aggressive drive (A. Freud, 1966, p. 59). In fact, 'with regard to the aggressive drive we are already less precise and are usually content to correlate specific aggressive expressions with specific libidinal phases' (ibid.), something which suggests a less than whole-hearted adherence to the dual-drive model. With regard to the ego, 'the analytically known stages and levels of the sense of reality, in the chronology of defence activity and in the growth of a moral sense, lay down a norm' (ibid.). However, this study of the various aspects of id or ego development is insufficient for a full understanding of the paths which a child takes to maturity. A more holistic scheme is required:

> Without doubt we need more for our assessments than these selected developmental scales which are valid for isolated parts of the child's personality only, not for its totality. What we are looking for are the basic interactions between id and ego and their various developmental levels, and also age-related sequences of them which, in importance, frequency, and regu-

larity are comparable to the maturational sequence of libidinal stages or the gradual unfolding of ego functions. (A. Freud, 1966, p. 59)

Thinking of child development in terms of 'basic interactions between id and ego' produces the concept of developmental lines: sequences in which particular aspects of personality gradually unfold, always from a position of relative dominance by the id to relative control by the ego. Thus, even though numerous different developmental lines can be described (for instance, from infantile sucking to organised eating, from wetting and soiling to bladder and bowel control, or from erotic play to work) they all follow the same path.

> In every instance they trace the child's gradual outgrowing of dependent, irrational, id- and object-determined attitudes to an increasing ego mastery of his internal and external world. (A. Freud, 1966, p. 60)

Interestingly, the developmental line Anna Freud presents as a prototype for others is 'From dependency to emotional self-reliance and adult object relations'. This describes how the child moves from a complete narcissistic identity with the mother through gradual experiences of separation and frustration, culminating in the Oedipus complex, the latency period interest in people outside the family and, later, adolescent struggles around assertive independence.

Anna Freud's notion of developmental lines is an important addition to the psychoanalytic vocabulary. Descriptively, its assumption of continuities in development moves the theory away from the traditional Freudian concentration on fixations and regressions – that is, it is not so reliant on the idea that there is an undiluted retention of the past in everything that happens throughout life. Regressions do occur in this approach; in fact, they are predictable consequences of stress. But, more significantly, developmental lines are cumulative processes: at every point in her or his development, the child is shifting along a graduated course, each step produced by past steps and by the current state of the drives and of the environment. This approach has considerable practical attractions, for instance making it possible to offer guidance on particular children's developmental problems. Theoretically, it also presents a fuller psychological account of development than is possible from the pathology- and drive-oriented version of Freud. However, the theory also has drawbacks. Characteristically for ego psychology, Anna Freud's notion of developmental lines contains normative elements, in that the appropriate direction for development is towards greater ego strength, more successful 'adaptation', in Hartmann's (1959) terms. This contributes to the sequential logic of the approach, but at the price of neglecting the continuing irrationalities of mental life. It also reduces the acuteness of the account of subjectivity; that is, while Anna Freud is extremely clear in suggesting how a child's understanding of events might be determined by her or his position on relevant developmental lines, she is less attuned to the unconscious factors which, other psychoanalysts suggest, continually disrupt even achieved positions, Anna Freudians downgrade the possibilities of infantile mentation and subjective experience as part of a wider argument for the relative importance of ego activities. Their psychoanalysis is, in its emphasis on cognitive development and on adaptation, akin to conventional developmental psychology: it certainly has more space for emotion than the latter, but it is concerned primarily with normative stages, with prediction, and with remediation of blocks to progress. This gives it practical utility, but reduces its critical force.

There are numerous alternative formulations of development that contribute significantly to the psychoanalytic picture of the child and that clarify the comparison with developmental psychology. The work of Margaret Mahler, for example (e.g. Mahler *et al.*, 1975), has its roots in the ego psychology of Hartmann, but constructs a version of development centred around a process of 'separation-individuation' that prioritises the positioning of the child in relationships with others. Mahler's description of the various stages through which development occurs is one of the most detailed in all of psychoanalysis.

According to this theory, the infant's first few weeks are spent in a state of 'normal autism', in which she or he is impervious to the external world. This is followed by a 'symbiotic' phase in which the child experiences her or himself as omnipotently fused with the mother. It is from here that the process of separation-individuation begins, with the first of a number of sub-phases, that of 'differentiation' in which a sense of self as distinct from other begins to develop. There is then a 'practising' sub-phase, where the crawling and toddling child begins to explore the world, pushing away from the mother but continuing to use her as a secure base, until the child begins to feel autonomous. In the next sub-phase, that of 'rapprochement', the child's realisation of separateness produces an awareness of her or his lack of omnipotence, leading to anxiety and an increased longing for the mother, this time as a separate person. This culminates in a 'rapprochement crisis' at about two years, in which the child wants both to be independent of the mother and to cling to her, leading to difficult behavioural disturbances. If this crisis is negotiated successfully, it leads on to a phase in which individuality and object constancy are relatively achieved, continuing to develop throughout life. The child internalises a sense of the mother as real and continuing to be available, allowing the separation process to occur – the mother is emotionally present to the child, even when physically absent. In addition, the child's ego development continues apace, with the achievement of various complex cognitive abilities and the sense of a fully autonomous self.

There are several complications involved in Mahler's description of development, due particularly to her attempt to wed an account given in terms of the mother–child relationship to an underlying drive model of motivation (Greenberg and Mitchell, 1983). For present purposes, however, the significant point is that Mahler concentrates neither on the maturation of the sexual drive around various erotogenic zones, nor on the negotiations that occur between id and ego impulses. Although elements of both these lines of thought appear in her work, its primary thrust is towards a description of how the child develops a sense of self from within a formless and fused original relationship with the mother.

This is an idea that has been central to the work of many post-Freudians, especially those using object relations theory but also in the more recent 'self-psychology' of Kohut (e.g. 1977): that the child begins life psychologically absorbed in the other, with no sense of an independent selfhood, and that it is through the original support of the mother and then her unavoidable failures that a sense of independent selfhood appears. Despite a radical difference in underlying theoretical stance, this is, for instance, the model adopted by Winnicott with his notion of 'good enough mothering':

through the mother's original perfect meeting of the child's needs, a sense of omnipotence develops in the child; this gives way to a more realistic, separated and coherent experience of the self as the mother gradually fails to satisfy all the child's demands. For these theorists, the question that is central to developmental psychoanalysis is: how does the self arise? Their answer, on the whole, is that it arises out of the complex interchanges between infant and carer; that, subjectively, the child first experiences her or himself as absorbed in the other, with no boundary or distinction possible, and that subjectivity becomes more complex as a result of the more or less successful discrimination of internal and external worlds.

Of all psychoanalytic approaches, it is perhaps that of Melanie Klein that portrays most evocatively the internal dynamics of the child's mind. Like Anna Freud, Klein's clinical work was predominantly with disturbed children, providing her with a more direct experience of the emotional concerns of childhood than that available to Freud. For Klein, however, it was the functioning of the id that was of most interest, with biologically-given destructive impulses being of crucial significance for the explanation of the direction taken by child development. There are both exciting and retrogressive elements in Kleinian theory: it contains a provocative account of the intersection of internal and external forces, but at the same time is limited by a lack of explicit consideration of social processes and a commensurate over-emphasis on biological 'instincts' and their pre-given objects (see Frosh, 1987, chapter 5). In addition, as described in Chapter 1, it has a tendency towards over-literalism in treating psychological processes as concrete objects; it is also the psychoanalytic approach that seems to take most liberties with observational data. But Kleinianism does point clearly to the elements in psychoanalysis which are most distinctive and which supply the firmest base for a critical evaluation of other psychological theories.

Klein's developmental theory to some extent follows the libidinal stage theory of Freud, but concentrates much more on the way the child's subjective world becomes constructed, particularly in relation to anxiety. In brief, Klein postulates the existence of a basic Death drive that causes the neonate's incipient ego to experience anxiety. As a defence against this, both the destructive and loving impulses of the child are projected outwards on to the first external object, the breast. Because of the dual nature of the projection, the breast is then experienced as if it were two separate objects, a 'good' and a 'bad' breast; at this time, persecutory feelings from the bad breast are primary, with the child's mental life dominated by the 'paranoid-schizoid position'. The history of the early months of childhood is one in which the split object is internalised and, through experiences of real nurture and gratification, the effects of the child's constitutional destructive envy are overcome sufficiently to allow the object to be integrated as one whole. This brings the child into the 'depressive position' where the predominant feelings are of sadness, loss, guilt and – with some optimism – reparation, the desire to rebuild what has been damaged. The child continues to experience the external world through a screen of unconscious phantasies that always threaten to fragment reality, but the more secure the child's progression through the depressive position, the more integrated and stable the world subjectively appears.

What is evident even from this very schematic account, is that Klein focuses on the subjectivity of the child to such an extent that it often appears that she is making it causal of all that happens in development. While such an extreme position is probably untenable (the external world of parents and others have their own agenda for the child, and impinge powerfully on her or him), Klein's depiction of the contradictions and passions possessing the child is extremely valuable. First, it provides a developmental history of subjectivity which goes further than an account of the emergence of the 'self' from primordial absorption in the mother. There is no whole and perfect self in Kleinian theory, only an acceptance of one's own emotions that makes ambivalence relatively tolerable. More subtly, Klein postulates some sort of distinction between the internal and external world from the start of life (otherwise it would do no good for the infant to project her or his impulses on to the breast) while retaining the idea that there is an unconscious link between the two (or projection would not be possible).

But most important is the Kleinian notion of phantasy, an automatic unconscious registering of the drives which forms the starting point for all mentation. According to Klein, there is unconscious mediation of all internal and external experiences; that is, all the child's activities and experiences have a subjective element to them which is not just one aspect of the experience, but is absolutely central to it. Klein thus offers a developmental account of subjectivity emphasising the confusions, contradictions, desires and anxieties of the child's mind, and the way unconscious forces operate to produce a complex internal world in the light of which everything else is felt and perceived. Whether or not Klein is correct in the substance of her theory (particular criticism has been directed at her idea that representations of the self and of objects occur in the first few months of life – see Lichtenberg, 1983), she shows that such theories are possible and important; developmental accounts which omit subjectivity omit a central feature of development.

The distinctive contribution of psychoanalysis to theories of child development, then, is not just to remind theorists to include emotion somewhere in their scheme. Rather, it is to argue that a psychology which is concerned only with knowing and doing is one that deals only with secondary phenomena. Despite differences in the ways in which they use biological and social models, and in their vision of the capabilities and mental life of infants, psychoanalysts generally agree that at the centre of each infant, each person, is something which is constructed through experience and which develops through a complex series of interchanges with the environment. This 'something' is more often taken for granted than theorised, as 'the self' or 'the individual', but it requires theorising if one is to be able to speak about experience.

Psychoanalysts have devoted a considerable amount of energy to describing the way subjectivity unfolds, both structurally (in the sense of how the 'self' is formed) and in terms of its content – as centred around drives or particular object relationships, for example. The effect of this approach is a 'deconstructive' one: the notion of the individual or of the central self is taken apart and analysed, until the roots of individuality and subject-hood are exposed. What emerges is a realisation that the subjective structure of the child – the child's 'internal history' – is as much in need of theorising as are the more specific capacities and competencies which are the conventional focus of developmental psychology. Psychoanalysis provides a sample of just such theories, sometimes contradicting one another, frequently speculative and occasionally wayward in their observations, but always attempting to engage with the issue of how the child's inner world is formed – how meaning and experience intertwine to create a subjectivity that is both dynamic, in the sense of motivating, and relatively fixed in its structure. It is from this position of engagement with the issue of how the human 'subject' is formed, that psychoanalysis looks quizzically at psychology's focus on the development of cognitive and social skills.

In summary, just as it was suggested in Chapter 1 that an explicit account of subjective meanings is a necessary component of any complete theory of the mind, so the insights of psychoanalysis imply that the history of this subjectivity should be, and could be, the focus of a full account of development. With all its elegance of methodology and reliability of observation, it is not clear that psychology has been able to develop an account which is full in this sense; it is perhaps for this reason that psychoanalysis remains a critical touchstone implicitly challenging the insights of developmental psychology.

## Growing knowledge

The criteria for psychoanalytic interrogation of developmental psychology are now clearer. They relate both to the place given to affectivity in the general scheme of things and, more crucially, to the degree of recognition given to the construction of subjectivity during the developmental period. On this latter issue, the seminal work of Jean Piaget holds a curiously paradoxical position which, because of the influence of his approach, has permeated through much cognitive developmental psychology. In what follows, it is the general structure of Piagetian theory rather than its details (which have been criticised by many psychologists who nevertheless work within a loosely Piagetian framework) that is examined.

Piaget has characterised his theory as a 'genetic epistemology', an empirically-based investigation of the origins and nature of intellectual knowledge; psychology is the means rather than the end to this investigation. Piaget's argument is that understanding how something comes about supplies necessary insights into its nature. This is an area of congruence between Piagetian and psychoanalytic approaches: for both, any full account of the current state of a person, whether a psychological complex or a mode of cognition, requires the provision of a history of how that complex or cognitive mode came to be.

Both approaches also strive to identify normative routes for development, which can become general accounts of how all children acquire the skills and routines of adult life. It should be noted that this assumption, that understanding the current state of an individual (or any organism) depends on the production of a developmental framework, is not one shared by all theorists. Many would suggest instead that there may be alternative routes through which a phenomenon could arise, without its nature being changed. For instance, Hamlyn (1978) proposes in relation to the development of concepts that, 'while there may be typical ways in which a form of understanding may be arrived at there need be *no one* way in which it comes about. It depends very much on the background of understanding of the individual' (p. 42).

There are two separable points here. One concerns the significance of a developmental understanding of any individual in accounting for her or his current state; the other questions the viability of general or normative developmental frameworks as explanations of individual functioning. The psychoanalytic perspective suggests that while there are developmental tasks which are faced by all children (for instance, the separation-individuation process in Mahler's theory), knowledge of the particular idiosyncratic experiences of an individual is necessary before that person's current functioning can be understood. Moreover, it is because people consciously and unconsciously make sense of, and respond to, current events in the light of their past history that this history is relevant to explanatory accounts. In other words, the importance of the individual's developmental history is implicit in the psychoanalytic assumption of the determining power of subjective structures which are themselves formed through experience. In Piagetian thought, this logic is less compelling. Although later cognitive structures are always built upon earlier ones, it is not clear that knowledge of these earlier structures is necessary for explanation of current functioning. Piaget's own idea that each cognitive stage represents a transformation of a preceding one reduces the relevance of the developmental account: if something is completely altered, then knowledge of its previous condition cannot explain its current state.

A significant difference between the orientations of psychoanalytic and Piagetian work is revealed here, additional to the differences produced by the choice of affective versus cognitive focus. This is that psychoanalysis engages with explanations of *the person*: its aim is always to provide an account that makes sense of what an individual is doing or feeling. To this end, the history of that individual is crucial. Piaget, on the other hand, is interested in understanding how certain cognitive abilities arise: the histories which he provides are histories of concepts rather than of people. Piaget's developmental account does not show in detail how any single child gets to where it is; rather, it attempts to explain how certain mental operations can be acquired. Piaget's approach, therefore, is a further instance of the psychological tendency to fragment the object of its study, resulting in investigations of mental processes and (in this case) their development which do not touch the child's subjectivity even when they deal with her or his thoughts and experiences. This is, perhaps, a major source of the abstract and over-schematic readings of experience to which Piaget's theories are prone to give rise.

According to Elkind (1964), there are three 'themes' to be found in Piaget's work: logic, relativity and dialectics. Boden (1979, p. 18) also finds three 'key ideas' in Piaget, but they are rather different: 'wholeness, transformation and self-regulation'. The difference may reflect the preferred reading of Piaget adopted by these two expositors of his position, with Elkind emphasising the general epistemological framework and Boden showing more interest in the cognitive psychology involved (how children come to know things); in addition, Boden writes as an expert from within the context of recent cognitive science, with its use of the language of cybernetics. In any event, such differences indicate the openness of Piaget's writings to interpretative variety – another similarity to Freud. What Elkind draws attention to in his reference to the theme of 'logic' is Piaget's fascination with the structure of knowledge. Whenever something is rule-governed it can be said to obey a logic of a kind, so children of all ages are logic-users to the extent that their ideas are rule-governed. On the other hand, *correct* logic (the set of rules which accurately describes events and objects in the world) only gradually develops, through the series of stages that Piaget has made famous and others have contested (sensori-motor, pre-operational, concrete operational and formal operational intelligence). This idea, that children's knowledge is always organised into structures with a recognisable logic of their own, has perhaps been Piaget's greatest single contribution to psychology, suggesting that cognition and learning are not just cumulative procedures (the child as an ignorant version of the adult), but active processes which involve the child in speculations about the world and in attempts to organise these speculations into a coherent framework. Understanding the child then becomes a matter of understanding these gradually unfolding frameworks, the grammar of the child's mind. It is from this idea that much of Piaget's practical influence has derived, as educationalists have attempted to gear their teaching methods to the child's current stage of cognitive organisation; it has also produced reams of psychological research attempting to clarify the nature of the cognitive stages and the events determining the transition from one to another. Finally, the emphasis on structure is what Boden refers to as the idea of 'wholeness', that intelligence can only be understood as a complete system, in which all parts are related to the whole.

In addition to producing the notion of structure, Piaget's concern with logic is connected to his wide view of the way biology is implicated in development. For Piaget, the construction of intelligence is a 'natural' process in the sense that it is part of a biological scheme to produce adaptation of the individual to the environment. 'For Piaget . . . logic presupposes both "given" facts of environmental and biological embodiment, and "autonomous" activity in the self-regulated exercise of biologically based capacities' (Boden, 1979, p. 58).

More formally, Piaget (1971, p. 54) claims that 'cognitive functions are an extension of organic regulations and constitute a differentiated organ for regulating exchanges with the external world', implying an in-built biological link between the gradual unfolding of cognitive capacities and the adaptations required by the external world. For Piaget, it is a biological fact that humans strive to adapt; part of that process involves the production of knowledge, with the organisation of information into structures being a tendency inherent in the human mind. In some lights, this reads like a cognitive version of Freud's description of the ego and of the reality principle; it is also akin to the suggestion of ego psychologists that people are biologically programmed to adapt to their environment, with the reality principle being the means through which this occurs (see Hartmann, 1959). In its strongest form, Piaget's theory proposes that cognitive development proceeds in a particular sequential order because the nature of adaptation to reality requires the attainment of a certain end point (at least concrete operations, with formal operations being a fuller development not achieved by everyone), and because each stage leading to this end point is built on the achievements of the preceeding stages. Thus, there is a normative goal for development, and both the form and the order that development takes is biologically given, with experiences serving only to impede or advance it, not to change its nature. Stated like this, Piaget's is a biological theory of cognitive development.

In tandem with the biologism of Piagetian theory there rides a component which has much in common with more socially-oriented approaches. This is the element that Elkind (1964) refers to as 'relativity', apparently meaning the recognition that all our perceptions of the world are mediated by internal processes which half-construct what we see.

> If, as Einstein had shown, conceptual judgements were always relative to the position of the observer making those judgements, then the observer could never be left out in the construction of concepts. This contention reinforced a pre-established Piagetian conviction – derived from Kant and perhaps from Marx – that reality always involved a subjective element, in the sense that it was always, at least in part, a projection or externalisation of thought or action. (Elkind, 1964, p. xi)

The relationship between mind and reality is governed by this kind of relativity, wherein the individual makes interpretations in the very act of perceiving the world – again a seminal notion for educational and cognitive psychology. In Piagetian terms, the mechanisms through which this occurs are those of 'assimilation and accommodation', the former referring to the way information coming into the mind is modified in order to fit in with the existing cognitive structure, while the latter describes the alterations which take place in that structure to deal with information that is discrepant with what the structure expects. This 'dialectical' process is therefore one in which reality can never be comprehended absolutely, without mediation, but also one in which there are gradual approximations to more accurate readings of the world. There are obvious similarities here with psychoanalytic models of the mind, particularly that of Klein in which all perceptions are mediated by the unconscious workings of phantasy; although Kleinians focus on the continuing distortions imposed by these phantasies, their model of normality is, like Piaget's, one in which more realistic appreciations of the world gradually emerge.

The final element of Piaget's basic approach requiring mention here, is the mechanism postulated to explain the transitions which occur from one stage to the next. Assimilation and accommodation are continuous processes – we are always adapting the world to our ideas of it and vice versa – but at particular times the amount of conflict produced by the discrepancy between prediction (due to cognitive structure) and feedback (due to the environment's response) is so great as to force not just slight changes in the structure, but a total reorganisation. This conflict is experienced psychologically, but its underlying dynamic is again a biological one: the 'desire' of all living systems for homeostasis, balance or equilibrium – a desire expressed in what Piaget refers to as the process of 'equilibration'. Simply, equilibration is at once the motive force behind, and a description of, transitions from one state to the next: it is why and also how a system that threatens to get out of control (too disequilibrated) returns to a situation of relative balance. This balance is not static – as noted above, there are always alterations to the system as new events occur – but it is one which does not threaten the basic integrity of the underlying cognitive structure. To borrow terms from Kuhn's (1972) model in *The Structure of Scientific Revolutions*, the developmental process is one in which long periods of 'problem-solving science' are interspersed with revolutionary transitions from one way of understanding things (a paradigm) to another, when the old paradigm can be adapted no more.

Piaget's neglect of emotional development has been commented upon many times. A common defence is simply to argue that no one can be expected to do everything, and that as Piaget was concerned with understanding the growth of knowledge one should not be critical of him for failing to produce a theory of emotions as well. This argument has its strength – it is all too easy to attack great innovators for what they have not done, when one cannot improve on what they have. The drawback to this lies in the issue of whether, in neglecting emotionality, Piaget has actually omitted something which is important even to the material that he has attempted to theorise. In this respect, psychoanalysis and Piaget cannot both be right, for the former proposes that affective events determine development, including cognitive development, while the latter sees cognition as a 'wired in' function of the human mind, self-motivating and requiring no further explanation in terms of drives or emotional needs. Emotion, in Piaget's scheme, does have an 'energetic' function, but this is limited to slowing down or speeding up cognitive development; it does not enter into the construction of cognition itself, which is pre-determined by adaptational needs (see Urwin, 1986). In contrast, psychoanalysts assume that knowledge takes the form given to it by the pressures of underlying drives (e.g. scopophilia) or anxieties; that is, cognition is not just mobilised by emotion, but its content is affectively determined. For instance, as described in Chapter 1, Klein's (1928) concept of an 'epistemophilic impulse' suggests that the pursuit of knowledge is intimately bound up with the infant's sadistic and controlling desires around the mother's body; similarly, the child's forays into symbolising and language derive from the unconscious workings of anxiety (see below, Chapter 3). Even if, as seems likely, those psychoanalysts are wrong who assume that cognitive development is derived totally from emotional needs, they argue a powerful case for the emotional significance of knowledge.

Thus, psychoanalytic investigations and treatments of learning inhibitions in children usually begin from the premise that acquiring knowledge of certain kinds has an impact on the child that, under certain circumstances, can increase anxiety. For example, a child who fails to learn to read might be doing so for fear of finding something out, or learning may be inhibited by sexual anxieties (Klein, 1955). On the other hand, acquiring certain cognitive skills may enable a child to deal with feelings or situations that were previously disturbing (Urwin, 1984), fuelling further cognitive development. Theorising affect and cognition separately, as psychologists tend to do, defuses the dynamic linking the two spheres, impoverishing the overall account.

It was argued previously that it is in the provision of a theory of subjectivity that psychoanalysis interrogates developmental psychology most searchingly. Piaget does, in fact, have such a theory, although as usual it is secondary to more purely cognitive

concerns. Piaget and Inhelder (1969) provide an overview of their
ideas in the following paragraph, which links the differentiation
of the self and the formation of relationships with other people to
the famous 'decentring' process, whereby a child comes to
understand that things can be seen from perspectives other than
her or his own.

> We have assumed that affective decentring is a correlative of
> cognitive decentring, not because one dominates the other, but
> because both occur as the result of a single integrated process.
> Indeed, when the little child ceases to relate everything to his
> states and to his own action, and begins to substitute for a world
> of fluctuating tableaux without spatio-temporal consistency or
> external physical causality a universe of permanent objects
> structured according to its own groups of spatio-temporal dis-
> placements and according to an objectified and spatialised
> causality, then his affectivity will also be attached to these
> localisable permanent objects and sources of external causality
> which persons come to be. Whence the formation of 'object
> relations' in close connection with the scheme of personal
> objects. (p. 26)

Decentring is a crucial cognitive process: the child begins life
solipsistically, believing and feeling her or himself to be the centre
of all things; gradually, through experience of the world of objects
and, equivalently, the world of other people, she or he recognises
the existence of other centres of consciousness. In the quotation
given above, Piaget and Inhelder suggest that the cognitive and
affective sides of this go hand in hand 'as the result of a single
integrated process'. What this seems to mean is that as the child
discriminates separate objects, both human and inanimate, so she
or he forms affective links with them, possibly of the kind called
'object relations' by psychoanalysts. What this obscures, however,
is that Piaget postulates a completely different motivational origin
for the decentration process than those hypothesised by analytic
theorists when they consider the emergence of the self from a
symbiotic state. For the latter, the boundaries of the self are
formed when the child's early anxieties are modified by the
presence and actions of the parent, leading to more integrated
feelings; at the same time (through repression or splitting) a

division is made between consciousness and the unconscious. Piaget, in contrast, formulates decentration as a cognitive process which makes it possible to attach emotions to distinct others. Even more importantly for this discussion, cognitive decentration allows the child to begin to construe her or himself as an autonomous being. This is not so much a question of feeling, but of self-cognition: more precisely, 'the self and the personality are simply those conceptual systems concerned with personal and interpersonal realities' (Elkind, 1964, p. xiv).

Piaget here is at the source of modern theories of social cognition, which regard the self as an object in a conceptual space, gradually becoming more complex and differentiated as development occurs. But this is not, after all, a theory of subjectivity of the psychoanalytic variety; instead, it treats 'the subject' as if it were an object, directing attention to the way people describe their selves and away from what they feel. This limitation relates to a further element in Piaget's solipsistic view of the child, his neglect of the possible social origins of subjectivity. Viewing each individual as a system biologically attuned towards adaptation, Piaget formulates development as a process whereby the child is shut off in a separate, asocial world until, through the results of her or his experimental manipulations of objects (including people), she or he discovers that others exist and reasons that she or he, too, must have a self. However, many contemporary developmental psychologists have produced evidence to the effect that children are more socially oriented and socially driven than is allowed for in this approach. For instance, Dunn (1986) reviews data suggesting that children are sensitive to the needs of their parents by the age of two, far earlier than proposed by Piagetians. More importantly, she argues that the salience of children's social relationships is reflected in their earliest causal questions, which tend to concern the behaviour of people rather than of things, and is also evidenced in a series of emotions which may be intimately connected with cognitive social perceptions.

> Paralleling the changes in social understanding are dramatic increases in the anger and distress that children show: the very exchanges in which children begin to 'read' the emotions and intentions of others are often those which include tantrums, self-abuse and deliberate destruction of objects. (Dunn, 1986, p. 103)

This suggests that Piaget may have underestimated the motivating and organising power of sociality, in particular in producing the differentiations that organise the self. Butterworth (1984) points to this as the terrain of Vygotsky's critique of Piaget, with Vygotsky proposing that all those mental functions depending on speech and language occur first on the social level, between the child and another, and only subsequently are internalised. With all their variety of ideas, psychoanalysts would generally agree: it is through the internalisation of object relations that the child's inner world is structured and the pattern of the self laid down.

Numerous criticisms from within psychology have been made of Piaget's work, many of which relate to this point concerning the primacy of social experience. On a relatively straightforward level, Piaget's interpretation of his experimental results have been questioned, with ingenious replications undertaken to demonstrate that children are capable of such cognitive functions as conservation from an earlier age than that postulated in the original theory (e.g. Bryant, 1982). On the whole, these results do suggest that Piaget has underestimated children's capacities and has also neglected to consider the role of perceptual conflict in causing children to produce confused responses to his tests. In addition, the variation between children on these tasks, and the variation within children in the degree of success they have with tasks supposedly testing related abilities, suggest that Piaget has overstated the significance of clearly distinct stages, and underestimated the amount of gradual change that takes place in children's cognitive abilities (Boden, 1979).

Importantly, it seems that when Piagetian tests are restructured so as to deal with issues that are familiar or relevant to children, test results can be strikingly improved, for example in showing increased decentration in fictitious social situations (e.g. Hughes and Donaldson, 1979, who replaced the Piagetian 'three mountains' perspective-taking test with one involving a doll hiding from a policeman). Light (1986) argues that the greater success of young children on tasks which make 'human sense' has to do not so much with the familiarity of the materials, but with the intelligibility (to the child) of the social exchange with the experimenter. In support of this suggestion, he gives examples of 'incidental transformations' in which the experimenter's question to the child about the equivalence of amounts (the conservation situation) can be understood as checking rather than interrogating. Urwin (1986) suggests that this work might also relate to the general argument that children's emotional concerns are often determinant over their cognitive abilities, fitting neatly with her pro-psychoanalytic explanation of cognitive development. Thus, these empirical considerations again raise the issues of the significance of social relations and of emotion in cognitive development. Bruner and Haste (1987) summarise the direction in which this and related work are going:

It is not only that we have begun to think again of the child as a *social being* – one who plays and talks with others, learns through interactions with parents and teachers – but because we have come once more to appreciate that through such social life the child acquires a framework for interpreting experience, learns how to negotiate meaning in a manner congruent with the requirements of the culture. 'Making sense' is a social process; it is an activity that is always situated within a social and historical context. (p. 1)

There have also been a number of theoretical critiques of the general Piagetian enterprise, which can provide a conclusion for this section, as they converge on some central assumptions that mark the distinction between this form of developmental psychology and psychoanalysis. As with the empirical data outlined above, the main objects of criticism are the Piagetian attitudes towards social relations and emotion; in their more general form, these become aspects of the Piagetian assumption of normative rationality. Hamlyn (1978) expresses the social side of this as follows:

When . . . it is said that Piaget seriously underestimates the social in his approach, it is not just that he underestimates the efficacy of social factors in producing deviations from the normal pattern of development . . . ; it is also that he ignores the necessity of bringing others into the picture as part of the context in which alone the concept of knowledge can get a purchase. (p. 59)

Knowledge is something which is constructed between people; it does not have an absolute form, but an agreed form which makes the social world comprehensible, and which is institutionalised in the formal curricula of schooling. Piaget produced ideas which have led to educational reforms, but in part this was possible because these ideas take for granted the procedures and modes of understanding which are characteristic of our social world – including the privileging of rationality over emotion, of logic over creativity. Whereas psychoanalysis sees rationality as a kind of necessary evil, Piaget idealises it, as the normal and desirable end point of development.

The more general strand of argument relevant here has been articulated by Walkerdine (e.g. 1984; Venn and Walkerdine, 1978) and Urwin (1986). This concentrates on the assumption of core rationality that is present in Piaget's theory and that renders it essentialist in a manner militating against the possibility of theorising subjectivity. To a considerable extent, this assumption is present in Piaget's biological approach to cognition; this theorises cognitive development as a naturally unfolding process which is internally driven (by the maturation of the child) and that simply takes the external world as a collection of objects of knowledge. Walkerdine (1984) shows how this idea is linked with the development of 'apparatuses of normalisation' producing 'a model of naturally occurring development which could be observed, normalised and regulated' (p. 170), and Urwin (1986) traces its roots to the Child Study Movement of the nineteenth century, with its evolutionary view of how development 'unfolds according to predetermined biological principles' (p. 267). The important point, however, is not so much the origin of this view of child development, as its implications and limitations. Here, what is crucial is its assumption of a pre-given core rationality that defines the individual's subjectivity. This assumption is very widespread in psychology (see Banton *et al.*, 1985, for its role in theories of mental health); it produces a view of individuals as integrated subjects, whose history is one of the gradual accretion of more and more sophisticated abilities and knowledge of social roles.

One limitation here is that this approach takes as given that which is most in need of explanation – the experience of subjectivity and selfhood that each of us either has or strives towards. By calling this 'biological', it is explained away; it is not analysed. In addition, approaches which share this assumption and also downgrade irrationality, as Piaget's does, tend to produce theories of development that either ignore conflict or view it as something which can always be resolved into a rational, acceptable result. In contrast, one thing which psychoanalysis has documented extremely persuasively, is that conflict is characteristic of personal functioning; this point will be discussed again below. More strongly in the present context, the phenomena with which psychoanalysis deals suggest that the rationality taken by Piagetians as central may in fact be quite a fragile achievement, always liable to be undermined by the contradictions and disturbances of emotional life. Psychoanalysis argues that no assumption of a pre-given rationality is possible and that a historical account of a child must investigate where her or his selfhood comes from and what it means. Piaget's theory, with all its useful insights into the cognitive strategies adopted by children as they grow up, can offer no way into this.

## Creating a social being

In the area of developmental psychology that most explicitly theorises sociality, that of 'socialisation', there have been enormous advances in the past twenty years. From a position where the dominant non-psychoanalytic theory was behaviourism, emphasising the role of reinforcement processes in structuring the child's social behaviour, a far more complex and interactional approach has developed. Much of the impetus for this has come from the work of John Bowlby, whose attachment theory has the virtues of linking psychoanalytic observations and biological explanations, and of forcing investigators to look seriously at their empirical findings before airing their favourite hypotheses. Bowlby's approach, particularly as developed in the first volume of the 'Attachment and Loss' trilogy (Bowlby, 1969), is consistent both with object relations theory and with much contemporary psychology, in that it emphasises the significance of social relationships in child development, making that particular kind of relationship which he calls 'attachment' a fundamental building-block of development. Where he differs from some theorists and goes further than others is in arguing that the power of the attachment relationship (the specific emotional link that a child makes with her of his primary caretaker, usually the mother) derives from its biological function.

Attachment behaviour is regarded as a class of social behaviour of an importance equivalent to that of mating behaviour and parental behaviour. It is held to have a biological function specific to itself and one that has hitherto been little considered. (Bowlby, 1969, pp. 223–4)

The complexity of attachment as a concept is that it refers to a number of phenomena at different levels. These include, for example, a set of behaviours by which children show that they desire or have a relationship with an adult (e.g. clinging, following, reduction of distress in the presence of the adult), an underlying emotional link explaining the observed behaviour, and a set of object relational experiences which are internalised by the child and, in a relatively traditional psychoanalytic manner, are thought to form the child's inner world. But at its simplest level, attachment is a biological concept, an evolutionarily-determined drive arising out of the necessity of protecting human young against predators, and paralleled by a similarly evolved pattern of maternal activity which is reciprocal to the child's needs. Thus, fulfilment of the attachment drive is a biological as well as a psychological necessity; or, rather, these two levels are not distinct, for psychology is read by Bowlby as part and parcel of the biological system that is the human individual.

This is, subtly, not as reductionist as it seems: although it is at the biological level that the explanation for the significance and ubiquity of attachment can be found (e.g. the motivation for attachment is inherited as an instinct; failures of attachment are equivalent to the thwarting of a drive and always have severe developmental effects), the impact and meaning of the attachment relationship is given psychologically and psychodynamically. Biology preordains that the mother–child couple performs as a kind of cybernetically balanced system, the child displaying proximity-seeking behaviours and rewards for maternal attention, the mother reciprocating with food, comfort and supervision of the child's safety. This biological system has the characteristic of producing intense contact between child and mother, as a result of which a deep psychological bond grows which is then internalised by the child into a sense of security and a knowledge of social relations. Secure attachments produce secure children who are well socialised because they understand about human relationships and because they feel safe enough to explore their social environment in an active and risk-taking way. Thus, a developmental process which has been activated by biology merges into a socialisation process expressible in fully psychological terms.

Bowlby's attachment theory has generated a vast amount of critical discussion and investigation over the years, which it is not relevant to review in detail here. The main points of the critique, however, have been that Bowlby overstates the biological determinedness of the attachment relationship, focuses too strongly on the biological mother to the exclusion of other attachment figures, places too much weight on the aetiological significance of disrupted attachments and separations in his explanation of psychopathology, is ethnocentric in generalising too widely from observations of western infants, and neglects to consider the impact of wider social factors on child development. In addition, the conformist implications of Bowlby's argument that separations from the mother are always destructive, usually permanently so, have not been lost on governments anxious to remove women from paid work and reduce the provision of nursery and other child-care resources (see Riley, 1983; Scarr and Dunn, 1987).

Empirical investigations have generally produced results supportive of the critiques; for instance, they suggest that children characteristically form a number of different attachments which differ in strength rather than in kind; that the biological mother is not necessarily the primary attachment figure; that separation experiences do not always cause marked distress; that current rather than past social relationships (especially parental relationships) are the most important aetiological influences on childhood disorders; that the impact of poor attachment relationships in early life can be alleviated by later improvements; that substitute care can be beneficial; and that wider social factors have a substantial impact on children's development (see Rutter, e.g. 1982; Wolkind and Rutter, 1985, for a series of comprehensive and persuasive reviews). Nevertheless, the notion of attachment is retained throughout this work as a major descriptor of the quality of a child's relationship with her or his carers, and continues to be seen as a (or *the*) primary source for a child's internalisation of the possibilities and values of the social world. For although it is recognised by most researchers that simple 'conditioning' and role learning does operate under some circumstances (e.g. in moderating or accentuating aggressive behaviour), psychologists have joined psychoanalysts in suggesting that the most powerful socialisation forces operate subtly from within the context of intense relationships, usually with parents. Understanding the form of these relationships and the manner in which they have an impact is therefore crucial for theorists of child development.

One of the attractions of Bowlby's approach and the work that has branched off from it, is that it is congruent with the impressive research evidence demonstrating the remarkable cognitive capacities of neonates and, in particular, the way in which these abilities seem to be attuned to social interactions. Thus, from the start of life there are perceptual attributes of faces and voices which appear to be particularly attractive to children, who show interest in topographical representations of facial features (e.g. Fantz, 1967; Goren *et al.*, 1975) and who also seem to show considerable ability to discriminate familiar voices from as little as three days old (DeCasper and Fifer, 1980). This clearly suggests some form of in-built social ability in the child. It also has another consequence for theories of socialisation. In the traditional Freudian account of how children come to repress their desires in order to make it possible to live in a social world, and also in the 'social learning theory' version of how they develop constraints on impulsiveness, aggressivity and the like, there is an assumption of basic incongruence between the child's inner desires and the requirements of social adaptation. Presumably, this assumption derives from the everyday experience of millions of parents trying to control their wayward youngsters, but it does not make much sense within a framework that supposes a biological propensity towards the formation of positive social relations. If attachment theory is correct, an implication is that normal development is a process of cooperation and mutuality between parent and child, not one of conflict at the end of which the child's desires are controlled or repressed. This is precisely the argument used by many modern socialisation theorists, based both on the theoretical and empirical considerations mentioned above and on evidence that compliance with parental requirements is generated most effectively from within contexts of cooperation and support rather than strict controls or conflict situations – data which derives from studies of both normal and disturbed child populations (e.g. Wolkind and Rutter, 1985). Drawing on both developmental psychology and psychoanalytic literature, Lichtenberg (1983) proposes that,

> from the beginning both the newborn and the mother are primed to participate in a social interaction rather than to act as two individuals sending discrete messages. Their attachment is based on this mutual reciprocity. (p. 18)

From a somewhat different perspective, Schaffer (1984) also notes that, 'Far from seeing the parent–child relationship as a never-ending battle investigators have come to be impressed by the "fit" of the two individuals' sets of behaviour patterns' (p. 169). For him, 'mutual adaptation, not conflict, is the basic theme that runs through the course of parent–child interaction' (ibid.). It is not that the parent does not control the child, but that socialisation pressures (which 'are brought to bear on the child from the moment he is born' – p. 181) operate smoothly and indirectly, with the child gradually absorbing successful and positive social attributes as the parent equally gradually supplies guidelines.

Schaffer is one of many socialisation theorists who focus upon the supposedly inherent fit between child and carer (usually the mother in this literature), and devote their attention to charting the course which the dyadic relationship takes. For Schaffer (1984), 'Individuality . . . is a secondary phenomenon; social relationships are primary' (p. 2) – a tenet with which many object relations theorists might agree. The child certainly brings some inbuilt propensities and potentialites to the situation, and some of the child's inner maturational changes are likely to call for a reorganis-ation of the concerns of the mother–child dyad at various times. But these researchers go further by proposing that infants and mothers are pre-programmed to stimulate and respond to one another and thus that social relationships exist from the moment of birth. The quality and concerns of the primary relationship change from time to time as a product of new competencies that emerge in the child (Schaffer postulates a stage or 'step-like' pattern of development rather than a steady accretion of new knowledge or more complex interactional forms), but at each point healthy development is marked by successful mutual accommo-dation between child and adult. The child learns the skills of social interaction and the structure of social life from within the reciprocal but asymmetrical relationship with the carer, who props up the child's inadequacies in a supportive way, allowing her or him to perceive and absorb the grammar of interpersonal relationships. Throughout this process, and however many periodic changes of course there may be, the context is one of a harmonious dyad informed by expectations and capacities that can only have biological roots.

> Parent and child may be regarded as a mutually accommodative interactive system, but how that accommodation is achieved varies from phase to phase according to the particular circumstances prevailing at that time. Of these circumstances, the most marked are the new competencies that periodically emerge in the child; these refer to universal achievements evident across a wide range of child rearing practices, resulting in some specific extension of the child's ability to interact with his environment generally and the social partner in particular. (Schaffer, 1984, p. 15)

There are a number of similarities between the attachment and interactive accounts of socialisation and some aspects of psychoanalytic theory, particularly of the object relations variety. There is the same prioritising of social relationships, the focus on the mother–child dyad (although, to be fair, Schaffer acknowledges the limitations of this focus and devotes considerable space to what he terms 'polyadic settings' such as those in which children interact with peers), and the argument that it is through the early mother–child encounter that the child's consciousness of sociality develops. In all these respects, the evidence that these theorists marshal and their general empirical approach has been immensely productive in increasing understanding of the interactional component to children's learning about social skills, their social world and their interpersonal position. What is not considered, however, is what is characteristically omitted in psychology: not so much the emotional component of development (for this is either mentioned or can be extrapolated from what is described, and it is quite central to Bowlby's attachment theory), but the constructionist element – the relationship between social events and the formation of the child's internal, subjective world. Approaches such as that of Schaffer, with their assumption of a harmonious social environment serving to prop up the naturally unfolding capacities of the child (which emerge irrespective of the particular social setting in which the child is to be found, hence making conceptualisation of the social world unnecessary), remain cognitivist and rationalistic in their attitude. What they see happening in social development is the gradual learning of the way in which the social world operates, and of how to take up a position within it. This presumes the existence of internal structures that can learn these things; once again, it leaves the origin and nature of these structures untheorised.

It is, however, precisely the formation of such internal structures that is the problematic for psychoanalysis, paradoxically making it *more* social in orientation than is developmental psychology. This is because social experiences, particularly microsocial ones between infants and their parents, are made constitutive of the child's psyche; socialisation is, therefore, not just a matter of learning the rules of social engagement, but of having one's subjective space moulded and structured along lines given in encounters with other people, who are themselves the carriers of social 'messages' (Frosh, 1987). In this way, psychoanalysis suggests that consciousness and the unconscious become organised in response to social experience – some would say, along social axes such as those implicit in discourses on gender and race. Once more, psychoanalysis offers a critique of psychology suggesting that the latter does not dig deep enough in its exploration of the formative factors of the mind.

As well as neglecting the mechanisms whereby subjectivity is constructed in a social context, the socialisation theories mentioned here undervalue the impact of social forces – not just 'polyadic situations', but the social structures that manage the shape of all interpersonal encounters, whether dyadic or polyadic, structures that give rise to the pervasive social rules (such as gender differentiation) lying behind much of what a developing child 'learns'. This is linked to their presentation of a view of the world as naturally harmonious, and of the child as a being whose gradually unfolding rationality makes adaptation to this world normal and predictable. Yet, what seems apparent from both clinical and theoretical psychoanalysis – and from everyday observations, if these be methodologically acceptable – is that conflict, both internal and between the child and the environment, is something which is widespread during development and deep in its origins and effects.

Neither rationality nor adaptation is all that subjectivity consists in; they may not even constitute the larger part. Urwin (1986) summarises these points effectively:

> This rationalised view of the young child is coupled with an idealised but also grossly impoverished view of mother–child relationships. Turning to the infancy work, before the child goes to school, we are presented with the mother–child dyad as a unit of perfect harmony, in which adults' readings scaffold the child's intentions within an increasingly familiar world. Not only is the social world limited to the dyad, but in this world there appears to be little room for pleasure and distress, or for conflict or aggression. (pp. 264–5)

The reference to 'scaffolding', a process whereby adults provide guidelines and shaping messages by means of which a child makes sense of what is going on, links this material to the cognitive work described earlier. There it was noted that some critiques of Piaget arising from within psychology have taken issue with his tendency to diminish the importance of social factors in development, and have argued for recognition of the social embeddedness of cognitive growth. From the studies of socialisation, an image of what this social context might be has arisen: it is a context of purely supportive actions and communications that enable the child to smoothly learn the rules and procedures for cognitive understanding and social interaction. This is an explicitly adaptationist vision which is congruent with some psychoanalytic work (that of ego psychology) emphasising the importance of adjustment to one's surroundings. However, alternative psychoanalytic readings of the impact of sociality on individual development contradict this vision: they suggest that 'socialisation' is a process of loss and of repression of inner desires, a process characterised by conflict and separation, by splitting and denial. In the Freudian view, socialisation is a matter of giving up the possibility of happiness and replacing it with strategies for avoiding pain; for Kleinians, it consists of learning to tolerate the ambivalence of internal impulses and external responses. In the Lacanian view, to be described more fully in Chapter 3, socialisation is a process of continuing alienation from desire, the production of a human 'subject' which is fixed in a certain position with respect to the structures of society, but which is riven within by the workings of the unconscious. From this perspective, psychologists' emphasis on the easy and pre-ordained meshing of infantile needs and environments is a further aspect of an ideological smoothing-out of the conflicts inherent in every social experience.

In summary, then, what psychology has produced, both in socialisation and cognitive developmental fields, are theories of regulation rather than of production, of how the child learns to act as a rational social being rather than of how the environment is experienced. This approach carries an implicit assumption that the world is rational, and that development involves the incorporation of the rules of that rationality until they regulate behaviour and thought effectively. This position, however, is not only subverted by psychoanalysis' revelations of internal conflict; it is also undermined by descriptions of the social world that do not accept its homogeneity and rationality, but instead explore its conflicts and aberrations. The conflation of these two traditions, psychoanalytic and sociopolitical, suggests that development is not just a matter of learning the grammar of adult action and regulating one's behaviour thereby; it also involves the production of a subjectivity which is as laden with ambiguities, ambivalences, irrationalities and conflicts as is the supposedly 'rational' world outside.

## Conclusion: the problems of linkage

This chapter began with a critical examination of the methodology that psychoanalysis employs when investigating the inner world of the child. The in-built unreliability of the psychoanalytic observational procedure came to the fore: the way in which it almost guarantees the infiltration of observations by theoretical and personal expectations, and the sheer untenability of many of the claims to accurate knowledge which it produces. Nevertheless, it was suggested that the clinical psychoanalytic situation can be a source of informative observations and hypotheses about children's inner worlds, despite the unreliability of the material that the analyst collects. This unusual situation, in which unreliability does not necessarily ensure invalidity, comes about because psycho-analysis enables analysts to observe their child patients in an intense and detailed way over a prolonged period of time, and in the context of a situation of maximum emotional involvement – a situation structured, therefore, to produce information on subjective, affective experience.

Perhaps because of variations in analytic practices and observational procedures, a range of alternative psychoanalytic formulations of development have been produced. These vary from the traditional Freudian description of the organisation of libido around a sequence of bodily zones, to the object relational concentration on the progressive internalisation of relationships with significant people. More generally, however, the psychoanalytic concern with the emerging subjectivity of the child, with the way in which 'selfhood' becomes constructed and organised, raises issues that are of importance for developmental psychology. These not only indicate the necessity of including emotion in any developmental account, but they also point to the limitations of views that take for granted the existence of a pre-given, rational core self. Underlying this 'egoic' self, psychoanalysis suggests, is a different realm of subjectivity that is just as much in need of developmental explanation. Piagetian theory, which provides an informative account of cognitive development that still dominates psychology, is restricted by its assumption of basic rationality as much as by its neglect of social considerations. The same criticism can be applied to psychological work on socialisation which, despite supplying a mass of useful empirical data and some guidelines for thinking about parent–child interactions, fails to theorise the significance of conflict either in the social world or within the child. Both these strands of psychological work produce a cognitive image of development, in which an individual with a pre-given capacity for understanding gradually learns more and more about her or his physical and social world, and the place that she or he has in it. Subjective experience here is displaced by intellect and action.

There have been numerous attempts to integrate psychoanalysis and developmental psychology. These have usually been unsuccessful, as they have often relied on a literal reading of the least tenable element of Freud's developmental approach, the stage theory. Bowlby's work is a relatively rare example of a theory that draws on psychoanalysis and empirical psychology in a manner which has proved productive for both. More recently, however, a few psychoanalysts wedded to the methods of developmental psychology have turned their attention to extending those methods to explore psychodynamic concerns; in particular, they have shown interest in the extent to which the observational data of developmental psychology can shed light on the child's subjective experiences. The argument of these researchers (e.g. Lichtenberg, 1983; Stern, 1985) is that neither developmental psychology, with its neglect of internal experience, nor psychoanalysis, with its unreliable methods, can alone provide an adequate approach to development. Some of this work has been very useful, in particular in documenting the consequences for psychoanalytic theories of psychological findings on the cognitive capacities of young infants (e.g. Chamberlain, 1987). Lichtenberg (1983) demonstrates how data of this kind can be used to elaborate and choose between various psychoanalytic possibilities; for instance, he argues that research indicates both that neonates are highly differentiated cognitively and that the task of developing an internal representational world is a complex one. This leads him to reject the Kleinian dating of mental development, but in a relatively sophisticated way.

Although the neonate begins extrauterine life primed to perceive and react differentially to a number of different objects, the evidence indicates that it is not until much later, probably during the second year, that the growing child gradually develops the capacity to represent self and others at a conceptual level. (p. 63)

It is perhaps Stern (1985) who has taken this procedure furthest. In brief, his argument is that both the methodology of developmental psychology and the interests of psychoanalysis are important for understanding children, in the former case because it is necessary to have a regularised structure for collecting information, and in the latter case because any complete theory needs to account for subjective experience – much as has been argued throughout this chapter. Stern's interest is in the emergence of selfhood: in contrast to the psychoanalytic theories described earlier, he suggests that children always have a meaningful sense of self from birth. This self, at first just 'emergent' and related to bodily activity, gradually becomes more structured and differentiated, but it is never lost in a phase of symbiosis or absorption in the mother. Thus, whereas for psychoanalysts such as Mahler the problem faced by an infant is how to become a separate, individuated psychological being, Stern suggests that children always have some self-awareness, and that recognition of the subjectivity of others is more nearly the task with which they are faced.

Stern's is an interesting and important account of developmental sequencing in its own right, as it goes against the grain of most alternative psychoanalytic views, from Mahler to Lacan. Indeed, of the theorists discussed in this chapter it is perhaps Piaget whose position is closest to that of Stern. But the significant point for present purposes is Stern's suggestion that observational data can be used to substantiate his position. An example here is what Stern calls 'affect attunement'. The issue is as follows: if Stern is correct in thinking that infants begin life with some subjective sense of their own selfhood, how do they come to experience others as having selves as well; that is, how do they come to comprehend *intersubjectivity*, the possibility of communicating between one's own subjective position and that of another? Stern suggests that this follows the discovery of the existence of motives and intentions governing the behaviour of others. One mechanism that is held to relate to this is the discovery by the child of the possibility of an empathic link between her or him and the parent, leading to a recognition that affective states are being shared. Stern argues that for the child to feel this the parent must not only accurately recognise the feelings that a child has, but must also demonstrate this understanding in a way that the child can comprehend. The demonstration alighted upon by Stern is a variant of imitation in which the parent does not so much produce an exact copy of the behaviour shown by the child, but picks up and enacts the affective tone of the child's behaviour, by copying its structure, intensity or rhythm. Many of these copies are not actually imitations at all, as they occur in a different modality from that used by the child: for instance, a mother may verbally echo her child's excited physical movement. The important thing is that somehow the adult recognises the emotional tone of the child's actions and performs an activity of her or his own that reproduces this tone in an observable and comprehensible way.

What is significant about Stern's approach, and that of the other developmental psychoanalysts mentioned above, is that it moves from a version of psychoanalytic theory to specific predictions concerning the observable consequences if this theory should be correct. The generation and testing of these predictions, however, remains problematic – more so than in conventional developmental psychology because of the difficulties of operationalising concepts which are concerned with internal representations of selfhood and with processes which are unspoken and sometimes unconscious. (The major investigation of affect attunement reported by Stern *et al.* (1985), for instance, is only a 'pilot study' and is undermined by serious methodological flaws, ranging from the very small number of children studied to poor definitions of observational categories and some cavalier interpretations of results.) This raises a question-mark over the viability of the procedure of using observational data to choose between psychodynamic theories. As Stern (1985) himself notes, psychoanalysis is forced to go further than what is visible in making its hypotheses about psychological processes. This is a characteristic shared with any approach that presumes the existence of underlying structures which cannot be measured directly: these will always have the status of hypothetical constructs, the existence of which can only be reasoned about or deduced.

The problem for psychoanalysis, however, is deeper, because of its emphasis on the disguised, partial, fragmented and confusing states that constitute subjective experience. The hidden nature of unconscious intentions and desires means that the form of their manifestation as observable behaviour can never be predicted; conversely, the 'over-determined' (i.e. multiply caused) origin of any external act means that its inner significance may be variable or speculative. Once again, this raises the difficulty of validating a theory that deals not just with subjectivity, but with its unconscious determinants. There must be some way to move from what one perceives other people to be doing to what one understands them to be experiencing, but if, as is claimed to be the situation in both the analytic and the mother–infant encounter, this way is through the unconscious of the observer, it is a difficult task indeed to construct a viable operational procedure to measure it. Whether this is a judgement on the limitations of developmental psychology or a criticism of the unscientific nature of psychoanalysis is, of course, a traditional and unresolved focus of dispute. It may mean, in the end, that the opposition between developmental psychology and psychoanalysis is too fundamental to allow integration of the approaches to occur.

# 3 Words and Meanings

Language is an object of central interest both for psychoanalysts and for psychologists. Psychoanalysis, after all, was dubbed 'the talking cure' by one of Freud's early patients because of the way it attempts to release psychic tension through verbal reminiscence of traumatic experiences. Despite the many alterations in analytic ideas and methods, the speech of analysts and analysands is still its primary mode of work and empirical data. More broadly, psychoanalysis deals with the symbolic world which is internal to each individual; this may be more extensive than language (a point disputed by some analytic schools), but language is a substantial component of it. Since Freud's *Psychopathology of Everyday Life*, investigations of the use and mis-use of language have consequently been both the main clinical method available to practising analysts, and a research tool used to increase understanding of the relationship between conscious 'discourse' and unconscious desire.

In psychology, there has been a long debate over the relationships between language and thought, revolving around the question of whether language 'determines' thought or should be viewed as its tool, allowing meanings to be coded and expressed. On the whole, it is the latter position that has prevailed, although language is usually conceptualised as a communicative medium rather than simply as a window on to the individual's internal world. This does not reduce the importance of language for psychological studies: as the main form of communication available to people, language can be represented as the interface between the individual and society. Hence, questions concerning the processes whereby children learn to 'use' language, to understand and be understood, become questions about social as well as psychological events.

It is already clear that there are numerous different issues surrounding the psychology of language; it may be that the almost total separation between the psychological and psychoanalytic

111

literature on the subject is a product of their concern with different groups of these issues, rather than of total incompatibility. As one might expect, those issues more characteristic of psychology concern the functions of language; those more closely linked to psychoanalysis concern its meaning. These different issues can be listed as a series of distinct questions:

(1)   How is it that all non-handicapped humans understand and use language? This can be called the 'genetic' question, as it is concerned with the basic human capacities which make language-acquisition possible. It is also linked to more neurological issues concerning the brain processes underlying language.

(2)   How does a child acquire language? This 'acquisition question' takes language as an object or skill which is learnt by each child through certain specifiable processes.

(3)   What benefit does language bring? How does it relate to thought? These are questions about the functions of language.

(4)   What is the relationship between language and social context? Although this 'social question' overlaps with both the previous questions, it also raises the specific issue of the impact of the social environment on the development and use of language.

(5)   What is the experience of 'having' language? This 'experiential question' is distinguishable from the functional one on the grounds of its focus on the emotional and phenomenological state of the individual.

(6)   What role does language play in constructing consciousness and individuality? Again, this 'constructionist question' overlaps with the functional one; the difference lies in the way it focuses on the degree to which language might play a formative role in creating the boundaries of selfhood, rather than on the uses to which language can be put.

As has been pointed out, these questions overlap, but they are sufficiently distinct to provide a guide through the territory of language studies. In what follows, psychological and psychoanalytic accounts of language development are described and evaluated in terms of their adequacy in addressing these questions. Language *development* is concentrated upon here not only because it has been the focus of most research (particularly in psychology), but also because it is in the context of descriptions of how infants come to be linguistic creatures that the social and constructionist issues are highlighted, and that boundary questions over language and thought can be explored with most clarity. The strategy adopted here is to present an outline of psychological approaches to language development, followed by a description of some psychoanalytic theories that, despite many inadequacies of their own, suggest a whole range of additional points which require consideration if a complete theory is to be formed. It will be argued that, perhaps more than is the case for the other topics considered in this book, psychological and psychoanalytic accounts of language development provide critiques of one another which are different in content, but roughly equal in force.

## Operants and universals

The history of modern psychological studies of language development is usually given as beginning with Skinner's (1957) ill-fated *Verbal Behaviour*. This book has the curious quality of always being read retrospectively, in the light of what is usually called Chomsky's (1959) 'devastating' critique, with the result that those elements in it which have been productive (for instance, its appreciation of the important role of specific experiences in determining the form that language development takes) are often neglected. Skinner's general claim is that language is something which has to be learnt by a child through experience, and that this learning proceeds wholly through operant conditioning, understood in a slightly extended sense. Thus, rather than view the child as an inherently active generator of linguistic forms, Skinner assumes that she or he is motivated by external forces, the desire to achieve more basic rewards, usually from the parents. Through selective reinforcement of the child's (innate) babbling, she or he learns both the meaning of words (in this case, the names that objects and actions have) and the correct (adult) syntactic forms necessary to communicate effectively. A particularly powerful method for learning these things is through imitation of adults' speech. The child's language is thus shaped through parental and other reinforcement, with gradually increasing demands until it approximates to adult usage.

Put in this bald way, it is perhaps not immediately obvious why Skinner's proposals have become the subject of such hilarity in the psychological community. In part, the answer to this is that they have been mis-represented: Chomsky's critique proceeds by way of *reductio ad absurdum*, giving the impression that Skinner is claiming that children can only learn grammatical forms, words and sentences by slavish imitation of parental utterances, with consequent rewards. As Chomsky shows, this is clearly not the case: children and adults alike produce utterances that no one has ever used before, and that may not even be 'in the language'. However, Skinner does not claim that every individual utterance is imitated and reinforced in this way; rather, his suggestion is that reinforcement is of gradual approximations to adult speech. To some extent, such an imitative-reinforcement process must be occurring, or no child would ever learn the specific verbal formulations and idiosyncracies of her or his language community. What the reinforcement model cannot deal with, however, is the complexity of the grammatical structures and linguistic rules which are shown by the child even in the face of impoverished input. More specifically, children routinely comprehend and produce linguistic forms of such sophistication as to imply the operation of an active process going further than the externally-motivated repetitions suggested by behaviourism.

Skinner's limited view here is linked with the way he theorises only one aspect of language, speech, which in turn is viewed as no more than verbal *behaviour*, originally emitted naturally as babble but then adjusted to the communicative needs of the child and her or his social world through the reinforcement process. This idea shares the defects of the passive view of socialisation characteristic of behaviourism, in which development becomes a matter of inserting social rules into the child's untheorised mental 'blank space'. More strongly, it provides at best a very impoverished account of meanings, reducing them to the desire for reinforcement. Skinner's operant account of language development makes language a procedure for naming objects and communicating demands motivated only by the desire for reward; aside from this desire, there is no inner world.

Before moving on from Skinner, it is worth noting two areas in which his work is productive. First, as mentioned above, it is clearly the case that in some sense imitation must operate in language learning, or else a child would never learn the particular codes of her or his linguistic community. At least, the child must copy the sound patterns around her or him to be able to communicate in words. Secondly, what Skinner's approach does do rather powerfully is to direct attention towards the social aspects of language development: language may not arise through simple reinforcement processes, but it does come about in the context of social encounters, with at least one of its functions being to serve and enrich the quality of those encounters. Although most post-Skinnerian theorists recognise this, not all of them have paid it due attention.

In some respects, Chomsky's contribution to the psychology of language (as opposed to his contribution to linguistics) derives from the force of his demonstration of the simplistic nature of operant theory when faced with the actual complexities of language. The linguistic and grammatical creativity of the child, the speed with which she or he could learn to communicate sophisticated meanings, the virtual universality of language within the human species – all these indicated to Chomsky that language development could not possibly be dependent on the crude vagaries of parental reinforcement. However, Chomsky's approach differs from Skinner's on more grounds than just the mechanisms proposed to explain language acquisition. They differ in their views of what language is, of the relationship between language and other mental systems, of the role of the environment in influencing language development, and of the basic questions which are worth asking of language development. To take the final point first: Skinner, alongside many other psychologists, prioritises what was earlier called the 'acquisition question', whilst also providing some answers to the 'social question' of the relationship between language and social environment. Chomsky, addressing the issue of the virtual universality of languge and the remarkable ability which children show in developing linguistic competence even when the information provided them is fragmentary and impoverished, is more concerned with the 'genetic question' of what the necessary prerequisites to language learning might be, than he is to spell out possible acquisition processes. In the course of his answering of the genetic question, Chomsky does, however, offer some provocative positions on both the acquisition and social questions; he also raises more general issues concerned with the relationship of innate processes to development in social contexts, and with the functions of cognitive events that are generated 'internally' by an individual.

Chomsky rejects the view of language as verbal behaviour, but also refuses to see it as defined by its communicative function. Rather, he argues that it is a cognitive process in its own right, separate from thought and communication, but utilisable to certain ends:

> Language serves as an instrument for free expression of thought, unbounded in scope, uncontrolled by stimulus conditions though appropriate to situations, available for use in whatever contingencies our thought processes can comprehend. This 'creative aspect of language use' is a characteristic species property of humans. (Chomsky, 1980, p. 222)

Language is, therefore, transparent in the sense that it can be used to 'carry' or express thought, envisioned as a separate cognitive modality. But language has a real objective existence of its own, too, and this is as *grammar*, which can be 'analysed in terms of a certain structure of rules, principles and representations in the mind' (Chomsky, 1980, p. 91). It is these 'rules, principles and representations' that generate linguistic forms; they are at the heart of language, with the task of psychologists (amongst others) being to explore the way the grammatical system interacts with other cognitive systems (such as those dealing with concepts) to produce observable language behaviour. Language, therefore, does not just 'have' a grammar; in its essentials, it *is* a grammar; to be precise, a 'generative grammar'.

> I have argued that the grammar represented in the mind is a 'real object', indeed that a person's language should be defined in terms of this grammar. (Chomsky, 1980, p. 120)

Grammar is internally represented in the mind; from it all knowledge of language is derived.

Chomsky makes a number of specific proposals as to what this generative grammar may consist of, but these linguistic details are not of concern here. Rather, the issue that has taxed psychologists has been his proposals concerning the mechanisms whereby the internal grammar is manifested as linguistic competence. For Chomsky, language is not part of a general cognitive system, arising (as the Piagetians claim) from specific experiences. Rather, the remarkable facility with which children become expert users of language on the basis of weak data suggests that the core of language is a powerful grammar of a universal kind, and that this grammar is innately known. This 'universal grammar' is seen by Chomsky as a genetic programme, specifying in great detail the possible ways in which a language may be organised, but also containing parameters that can be altered (within bounds) by experience.

Universal grammar is a system that is genetically determined at the initial state, and is specified, sharpened, articulated, and refined under the conditions set by experience to yield the particular grammars that are represented in the steady states attained. Looking at the question of the growth of language ('language learning') in this way, we can see how it is possible for a person to know vastly more than he has experienced. (Chomsky, 1980, p. 234)

The study of universal grammar is part of the study of biology: calling it innate does not mean that it cannot be specified in more detail (as noted above, Chomsky develops a number of hypotheses as to what this more detailed specification might look like); it simply means that it is a starting point for development, rather than a product of experience.

Although the child is theorised by Chomsky as possessing an innate grammatical facility, this has to be translated through experience into knowledge of a specific language. Chomsky argues that the fundamental structure of all human languages is very similar, allowing the universal grammar possessed by the child to operate within very restrictive principles. The gradual adaptation of this universal grammar to specific linguistic knowledge comes about through the operation of a hypothetical 'Language Acquisition Device' (LAD) which oversees a set of necessary transitions that differentiate between infant and adult levels of linguistic ('grammatical' and 'pragmatic') competence. LAD, which is basically the operation of the parameters built into the universal grammar, allows the child to match her or his internal representation of possible grammars against an analysis of the actual language to which she or he is exposed. By a process of hypothesis testing, various candidate grammars are proposed and selected between, until a steady state is reached that matches the child's inner grammar with what is actually characteristic of the language of the community (Chomsky, 1965, 1980; Gleitman and Wanner, 1982). In contrast to Skinner, but like Piaget, Chomsky proposes that the child is an active hypothesis-generator of linguistic forms which are then tested against the reality of the input received from other language users; because of the richness of the child's innate 'theory' (universal grammar) and the restrictions on what is possible, this process will be highly successful.

The most controversial element in Chomsky's formulation amongst psychologists, has been his emphasis on an innate, relatively abstract core for language. In Bruner's (1983) gloss, 'Syntax was independent of knowledge of the world, and of communicative function . . . Linguistic *competence* was there from the start, ready to express itself when performance constraints were extended by the growth of requisite skills' (p. 33). In a simple sense, there must be a biological component to language; that is, for language to be possible there must be present the brain structures that make it so. This says no more than that humans are biological creatures, unable to do anything which the structure of their bodies, including their brains, makes impossible. It is also presumably something about the human brain that makes language almost a universal phenomenon amongst non brain-damaged people, but absent in non-human animals (notwithstanding the words taught to chimps – see Walker, 1984). So it seems undeniable that humans must possess a species-specific inherited ability to develop language. However, Chomsky goes further than this in suggesting that it is not just the biological hardware necessary for language that is in-born, but also the most important elements of the software, the template-program from which all manifestations of language are generated.

There is some evidence which can be used to support this position. For example, Lenneberg's (1967) investigations provide influential backing for Chomsky's theories by apparently demonstrating that linguistic abilities are acquired in the same order and at roughly the same pace in radically different languages, and also that there may be a 'critical period' in which exposure to linguistic input is necessary if language learning is to be activated. On the other hand, more recent research has revealed differences in the patterns of language acquisition demonstrated by different children (Harris and Coltheart, 1986), as well as the development of linguistic abilities amongst children brought up in extremely deprived circumstances (Skuse, 1984) – although disproval of the critical period hypothesis is not fatal for the idea of LAD.

It is, however, at a more conceptual level that dispute over how to conceive of language development is mostly to be found. Chomsky's argument concerning universal grammar focuses attention on the child's active capacity to theorise about the world and to generate and adapt rules for the use of language. In this respect, his work has gone unchallenged by most psychologists (see below). Nevertheless, his promotion of the idea that universal grammar is an aspect of biology may be only one possible rendering of the data. Granted that the facility with which children develop language is striking and that this suggests the existence of a predisposition to linguistic competence, it could still be that the balance between innate and environmental influences is rather different from that proposed by Chomsky. Chomsky's nativism reduces the social world to minimal significance – a trigger for the activation of LAD, a set of signals for the adaptation of the paramaters of the universal grammar. It may, however, be possible to explain regularities in development in an alternative way if one recognises that there is enormous overlap in the rather limited range of environmental situations encountered by young children. Harris and Coltheart (1986) express this as follows:

> The kind of model which best accounts for individual differences is one which regards language acquisition as a process in which the child develops hypotheses and tests them out. While there will be underlying similarities in these hypotheses, the precise details will differ from child to child, although the nature of language itself, and its relation to the world, means that the range of hypotheses which the child will develop and test out will be circumscribed. (p. 70)

Whether the degree to which this occurs is sufficiently strong to explain language regularities without Chomskyan assumptions of innate determination is another point, potentially at least an empirical one. As will be described below, Piagetians and researchers on 'pragmatics' have produced accounts of children's experiences that provide some guidelines in this sphere. However, it can be stated here that the theme of language as an objective phenomenon in its own right, not arising in any simple way out of the experience of particular children, is one which recurs powerfully throughout the literature, in psychoanalysis as well as in Chomsky's work. Whether it is inherited biologically or embedded in cultural products, language may be structured from some other site than the child's consciousness; it may make the child a 'subject' of its development as much as the other way round. Chomsky's genetic reading of language development makes it an abstract force that is present in the child's brain but is related only in very complex ways to experience and to the specifics of particular linguistic usages. Other psychological theories attempt to describe in more detail how experience can become causal of the child's linguistic ability. But psychoanalysts, particularly Lacanians, are akin to Chomsky in their suspicion of experience: they too, if in a different way, have been impressed with the evidence that language operates outside the individual, and that it may surprise one with its materiality.

**Constructions and pragmatics**

Chomsky's view of the child as an active generator of linguistic structures was shared in the 1970s by an influential group of theorists supporting the 'cognitive hypothesis'. In its fullest form, this proposes that language develops as an element in general cognitive maturation. This is a contrasting position to that of Chomsky in that language is viewed not as a separate entity which interacts with other cognitive processes, but as an aspect of a more basic and general cognitive function. In the words of one of the most persuasive proponents of this position, Cromer (1979), the cognitive hypothesis suggests that,

the course of first language acquisition is determined by the developing cognitive processes in the young child. Both the pace of acquisition and the types of linguistic forms and even lexical items which are used by the child are constrained by the cognitive processes which determine what the child is capable of understanding. (p. 102)

The work of Piaget on symbolic operations was a particularly powerful theoretical influence on this work. In his view, language develops as one of a number of symbolic operations, a particularly important tool but no different in kind from other modes of thought such as visual imagery or symbolic play (Piaget, 1951). Certain cognitive abilities, particularly the achievement of a capacity for mental representation and an awareness of object permanence at the end of the sensorimotor period of development, are necessary precursors of language; given their achievement, acquisition of language follows. The child is thus a hypothesis-tester, as in Chomsky's theory, but one whose competence develops through experience of the world, rather than being generated by internal processes that are only triggered by the environment. As Chomsky (1980) argues, however, the exact relationship between language and thought remains mysterious in that the Piagetian approach is very vague on the details of how the child's sensori-motor achievements are determinant of linguistic structure.

There is a considerable amount of empirical evidence to support the suggestion that many cognitive abilities develop prior to knowledge of the linguistic means for giving them expression, and, more strongly, that cognitive competence is a necessary prerequisite of linguistic competence (Cromer, 1974; 1979). There is also evidence that while cognitive ability may be necessary for linguistic ability, it is not sufficient – that language has its own constraints and possibly its own roots (Butterworth, 1984). Hence Cromer's (1979) espousal of what he terms the 'weak form' of the cognitive hypothesis:

Cognitive development predisposes the child to encode certain meanings; how these are actually encoded in language depends on both underlying cognitive processes and specifically linguistic ones. The specifically linguistic processes are still little understood. (p. 125)

This version of the cognitive hypothesis has many attractions. It retains the notion of the child as active constructor of linguistic knowledge while recognising the real constraints that might be placed upon the use of language by the nature of that language (e.g. the difficulty of certain grammatical forms). It helps to separate the concepts of 'language' and 'thought' in a way that would be clarifying for other theorists (including psychoanalytic ones) to take up. Most importantly, by emphasising the role of cognition, the cognitive hypothesis reintroduces meanings into descriptions of language development. However, this is done in a very limited fashion. Meaning is envisioned as comprehension of experience, coded and stored internally within the child and only then expressed linguistically. It is thus *cognitive* development that is made the domain of meaning, while language is largely relegated to a naming process whereby these pre-given meanings are put into words. Where a role for language in producing meaning is allowed, as in the weak form of the hypothesis, this role is noted to be 'still little understood', but is generally seen as having to do with the ease with which the child's thoughts can be coded into the particular language of her or his community (Harris, 1982). An alternative argument here is that language development can aid the acquisition of meaning within a context in which thought and language have separate roots but interlacing developmental paths. In addition, the neglect of meaning in the cognitive approach is reflected in an impoverished view of the contribution of the social environment to linguistic development: there is simply the child, a self-contained cognitive organism, gradually developing her or his mental model to make sense of the world.

Dissatisfaction with the cognitive devaluation of language and its absence of a social perspective has led to renewed interest, amongst Western psychologists, in the theory proposed by the Soviet psychologist Vygotsky. Vygotsky (1934) suggests that language, specifically speech, has separate origins from thought, but that during development the two functions become linked. This occurs at the point when 'verbal thought' appears (at about two years of age); significantly, verbal thought is regarded by Vygotsky as an internalisation of social speech which then becomes partly directive of, and partly a vehicle for, thought. Thus, the child's speech automatically has social functions rooted in its communicative role, and gradually develops a self-controlling function in which it becomes directed more towards the self ('egocentrism'), until inner speech becomes established. Butterworth (1984) notes,

Hence, according to Vygotsky, verbal thought is the outcome of a prolonged developmental process in which the child transfers initially overt speech, which serves a social function and is of social origin, inwards to the mental plane . . . Since language is rooted in social relations, the direction of development is from social to private speech (rather than from private to socialised, as Piaget argued). (p. 160)

It is interesting to note how, in Vygotsky's theory, allowance of the possibility that language can have an objective existence which can enter into causal relations with cognition (as well as thought influencing language), is linked to a sharp awareness of how social relationships can become part of the child's inner world. The primary function of language is seen as social (communication); as the child becomes more sophisticated, so inner speech develops, incorporating the social structuring of language. In this model, although the child's thoughts have their own cognitive roots, there is a gradual strengthening of social influences over thought as language becomes established in the mind. Again, as with Piaget's theory, the exact mechanisms whereby language structure becomes established are sketched rather vaguely. Nevertheless, Vygotsky's assertion of the role of language as a carrier of sociality presents a challenge to nativist views and an opening for approaches that attempt to articulate the power of language to produce individuals as subjects of particular communities. In particular, Vygotsky's argument that language is a symbol system which is historically determined, makes the developing child subject to culture in a very similar way to that proposed by some psychoanalysts, particularly Lacan (see below). Bruner and Haste (1987) draw this issue out:

Vygotsky sees the culture changing through the accretion of concepts and representations that emerge historically – changes that, so to speak, reflect the plight of individuals living in a common culture. Over historical time, this changed state of cultural representations affects the dialogue into which the child enters as he grows up. (p. 17)

This reading of Vygotsky makes his a theory which addresses not only the 'social' question, but also the 'constructionist' one.

Through language, the assumptions, perceptions, priorities and history of the child's social group – in other words, its ideology – take a formative role in the construction of the child's selfhood. The meaning of reality is always a symbolised meaning: Vygotsky's suggestion is that the process of symbolisation is one which carries within it a social charge. To a considerable extent, this must be an 'unconscious' process, at least in the cognitive sense of lying outside ordinary reflective awareness: psychoanalysts would argue that the penetration of the child by sociality through the medium of language, is unconscious in the dynamic sense as well.

It is awareness of the importance of social context in constructing language abilities that has governed the last of the psychological positions to be described here. This is usually presented as a theory of 'pragmatics', focusing on the function of language as a method of communicating meanings.

> In this view, the central idea is communicative intent: we communicate with some end in mind, some function to be fulfilled. (Bruner, 1983, p. 36)

However, neither the content of the 'communicative intent' nor the form of its expression are pre-given; rather, they are developed through a process of social interaction that begins before language proper appears.

> The child's use of language rests on her ability to appreciate the perspective of others – that *you* mean *you* when you say *I*, and *I* mean *I* when I say it, which involves a working understanding of reciprocal relations. In relations with others the child early has the capacity to negotiate meaning and to interpret what is going on – even before her full powers of lexico-grammatical speech have matured. (Bruner and Haste, 1987, p. 2)

Hence, adherents of the pragmatic view emphasise the continuity between language and pre- or proto-linguistic forms of communication; more strongly, language and communication are often conflated as one and the same thing.

There is considerable evidence supporting the notion that some of the characteristics of linguistic interchange are also present in early non-linguistic communications between infants and familiar others. For instance, Schaffer (1975) has documented how early mother–infant vocalisations seem to have a turn-taking pattern, the mother filling in the pauses in the child's activity. Bruner (1983) points out how infants and their caretakers develop a number of agreed 'formats', a format being 'a standardised, initially microcosmic interaction pattern between an adult and an infant' (p. 120). These formats can be observed in repetitive games such as object exchange and 'peek-a-boo' and have a 'grammar' of their own which has language-like properties. In addition, it has become clear that children develop early a number of interactive abilities which may be necessary for language to be used in a communicative way. These abilities include some awareness of intersubjectivity (the existence of real others in the environment), a regulated turn-taking competence which may be embedded in formats of the kind described above, and non-verbal abilities to coordinate attention and control the joint activity of the participants in an interchange (Goodwin, 1980; Butterworth, 1984).

Evidence such as this has been interpreted to mean that there are continuities between the prelinguistic and linguistic communications of the child, and that great significance should be credited to those aspects of prelinguistic experience which are linked with, and which may be organised to serve the goal of, language development. Schaffer (1977) notes the significance of this claim:

> Instead of seeing language arising *de novo* at the beginning of the second year, it is now being related to the preverbal communication patterns that are already established between mother and infant in the early months of life. Language acquisition, in other words, has been firmly placed within a social setting. (p. 4)

The role of this 'social setting' in supporting the child's language learning is perhaps most coherently presented by Bruner (1983). His position is summarised in the following quotation:

> Language acquisition 'begins' before the child utters his first lexico-grammatical speech. It begins when mother and infant create a predictable format of interaction that can serve as a microcosm for communicating and for constituting a shared

reality. The transactions that occur in such formats constitute the 'input' from which the child then masters grammar, how to refer and mean, and how to realise his intentions communicatively. (p. 18)

Although Bruner accepts that there are innate aspects to language learning, his emphasis is different from that of Chomsky. Whereas the latter focuses on children's supposedly inherent knowledge of basic linguistic structures ('universal grammar'), for Bruner the starting point of language development is a set of inherited perceptual abilities. These offer the child 'ways of embedding his gestures and vocalisations into contexts of action and interaction' (p. 131), and hence impose restrictions on the rules that a child might generate in her or his search for linguistic structures and meanings. Such inherited abilities include a 'means-end readiness' which enable the child to tune in to the requirements of action, and a predilection for human voices, faces and gestures – that is, for social responsiveness. In addition, Bruner disagrees with Chomsky's downplaying of the environment; for Bruner, every LAD must have its LASS, a Language Acquisition Support System, consisting in the regularised series of interactions between adult and infant that allow order to be placed on the child's communications, conventionalising them and making them culturally appropriate. A major constituent of LASS is the collection of repetitive action sequences or formats, mentioned above; the crucial point is that it is through predictable, familiar social interactions and 'negotiations' that the child both develops some knowledge of the world, and employs that knowledge to make sense of communications and to emit her or his own. Children thus learn about contexts and hence, using Bruner's word, about 'culture' before they learn language; language learning consists in finding culturally appropriate linguistic ways for communicating one's intentions to others. For Bruner,

> it is the requirement of *using* culture as a necessary form of coping that forces man to master language. Language is the means for interpreting and regulating the culture. (p. 24)

Because of their in-built sociability and readiness to find order in things, children utilise the repetitive formats that structure their social interactions to learn about their social world and how to communicate their desires within it.

Bruner's work, and that of the other 'pragmatists', has provided a lively and provocative alternative to earlier psychological theories of language development. The account of the way early experience is structured through microsocial encounters makes sense of observable regularities in development and also provides some content to the rather vague claim that language learning is linked to earlier experiences. In addition, Bruner's postulation that what is inherited by the child is a readiness for social interaction and an ability and eagerness to make sense of the world, which is then applied to routine and regularised environments, provides a more specific elaboration of the general cognitive thesis. Finally, the focus on the social context in which language development occurs is of great significance, especially as it is connected in this theory to a wider view of language as a cultural tool. This aspect of the pragmatists' approach creates the space for a broadening of the cognitive position from its individualistic perspective to a view of language as a social accomplishment.

Despite these positive attributes, there are some significant drawbacks to the pragmatist stance, some of which link with generally problematic aspects of psychological accounts of language. Empirically, it remains unclear exactly what, and how important, is the relationship between early non-verbal communications and later speech. Golinkoff and Gordon (1983), for example, point to the dearth of evidence supporting any effect of early communication on later language acquisition. They go on to present a more refined version of the proposed link, arguing that it is not the early communications of the infant, which have an interactional purpose, that are significant for language, but the later (last quarter of the first year) instrumental communications. This implies that only some aspects of pre-linguistic communication are relevant. Specifically, it may be that the early interactions of infant and adult are built upon the *adult's* ability to support and elaborate the child's innate repertoire; the qualitative shift to intentional, 'instrumental' communications still needs to be explained (Butterworth, 1984).

In principle at least, empirical considerations such as that mentioned above may be resolved by more careful analysis of infant–adult interactions. The conceptual limitations of the pragmatist approach are more troubling, however. The first major one is shared with some other psychological theories: the tendency to reduce language to communication and thence to speech. By stressing the continuity between pre-linguistic communication and language, the pragmatist approach directs attention away from the child's cognitive competence and also tends to pre-judge the issue of whether there is anything special about language itself. Just as with some psychoanalytic theories, this threatens to make language, communication and culture all collapse into one concept, with a resulting loss of important differentiations. In focusing on communication as the context for language development, a theory is produced which is admirably social but which deals with only one aspect of language: language as output, as verbal speech.

The advantage of this position is that it provides a model for understanding the complexities of language use within the context of a child's particular linguistic community. However, rather as with Vygotsky, it assumes that the use of language parallels the child's linguistic *input-processing* ability; that is, that the internal capacities of the child to comprehend language, and the incorporation of linguistic structures into wider mental functions, are in some way produced by the internalisation of social communication patterns. The pragmatists' failure to examine language, as an entity in itself, rather than the child's growing ability to use language socially, follows from this – as does the similar failure of all approaches mentioned so far, with the exception of Chomsky's. Apart from the general argument that certain interpersonal communicative abilities are precursors for linguistic ones, the pragmatists supply few details of how language itself develops as an object of knowledge. Learning about the particular meanings embedded in one's 'culture' does not necessarily teach one grammar. More broadly, it is not the case that all communications are linguistic; nor, for that matter, is it likely that all linguistic utterances are communications; in addition, 'culture' consists in more than agreed modes of expressing intentions.

Finally, the pragmatists leave unsolved the problem of meaning. Despite Bruner's emphasis on social context, his work retains an assumption that meanings are pre-given, that what the child masters over time is a de-coding of the world and a knowledge of what linguistic forms to employ to give expression to her or his intentions. The intentions themselves, the content of the 'speech acts' to which Bruner refers, are left untheorised; social context regulates their expression, but their origin remains firmly within the individual child. Some other workers in this area have attempted to deal with this issue, for instance Halliday (e.g. 1979), who stresses the social nature of 'learning to mean' and the way it is through intersubjective processes that a child's understanding of her or his own intentions, as well as of the external world, start to take shape. But even in this work there is a strong tendency for 'learning to mean' to refer to the linguistic coding of pre-given meanings, rather than to the carving out of consciousness. As will be described below, it is in this area that psychoanalytic approaches to language present the strongest challenge to psychologists.

### Representation, structure and meaning

Many of the positive and negative aspects of psychological approaches to language development have been mentioned in the preceding discussion. Taken together, the psychological approaches provide a reasonably coherent description of the stages through which language learning progresses, of the extent to which language is learned like any other skill, of the cognitive competencies that are necessary for language production to be possible, and of the microsocial contexts in which language learning occurs. There are useful proposals concerning the nature of the inherited equipment that allows any particular child to extract and use the linguistic features of her or his environment, plus some recognition of the links between language, culture and socialisation. If one considers all this in the light of the various questions about language development posed at the beginning of this chapter, psychologists have offered solutions to those concerning *acquisition* (e.g. language is acquired through activation of a biologically given Language Acquisition Device, or through the generation of rules to cover more and more complex interpersonal formats), *function* (e.g. language is a tool that develops out of wider cognitive capabilities to allow thought to be expressed in a communicable form), and *sociality* (social context offers guidance to the child on the form that these communications must take, and also mediates experience to present it in a cognitively and culturally manageable way). The 'genetic question' is usually answered by assuming an in-built biological propensity towards communication and/or language, although Chomsky's theory is the only one to specify details. With the exception of ideas based on Vygotsky's suggestions concerning the impact of language on thought, there have been few attempts to consider the viability of the 'constructionist' question; the 'experiential' one has not been dealt with at all in the theories so far described. It will be argued in the next sections that the strength of psychoanalytic accounts of language lies precisely in their ability to provide answers to these latter two, relatively neglected, questions.

Although the psychological theories have many productive elements, they are by no means completely adequate. First, the exact processes through which social experience is translated into linguistic knowledge remains unclear – the mechanisms whereby the child selects relevant portions of her or his interactions with others and encounters with the physical world, and then generalises from these to produce broad and relatively abstract linguistic rules. Appreciation of the complexity of this process is one major source of Chomsky's proposal that knowledge of grammar is largely innate; the more environmentally-oriented approaches identify possibly important aspects of experience while remaining vague on their linguistic consequences. Especially if cognition is given as determinant over language ability, this vagueness can also lead to a neglect of the manner in which language might influence thought: language is viewed as a product of other cognitive processes, a useful tool for representing and communicating them effectively, but it is not theorised in its own right, as something with existence and potential objective power.

Secondly, the notion of 'social context', while a comparatively sophisticated one in Bruner's and Halliday's accounts, remains very limited, both in being restricted to extremely microsocial (mother–infant) interactions, and being simplistic – society, or at least 'culture', consists of a collection of rules allowing individuals to regulate their dealings and communications with one another. There is also a less theoretical sense in which the notion of social context is restricted. As has been pointed out by some psychologists, most approaches to language learning are very ethnocentric, assuming a universal pattern of experience and achievement that is not borne out by the data. For example, Golinkoff and Gordon (1983) suggest that a number of supposedly

'necessary' environmental influences on communication and language development 'may simply be artefacts of child-rearing in
Western culture'. They list four particular such 'universals' that
are now challenged by cross-cultural data: (1) the attribution of
intentions and feelings to pre-linguistic infants; (2) the prevalence
of baby-talk or of an adjusted speech register when adults address
infants and young children (an example here is the notion of
'motherese' as a special mode of talk addressed by mothers to
their infants – see Harris and Coltheart, 1986); (3) the primacy
and importance of a dyadic mother–infant relationship for communication development (a proposal that is very characteristic of
the pragmatist approach); and (4) the necessity for reciprocity of
affect in extended face-to-face interactions (p. 17). This neglect of
the cultural specificity of the processes that lead to language
learning occurs because of psychologists' rather crude theories of
society, and perhaps also of thought. The result is a collection of
theories which are not only ethnocentric in omitting to consider
non-Western modes of upbringing and language acquisition, but
which are also derived from class-based notions of what constitutes
a 'normal' developmental setting. In addition, the assumption of
a particular maternal role that can be found embedded in many
of the psychological (and psychoanalytic, for that matter) theories
is not just another example of ethnocentrism, but also a reminder
that most researchers remain blind to the need for an analysis of
the relationship between language and gender acquisition.

One of the recurrent themes in this description of psychological
approaches to language development relates closely to the alternative attractions of psychoanalysis. This theme concerns the limitations produced by psychology's conceptualisation of language as
a tool, the use of which is learnt by the individual child and which
is then applied to pre-existing cognitions. Language does not, in
this view, generate meanings itself; rather, it is a transparent,
albeit complex, medium for expression of the individual's internal
world. This conception of language can be analysed in relation to
three key notions: representation, structure and meaning (Clifford
and Frosh, 1982). Language is regarded as a system which is used
to represent the thoughts of its speakers and to convey information
to others about the world in which they live. It is able to be used
in this way through possession of a conventional formal structure
(a grammar) which governs the formation of statements and

determines the meaning expressed by them. The acquisition of language is, therefore, a process whereby the child learns the rules of representation and structure and thus learns how to convey meaning, itself conceptualised as a relationship between linguistic structure and the objects or ideas represented by words. Hence, language does not produce meaning, it conveys it; it does not construct consciousness, but is employed by it to name and communicate what is happening inside one's head.

The limitations of this view of language relate mainly to the experiential and constructionist questions posed earlier. First, it is essentialist. The individual and individuated consciousness is assumed to exist prior to the impingement of language, and language acquisition is a process whereby the already-existing but pre-social individual becomes socialised. There is no explanation of where individual consciousness or personal 'meanings' derive from; instead, they are simply assumed always to be in existence, if not easily communicable. This problem is compounded by the way language is theorised as a transparent vehicle for the articulation of rational consciousness. Such a view makes it difficult to explain the way language can take on a life of its own, as something which goes further than, or produces deviations from, the dictates of the user's conscious intentions. For instance, the problems that people characteristically experience in expressing emotions and desires, suggest that language is not just used to name thoughts, but also to create, modify and hide them.

This is linked to another limitation of this view of language – its inability to account fully for the creation of new meanings. In this approach, meaning is separated from its communication, making the two processes independent, with the former prior to the latter. Meanings arise from some unspecified processes, usually concerned with new experiences that are cognitively coded and then communicated linguistically. However, the semantic effectiveness of linguistic forms such as poems and jokes, suggests that language itself can operate creatively on meanings, that language may, at least under certain conditions, possess causal properties having specific and powerful effects upon consciousness.

From what has been said above, it is perhaps not surprising that psychology has fared relatively well in describing the external attributes of language learning – its 'stages' and some of the environmental influences upon it – but is unable to fully construe

its creativity and emotional power. It is here that psychoanalytic
theories enter to fill out the picture. Urwin (1984) supplies a useful
bridge to this work by pointing out how an emotional component
may be integral to language and may result in language changing
the child. Reflecting on Bruner's ideas she notes,

> the specifics of the social regularities in the child's life [will]
> emerge in the content of early linguistic expressions . . . But it
> is not simply a question of the relative frequency of different
> kinds of events in the child's life. It is the issue of relative control
> which matters, and the shifts in position which enable the
> child to move from preverbal communication to language via
> particular identifications. (pp. 309–10)

Language gives the child power, as well as allowing her or him to
take up a position as a subject in an adult system of communication
and interaction. This is not just power to communicate desires
more clearly; it is also power to symbolise and construct them, to
feel 'in control' of separations and of experiences, and to become
a person – to *become* an individual – relating to self and others
along the cultural dimension of 'I' and 'you'. Language operates
creatively not just in the dimension of thinking, but also in the
affective vein; the experience of 'acquiring' language is, according
to Urwin, one of achieving power.

Presentation of this argument, that language produces affective
changes which themselves at least partially determine the trajectory
that linguistic development takes, is a central way in which
psychoanalytically informed theories take up a critical stance
towards psychological ones. In many psychoanalytic theories,
emotional rather than cognitive experience is seen as the driving
force behind language acquisition. Moreover, language operates
as a powerful element in emotional space: that is, it is infused with
an affective charge that makes language important to the child.
The achievement of an ability to symbolise, particularly through
use of the flexible and communicable codes of language, is seen
as a major way in which the child develops the sense that she or
he can understand and manage emotion and desire – in traditional
terms, can control unconscious impulses by making them conscious.
In addition, the emotional power of language gives it an ability to
create meanings in a way that is unimaginable to adherents of

language-as-representation models. This makes language something that is, or at least can be, constitutive of the mind, producing mental contents at the same time as it 'represents' them more or, often, less accurately. That is: psychoanalysis suggests that the emotionally charged nature of language gives it the power to introduce new meanings into the individual's mental space; given its cultural embeddedness, this in turn means that language helps structure the mind along social lines.

In what follows, these claims of psychoanalysis are elaborated through description of some of the most provocative psychoanalytic approaches to language. It will be suggested that the challenge which is presented to traditional psychological theories is very strong, but that the cognitive naïvety of psychoanalysis produces some fairly fatal flaws in its argument. What remains are two disciplines, neither of which supply a complete understanding of language development on their own, but which show some promise of being amenable to creative combination in this area of work.


**Language and the unconscious**

From the very start of his psychoanalytic investigations, Freud understood language to be more than a transparent medium for thought. The convolutions, inadequacies, gaps and errors in linguistic production – both spoken and written – are all regarded by Freud as revelatory of the underlying intentions and meanings of the person; indeed, they are *more* revealing than well-organised discourse, which is produced by the repression of disruptive, unconscious forces. Language is thus no innocent device for communication, but a subversive medium to be explored as much for what it hides about a person's intentions as for what it reveals. Where language breaks down, there the true 'meaning' of an utterance may be found. Hence Freud's (1917) choice of parapraxes as the starting-point for his *Introductory Lectures*: parapraxes 'are not chance events; they have a sense, they arise from the concurrent action – or, perhaps rather, the mutually opposing action – of two different intentions' (p. 70). Moreover, 'intentions can find expression in a speaker of which he himself knows nothing but which I am able to infer from circumstantial evidence' (p. 92).

Language both hides and reveals, its 'surface structure' of sense masking its 'deep structure' of desire.

Freud presents a dual notion of the relationship between language and the unconscious. On the one hand, it is precisely the absence of language that defines something as unconscious. In his discussion of psychosis in the metapsychological paper in *The Unconscious*, Freud (1915) makes the clearest possible statement that language is excluded from the unconscious, and that it is the formulation of something into words that transfers it to consciousness.

> We now seem to know all at once what the difference is between a conscious and an unconscious presentation . . . The conscious presentation comprises the presentation of the thing plus the presentation of the word belonging to it, while the unconscious presentation is the presentation of the thing alone . . . A presentation which is not put into words . . . remains thereafter in the Ucs. in a state of repression. (p. 207)

The unconscious possesses no language in the ordinary sense, nor any of the conditions that make language possible: its absolute negativity (no order, no time, no negation) precludes the organised structure by which language is partially defined. However, there must be a way in which language has access to the unconscious, or the attachment of words to things would be impossible, as would be the whole psychoanalytic project of making sense of desire through the speech of analyst and analysand. The language of the unconscious may be 'psychotic', concrete language, but it cannot be totally impervious to symbolising in the terms given by reality. Language itself, then, is a point at which the unconscious makes itself known. Although it is a secondary-process phenomenon, organised according to rational principles, it is continually infiltrated and undermined by primary-process thought, resulting both in aberrations (such as parapraxes) and in creativity. On the other hand, under some conditions language has a capacity to modify primary process thought, to release the analysand from the control of unconscious forces. Forrester (1980) expresses this paradoxical relationship between language and desire in Freud's work through a discussion of the way speech dissolves symptoms by displacing repressed memory, reversing the usual view that language is the support of all symbolic permanence.

> In some manner that is still unclear, speech is the agent by which permanent marks that lead to the suffering of the symptom are dissolved, forgotten . . . If language is the means by which permanence and memory *qua* insistent reminiscence come to be found at the heart of the symptom, it is via the ephemerality of speech-consciousness that a symptom can be dissolved, worn away – and forgotten. (p. 137)

Language both expresses the symbolism of the unconscious and is the means of unravelling it. It therefore embodies subjective experience but also provides a route to the source of that experience – the construction of subjectivity itself.

Freud's identification of a special role for language as mediator of unconscious ideas and of therapeutic interventions makes it of special concern to all analytic practitioners, even those who, working for example with children, are alive to other modes of symbolic expression. However, with the exception of Lacan, whose views are described below, psychoanalysts have not produced particularly powerful theories of language development, but have focused instead on the way in which language operates within the analytic environment. Where language development is theorised, it is generally in the context of a wider view of the growth of *symbolism* and its role in mental life. This risks obscuring the specificity of language, making the rather Piagetian assumption that language is simply a particularly powerful example of a more general semiotic function. Nevertheless, there have been some theoretical developments which, through a general account of the growth and functions of symbolism, have supplied insights into the role language may have in a child's emotional life, and articulated the potential source of its therapeutic action. Amongst the various non-Lacanian schools of psychoanalysis, it is Kleinians who have contributed most in this regard.

According to Klein, the motivating energy for the accomplishment of symbolism is anxiety, especially that early anxiety caused by the child's own destructive impulses, which are defensively projected on to an external object. This object then becomes threatening, leading the child to make a series of symbolic substitutions to lessen the experienced force of the external and internal threat. As each object is symbolised, so it too becomes invested with persecutory powers, consequently generating anxiety and producing a shift to a new symbolic object. It is thus negative feelings – sadistic phantasies – that are the origin of symbol formation, continually driving the child to find more roundabout and tolerable ways to represent the significant objects that make up her or his world. The starting point for this is congenital envy and hatred; its fuel is the anxiety that this negativity produces in the infantile ego.

> Since the child desires to destroy the organs (penis, vagina, breast) which stand for the objects, he conceives a dread of the latter. This anxiety contributes to make him equate the organs in question with other things; owing to this equation these in their turn become objects of anxiety, and so he is impelled constantly to make other and new equations, which form the basis of his interest in the new objects and of symbolism. (Klein, 1930, p. 97)

Symbol formation and the anxiety it is built upon are thus crucial components of early development, 'the foundation of all phantasy and sublimation' (ibid.), and also the source of the child's relationship to reality. For the earliest experiences of the child are wholly phantastic, with no differentiation between objects of anxiety in terms of their reality and power; the formation of new equivalences alongside the ego's growing capacity to tolerate anxiety are the central components of the child's ability to relate to reality. Symbolism, in this theory, is a chain that links internal phantasy with the external world.

Segal (1957) has provided a useful clarification of the Kleinian theory of symbolism which also points out its implications for language. First, she follows Klein's argument that symbol formation is fuelled by anxiety, but also draws attention to the intrinsic link between the ego (which 'does' the symbolising), the object (which is translated into a symbol) and the phantasy (which motivates the symbolisation). Symbol formation is thus always a three-term relationship, its context set by the ego's relations with its objects. Most importantly, symbol formation has a reparative role, lessening the sense of guilt and loss that derives from the child's envious aggression towards the object. Creating an internal symbol is a

way in which this destructiveness can be made good by repairing
the 'damaged' object – this being a first stirring of the creative
process that has its apotheosis in art. Hence, symbolisation proper
is not the same as early phantasy; it is a process that flowers fully
only in the depressive position, when the links between aggression
and loss can be felt by the child. In explaining this, Segal employs
a distinction between the symbol and the object that parallels
Freud's earlier account of the relationship between thing-presen-
tations in the unconscious and their preconscious word-presen-
tation. In Segal's account, the important distinction is between
'symbolic equations' and symbols proper. Symbolic equations are
characteristic of early development of the paranoid-schizoid kind;
in symbolic equations 'the symbol-substitute is felt to *be* the
original object' (Segal, 1957, p. 57). This is a restatement of the
usual psychoanalytic understanding of psychotic thought, that it is
constituted by a confusion between words and things. In contrast,

> the symbol proper, available for sublimation and furthering the
> development of the ego, is felt to *represent* the object; its own
> characteristics are recognised, respected and used. It arises when
> depressive feelings predominate over the paranoid-schizoid
> ones, when separation from the object, ambivalence, guilt and
> loss can be experienced and tolerated. The symbol is used not
> to deny but to overcome loss. (Segal, 1957, p. 57)

Symbols are used to reparative ends, to make damage good by
recovering and reinstating the lost object in symbolic form. In
addition, once the capacity to symbolise has been developed,
early, pre-depressive conflicts and anxieties which could not
previously be dealt with because of their absolute concreteness,
can begin to be alleviated by being translated into symbolic form.
Thus, the increased strength and integrity of the ego in the
depressive position both supports and is enhanced by symbolic
resolution of earlier conflicts and anxieties.

Finally, symbols are also used for purposes of communication,
both to other people and to oneself. It is here that the origins of
verbal language reside: it emerges from the ability to symbolise
which in turn is a product of the rapprochement between phantasy,
ego and object that is the achievement of the depressive position.
Language is therefore a major way in which anxieties can be

resolved and drives satisfied, both in the present and in the past, through integration of early emotional states into later developmental stages. This is, presumably, one source of the therapeutic impact of the 'talking cure'.

In an evocative and compelling 'postscript' to the 1957 paper, written in 1979 and showing the influence of Bion's work, Segal brings together the interpersonal aspects of language learning with its emotional significance.

> Verbalisation can be looked at from the angle of the relation between the container and the contained. Unlike the unconscious forms of symbolism, speech has to be learned. Though the baby begins by producing sounds, these sounds have to be taken up by the environment to be converted into speech, and words or phrases have to be learned from the environment. The infant has had an experience and the mother provides the words or phrase which binds this experience. It contains, encompasses and expresses the meaning. It provides a container for it. The infant can then internalise this word or phrase containing the meaning. (Segal, 1979, p. 63)

In this striking image is expressed much of the strength of the psychoanalytic position on language development. The child uses symbols and words to deal with anxiety, to make translations and reparations as necessary. But this is not simply an internal process: language is an essentially interpersonal event. Again, this does not refer only to the obvious fact that a major function of language is to allow communication of meanings between people; it also has reference to the affective components of early development. The unknown, inexpressible and potentially terrifying experience of the child, whether internal or external, is taken in by the mother, made meaningful and safe, and then given back to the child in an expressible and manageable form. The uncontained has become contained; the child's unshaped desires and anxieties are given form and meaning through being moulded in the mother's holding response. Language learning is not just a process of learning the names for external objects and for things that happen inside one's head; it is also a process of giving and receiving, of discovering meanings and of becoming powerful and safe. This image, of course, does not only apply to early language learning; it is also an image of psychotherapy – of having one's anxieties named, contained and returned in a manageable and meaningful way.

This form of psychoanalysis provides answers to most of the questions posed at the beginning of this chapter. In answer to the question of how a child develops the skills required for language, Kleinians stress the need for a relatively integrated ego and an ability to symbolise the relationship between ego and object in a constructive form. The functional and experiential questions are run together to suggest that language is a way of creating meaning out of uncertainty, and of dealing with anxiety; in the process, it produces a stronger sense of integrity, stability and power. There is less that is explicit on the social question, but as much as is present in most psychological theories: it is in the microsocial, mother–child context that psychoanalysts see language learning taking place, with the success of the mother in symbolically containing and naming the child's experiences being a crucial variable in determining linguistic progress. Finally, although not specifically addressed in the theory, there are Kleinian implications for the constructionist question. If the balance between ego and anxiety is a major factor in helping the child's mental structure to develop, then the linguistic containment provided by the mother will be a contributory influence of some importance. It will make a difference to the progress of the depressive position and hence also to the integration of earlier concerns, having an impact on the personality structure of the child.

Despite the richness of the suggested 'answers' described above, they cannot go unchallenged. First, the Kleinian account of language and symbolism suffers from the usual drawback of psychoanalytic theories – uncertainty concerning its evidential basis. There is some observational evidence suggesting that children feel more powerful and secure when they have become able to linguistically articulate a distressing event such as separation (Urwin, 1984). However, there are no clear empirical demonstrations that the success of the mother in 'naming' the child's anxieties is connected with linguistic development in any ascertainable way. Secondly, Kleinianism is less explicit than the psychological approaches on the exact patterns of linguistic interaction that proceed between parent and infant, the cognitive mechanisms active in a language-learning child, and the progression of linguistic stages that can usually be observed. This is not simply a descriptive problem, but also reflects an uncertainty about psychological processes. For instance, it is difficult to see how a child will comprehend that her or his mother is naming the particular experience or emotional state which is causing anxiety. The child may indeed feel comforted and helped by the mother's general ability to offer a stable and 'containing' presence, but this is different from learning the specific linguistic features of language.

It is here that Kleinian theory, and the psychoanalytic approach in general, is at its weakest. While it presents a persuasive (if empirically contentious) account of how a child might benefit emotionally from an ability to use language, it speaks only very vaguely and rather mystically of the cognitive processes enabling that child to develop this ability. Somehow, exposure to a containing 'environment' leads the child to develop linguistic abilities to symbolise and express feelings; but in this 'somehow' lie many of the most important questions concerning the acquisition of language.

It is clear from this discussion that the main strength of the Kleinian account lies in its answers to the 'experiential' and 'constructionist' questions, its portrayal of the emotional impact of learning language and the effect of this on personality development. As noted earlier, these are the aspects of language development neglected most completely by psychological theories. Indeed, it is because psychological and psychoanalytic approaches focus on different aspects of the growth of language that they may not be as incompatible as they are in some other spheres. Psychologists have presented descriptions of the stages of language development and, to some extent, accounts of the cognitive processes that are involved. Psychoanalysts, particularly Kleinians, have presented a clinically-based theory of the significance that language development has for the child's emotional life, and have also suggested that linguistic development may be motivated not just by the requirements of communication, but also by the need to overcome internal states of anxiety. Together, the two accounts supply a much fuller image of language development than either do separately: language is a cognitive process of considerable complexity, but it also has an impact on, and a place in, a child's feelings about her or himself and the world.

One limitation that the Kleinian account of language development shares with most psychological theories is its failure to consider cultural processes that go further than mother–child interactions. This makes it vulnerable to the same charges of ethnocentrism, classism and sexism as can be levelled against psychological theories; indeed, psychoanalysts have been even more normative in their assumptions and less open to evidence from other cultures than have psychologists. More generally still, the focus on mother–child interactions makes language a product of the microsocial environment, thus neglecting the possible role of features of the wider social world. This is a problem with Kleinian and object relations theory in many fields (Frosh, 1987), but the way language automatically refers to a community and to shared patterns of reference and communication makes it a particularly important test case. In recent years, one psychoanalytic school of thought has increasingly come to dominate discussions of this kind, although there are as many analytically-inclined authors who oppose it as welcome it. This school is that of the French analyst Jacques Lacan.

### Language and desire

The weight Lacan places upon language as the core of human functioning can be seen from the following passage:

> It is the world of words that creates the world of things – the things originally confused in the *hic et nunc* of the all in the process of coming-into-being – by giving its concrete being to their essence, and its ubiquity to what has always been . . . Man speaks, then, but it is because the symbol has made him man. (Lacan, 1953, p. 65)

This seems like the strongest envisionable form of an influential approach in psychology, the 'Sapir–Whorf hypothesis', which postulates that it is only through the codes provided by a particular language that thought processes can become organised to divide up the confusion of the world in a manageable way. Without words there is just an incomprehensible flux; the words one has determine the sense one can make. However, there is a crucial difference between the Sapir–Whorf hypothesis and Lacan's theory. For the former, it is the particular words made available by specific languages that determine the order placed upon the world. For Lacan, in contrast, it is not the particular language that one speaks that is at issue; rather, it is language itself that, through the alienation it incorporates into the psyche, creates the splits and flows of subjectivity.

Lacan's understanding of language is founded substantially on a reading of linguistics that derives from the work of Saussure (Clifford and Frosh, 1982). Archard (1984) identifies one of the central attractions of this approach:

> Saussure's innovation was to define *language* as a system – in distinction from actual speech. From such a perspective, it can be seen that language possesses a structure which is beyond the control and consciousness of individual speakers, who nevertheless make use of this structure in their sensible utterances. (p. 60)

In Saussurian linguistics, language is viewed as a system of signs which, through convention rather than any intrinsic property they might possess, have acquired a meaning – a connection with the world. Within this general conception a distinction is made between the 'signifier' and the 'signified', similar to the everyday distinction between the form (sound or spelling) and the sense of a word, but with one important clarification. This is that the distinction between signifier and signified includes no notion of the thing referred to: the signified is not an actual object, but the *mental representations* produced by the activity of the signifier. Meaning is created not by naming a pre-existing thought or an external object, but through the 'play' of signifiers: the meaning of a signifier or a set of signifiers is defined by its relation to, and difference from, other signifiers. For example, what is said can only be interpreted through its implicit relation with what is *not* said: the reply 'yes' to a question has meaning only in that it can be distinguished from 'no'. Language and the communication of information necessarily involves selection out of a set of elements, as Laplanche and Leclaire (1966) explain:

> If a signifier refers to a signified, it is only through the mediation of the entire system of signifiers: there is no signifier that does not refer to the absence of others and that is not defined by its position in the system. (p. 154)

Words do not stand for objects or ideas: they define what else could have been said, and hence differentiate reality in a meaningful way. The usual formula is inverted: language does not acquire meaning through the relation between words and objects – rather, it is through the relation between signs that we are able to refer to the world.

In the description just given of some elements of Saussurian linguistics, there is already an implicitly Lacanian gloss. What Lacan does is to take up the idea of the systemic properties of language and to explore its implications for human psychology. First of all, the conceptualisation of language as a structured system produces the notion that the site of language is not in the consciousness of each individual; rather, the individual is *subjected to* language, which exists as a system outside her or him, into which she or he is incorporated. Language is thus always something alien to the individual, an aspect of the social world that has material existence and that is never fully controlled by the desires of any one of us. Indeed, language is formative in its effects, dictating the patterns of relationship that arise between the subject, the ego and the structures of society. From the individual's point of view, this is experienced as a form of castration, of being cut off from the sources of power.

> Castration for Lacan is not only sexual; more important, it is also linguistic: we are inevitably bereft of any masterful understanding of language, and can only signify ourselves in a symbolic system that we do not command, that, rather, commands us. (Gallop, 1985, p. 20)

Benvenuto and Kennedy (1986) locate this in structuralist terms:

> One could say that the subject-to-be already has a place in the kinship structure before he is born. He is already situated as an element in a complicated, mostly unconscious, network of symbols. (p. 88)

This provides a link, to be more fully explored below, between the symbolic structures of language and those of the Oedipus complex; here, the important point is its reiteration of the primacy of language – the subject, one might say, is spoken rather than speaking' (Lacan, 1953, p. 69, referring to psychosis). Because of this primacy and because of the essential otherness of language, the way it enters into each individual as something from the outside, something alien, there is always a gap between what is expressed in and through language, and what actually exists for the individual. From this arises the project of psychoanalysis, to explore the errors and omissions of language for what they reveal about the 'truth' of the individual subject, that which underlies and disrupts ordinary linguistic activity. Lacan called this procedure 'La Linguisterie', referring to something which might be termed the 'language of the unconscious', which psychoanalysis pursues. 'La linguisterie is, as it were, the science of the word that fails, and thus Lacan was concerned with what one could call the "margins" of ordinary language' (Benvenuto and Kennedy, 1986, p. 17).

It should not be assumed that because Lacan emphasises the alteriority of language and the way it is imposed on the individual, he is also suggesting that the 'meanings' available to every individual are completely fixed. In fact, Lacan takes the Saussurian idea of the arbitrariness of the sign and extends it to suggest that meaning is always slipping away, that it can never be pinned down in any final form. There are two principal examples of Lacan's theorising in this connection. The first is what might be termed the *primacy of the signifier*. For Saussure, the signifier and signified are simply different aspects of the sign; for Lacan, there is a relationship between them in which the former has priority over the latter.

> For the signifier, by its very nature, always anticipates meaning by unfolding its dimension before it . . . From which we can say that it is in the chain of the signifier that the meaning 'insists' but that none of its elements 'consists' in the signification of which it is at that moment capable. We are forced, then, to accept the notion of an incessant sliding of the signified under the signifier. (Lacan, 1957, pp. 153–4)

Paradoxically, this relationship is both determinant and elusive: there is no necessary link between a particular signifier and a particular signified, rather, the latter are continually evoked by the movement of the former. Meaning is embedded in the movement of the 'chain of signifiers', altering from moment to moment as the chain moves. The signified is consequently relegated to a position in which it is an 'effect' of the signifier. There is no locality of 'pure meaning' or untrammelled thought: the signifying order predates consciousness, infiltrating and organising it.

The second notable element in Lacan's vision of slippage is his understanding of the mechanisms that operate within language and thought. The linguist Roman Jakobson (1962) argues that meaning is expressed in language through two basic processes – 'metonymy' (in which the name of an attribute is substituted for that of the thing meant – for example, 'sails' for 'ships') and 'metaphor'. Lacan suggests that these are formally equivalent to the processes that Freud believed characterised dreams and were basic to unconscious functioning: displacement and condensation. Metaphor and metonymy, fundamental aspects of language, can therefore be understood as the effects of the unconscious on consciousness. Meaning is thus produced through the play of linguistic signifiers; desire is constantly shifting through the signifying chain through a process of metonymic displacement, while each signifier is also constantly representing others through the operation of metaphoric condensation. Once again, there is no fixity of meaning here, only its production in an endlessly variable and untrappable way. More fully, Lacan's linguistic reading of the unconscious bolsters the view of language as something which becomes internally constitutive of the individual human subject, rather than an external system which an already-formed person can learn:

> The issue is not man's relationship to language as a social phenomenon . . . It is a question of rediscovering the laws governing that other scene which Freud designated, in relation to dreams, as that of the unconscious, the effects discovered at the level of the materially unstable elements which constitute the chain of language . . . (Lacan 1958, p. 79)

Before looking at Lacan's ideas on the developmental aspects of language (which in his case is the impact of language on development, rather than the converse), it is worth considering briefly the value of his general view of language. First, its focus on the productive power of language is an important counter to the tendency observable in psychological theories to reduce language learning to a kind of naming exercise. For these approaches, meaning is given by experience; that is, it consists in a correspondence between experience and a specific signifier or set of signifiers. In contrast, the Lacanian account makes meaning a complex and elusive product of the signifying chain, which is not linked in any direct way with experience. Indeed, language is inherently separated from experience by its location as a structure which is external to the individual, operating according to its own laws. It makes the individual its subject because it acts causally at a level which is beyond the conscious awareness of the individual; that is, it dictates to consciousness from a position of otherness.

As will be seen in more detail below, this view of language suggests a particular approach to development: the construction of the individual is seen as a gradual process of differentiation and organisation in which the *production* of meaning is central. The set of differences that constitutes language simultaneously differentiates the individual and differentiates the world and other people for her or him; language development is thus the process of creation of an individual standing in a certain set of relations to others. In addition, by refusing to take meaning for granted but instead investigating the way in which it is continually produced and subverted, Lacanian theory shares the general psychoanalytic interest in creativity, consciousness and irrationality – topics which are peripheral in traditional psychological accounts. Finally, because of the view of language as a system that originates outside each individual and has a constructing influence on subjectivity, Lacan opens the way for a fuller understanding of the impact of social structures on individual consciousness.

There are many difficulties with the Lacanian account of language which are also complicated by the awkward and inaccessible way in which it is usually presented. The most important of these has to do with the idea of the 'arbitrariness' of the sign, in particular the claim that there is no fixity to meaning, but that meaning is produced and reworked through the slipping of signifiers that carve out a signifying space. The problem here is to explain how it is that certain meanings come to predominate – that particular 'readings' of signifiers develop a power which is hard to shake. Laplanche and Leclaire (1966), in an interpretation of Lacan that was originally thought to be orthodox but was then repudiated by

Lacan himself, suggest that meaning is in fact fixed in certain positions. These positions are given by 'points de capiton', the 'buttons' or nodal points at which the order of signifers and that of signifieds are sewn together. At these points, the slipping of signifer over signified is arrested because of the formal intrusion of the metaphorical operation of a 'vertical' chain that leads down to a set of particular unconscious meanings, in the last resort formed during the process of primal repression, the original separation of the unconscious from conscious thought (Thom, 1981; Archard, 1984).

This suggests that there might be some meanings that are pre-set by biological or possibly social processes; however, Lacan's disavowal of Laplanche and Leclaire's work removes this prop from this theory. As Archard (1984) points out, what is left is a relativistic vision that, despite its insistence on the social nature of language as a system, neglects the way in which particular social meanings may have determining, ideological force. For example, although there may be an absolute sense in which the link between signifier and signified is 'arbitrary', in practice this link is given by the conventions of a particular linguistic community. These may well shift over time, but they do not shift from moment to moment as Lacan suggests can happen: with such continual slippage, communication of any kind would be impossible. Similarly, if signifiers are defined only in terms of other signifiers and with absolutely no reference to any signifieds, it is hard to see how any meanings at all could ever be generated. There must be some connection for signification to occur. In addition to these points raised by Archard, there is the important social one that the organisation of signifiers and the meanings they produce are not completely arbitrary. In each society, some readings of the world have dominance over others; these readings are embedded in the way language is used to order and express experience. Lacan's neglect of the social determination of meaning is seen most fully in his assumption that culture is always phallocentric, rather than that it becomes so through processes of power; but this neglect of social meanings is also at variance with other aspects of his theory, notably his view of the Oedipus complex.

Lacan's account of child development shares with Freud's a concentration on the Oedipus complex as the crucial determinant of human socialisation. Prior to the Oedipus complex, there is first a state of undifferentiated partial drives, and then a period in which the child is absorbed in the imaginary identifications of the 'mirror phase' (see Frosh, 1987, for a fuller description of this theory). In the mirror phase, the child develops an image of her or his 'self' as a unified entity, an integrated ego; the irony is that this awareness is based on an idealised and mistaken reading of the messages conveyed by others – by the 'mirror'. In effect, the child's sense of unity is something spurious, given from outside, an acceptance by the child of another's view. There are a variety of readings of the implications of this state for language development. Most commentators see the mirror phase as pre-linguistic, with some suggesting that language is impossible in such a narcissistic position. For instance, Achard (1984) sees language as that which breaks up the Imaginary order of the mirror: 'The Imaginary is characterised precisely by an inability to differentiate between its two essential terms: self and image, subject and object. What is needed to mediate this dyad is language' (p. 66). It is language that enables or forces the child to differentiate between I and not-I, self and other, so allowing communication to occur. For other writers, the mirror phase already involves language. Thus, Urwin (1984) proposes that the mirror phase does not just involve absorption in the other, but is also a time when the whole issue of separation is dealt with, a process which is intimately connected with the symbolising power of language.

> It is in the mirror phase that the child begins to acquire language, as he or she attempts to come to terms with the experience of the presence and absence of satisfaction . . . language allows the child some detachment from immediate sensation and the pain of separation, providing a relative increase in autonomy. (p. 277)

However, at this stage the child is caught up in a set of imaginary identifications with her or his own alienated image, unable to symbolise self and other in an adult way. So the change that occurs to full linguistic competence is a qualitative as well as a quantitative one: the language of the Imaginary is not the same as the language of the community. Put in more Lacanian terms, there is one kind of language (reproduced often in analysis) in which the ego (an empty, alienated entity) speaks to an other which cannot answer, which is the Imaginary source of its own alienation.

> On the other hand, [Lacan] described full speech, addressed to the Other, which is beyond the language ordered by the ego. The subject of this speech is the *subject of the unconscious*, which speaks most clearly in dreams, jokes, etc . . . Thus, Lacan stated, the unconscious is the discourse of the Other. (Benvenuto and Kennedy, 1986, p. 87)

The distinction here is clarified by Forrester (1987) as being between a set of relationships that the ego develops with its imaginary counterpart (the 'other'), and the impact of the 'Other', 'the *principle* of otherness that any act of speech presupposes'.

> This last, or 'big Other', is the locus of the linguistic code, the guarantee of meaning, the third party in any dual relationship – whether it be analysis or love. The subject's speech is vouched for by his Other . . . Yet it is transformed in having to pass via the fantasy structure in which the ego and its (fantasy-) relations to its objects predominate. The relation of the subject to the Other is thus the main line of the unconscious, for which analysis aims to clear the way. (Forrester, 1987, p. 71)

Thus, there is a proto-language in the mirror phase, because with all its mystifications the mirror phase contains in it a moment of separation – the child's selfhood becomes constituted by something outside it. However, because the child's experience is still one of absorption in an other, of narcissistic oneness, there has to be a further, radical shift for language proper to be created. This shift is marked by the introduction of splits into the consciousness of the child, forming the 'subject of the unconscious', a process which Lacan portrays as occurring in the accession to the 'Symbolic order' which takes place with the Oedipus complex.

For the child to take up a position as an apparently autonomous subject in the adult world, the sense of aggrandised unity with the other that characterises the Imaginary order has to be broken. Just as in conventional psychoanalytic theory the pre-Oedipal bond between mother and child is interrupted on the insistence of the Oedipal father, so in Lacan's thought it is the introduction of a third term into the self–other relationship that dissolves – or, rather, disintegrates – its fantasised wholeness. This third term is the 'Name-of-the-Father', the paternal indictment that forbids the fulfilment of the child's desire in the mother. This is the classical Oedipus complex, but it is re-written by Lacan in cultural and linguistic terms. Culturally, Lacan emphasises the force of the Law: it is not that each individual father breaks up an incestuous mother–child link, it is rather the Name-of-the-Father that operates, the symbolic position in which all human relationships are regulated by something outside them that has the force of law – the 'big Other'. What fragments the Imaginary here is its context: it is imaginary precisely because there is no absolute oneness, but everything is constructed through processes that operate from outside. Recognition of this determined fracturing, of the impossibility of unity, is what constitutes the Symbolic.

The child 'enters' the Symbolic order when social reality smashes the Imaginary self–other/mirror unity. For Lacan, it is a cultural law that is operating here, but it is also a linguistic fact. On one level, this is simply a statement of the necessary conditions for language: communication is not possible if no division is experienced between self and other, subject and object. So the division that enters into the unity of the Imaginary is also a mechanism whereby the child takes up a position in the linguistic community, upon which speech can be built. Secondly, linguistics operate in that it is through language that the cultural law of the Symbolic is coded. Sometimes this seems only to be a repetition of the conventional Structuralist notion that all social processes have a 'grammar', following the same kind of generative rules that language follows. More strongly, however, it refers to the idea that the laws of the Symbolic are written into language – the 'Non' of the Father – and that it is through the operation of the linguistic code that the rules of social living are received. Finally, it is through language that the individual 'subject' continually attempts to bridge the divisions which language itself beings into the psyche: language is built on a fragmentation of fantasised unity, but it is also the way in which unity is striven for, in which something which is absent can be symbolised and hence fantasised again as present. According to Lacan, all speech is a search for something absolute, a reconstruction of oneness, an attempt to reach an other to rebuild a state of lost, imagined integrity.

The function of language is not to inform but to evoke. What I seek in speech is the response of the other. What constitutes me as a subject is my question. (Lacan, 1953, p. 86)

Language has its location in the Symbolic, as something standing outside the subject as a source of meanings, but it is experienced through the Imaginary relationship between the ego and the other. In this way, language is both the core of truth and the medium of 'misrecognition'.

In the Lacanian account, it is through learning language that the child becomes a human 'subject', taking up a place in the adult community. But it is also through the operations of language that the child becomes internally split, as at one and the same moment language induces a search for integration and precipitates a complete and constant fragmentation. This introduces the notion of 'desire', which in Lacan's thought is something that is always striven for and always unobtainable. The desire of the child for the mother is replaced and obscured or repressed by the operations of language (the Name-of-the-Father). Hence language becomes both the means for the search for oneness, for reconstitution of the desired but lost object, and a division within the essence of the individual. This division is that of the unconscious: the fragmentation of the Symbolic makes all desire impossible to achieve; desire therefore becomes repressed, hidden behind a screen of language, to recur only in its interstices – the errors and gaps that are the focus of psychoanalytic interrogation. Desire becomes metaphor; metonymy creates meaning; the unconscious is created by language. Rose (1982) summarises the process as follows:

> Symbolisation starts . . . when the child gets its first sense that something could be missing; words stand for objects, because they only have to be spoken at the moment that the first object is lost. For Lacan, the subject can only operate within language by constantly repeating that moment of fundamental and irreducible division. The subject is therefore constituted in language as this division or splitting. (p. 31)

Even that great achievement of the Symbolic, the differentiated use of the personal pronoun 'I', is spurious in that the *word* 'I' replaces any possible integration of the self, becoming a signifier with its signified lost somewhere underneath. Once 'I' appears, the subject is alienated and split.

It will be clear from the description above that Lacan's theory of language development centres on loss. The child's identity and membership of the adult community is based on accession to the (linguistic) Symbolic, but this also involves renunciation of the fantasy of oneness that is the child's desire. Language produces the individual as a human subject, in the same process making this subject alienated and split. Language thus appears to unite people through speech, but its divisive qualities make real communication between subjects impossible. The operations of language construct the subject as a cipher: there is nothing real there, only the process of construction and loss.

Some of the difficulties with Lacan's account of language have been debated above. There are, however, additional psychological problems which arise from his use of language as a determining principle of development. First, as with all psychoanalytic theories of language, the linguistic details of what occurs is left extremely vague. For example, although the notion of the 'Name-of-the-Father' is clear in its reference to the symbolic power of patriarchy, there is a lack of specificity as to how this 'Name' is translated in practice – how the child 'hears' it linguistically. Similarly, although there have been some elegant Lacanian portrayals of children's 'symptoms' as embedded in words and silences (e.g. Mannoni, 1970), the child's *production* of language is theorised only at the level of the use of words to stand in for lost objects – that is, only in terms of its functional and experiential content. How children acquire particular signifiers (especially when they are constantly shifting) is a question to which no solution is offered that goes further than Freud's 'fort-da' game (Freud, 1920).

In response to the criticism of vagueness, it can be argued that Lacanian theory is not concerned with how children develop language, but with the impact of language on development – specifically the construction of the psychological 'subject'. However, there appear to be problems here too, which have to do with the dual levels on which language is taken to operate – the levels of the Imaginary and the Symbolic. As discussed above, Lacan's theory is in part an attack on the idea that meanings are given automatically by experience, that an already-formed human subject

observes the world and learns to name it. The great strength of
the notions of the 'chain of signifiers', of differentiation rather
than identification, and of the impact of the Other in the Symbolic
register, is that they emphasise the production of meaning as
something that arises from outside the subject, inserting the
external order into the process of subjectivity. However, as
Williamson (1987) discusses, the way in which language is theorised
in the Imaginary order – particularly in the mirror phase – owes
more to traditional ideas of experience than to this more radical
vision. For one thing, the 'hailing' of the image by the ego in the
mirror phase raises the question of what it is that does this hailing –
who is looking in the mirror – and at how it comes about that the
image is perceived as real. What the theory of the mirror phase
seems to suggest is that the *experience* of the child, her or his
perception of the self in the mirror, is productive of an internal
psychological state, the ego-other identification. More linguistically, the idea that words can, as Rose (1982) suggests in the
quotation given above, 'stand for objects', reintroduces the representational status of language into a theory which purportedly
opposes such views. Williamson (1987) notes,

> The problem with retaining this concept [of language as represen-
> tation] is, of course, that signs are assumed to have the single,
> essential function of reflecting the object to the subject, while
> no criteria are provided for how either the object or its
> representation are rendered intelligible, other than an idealist
> assumption of cognitive powers natural to consciousness. (p. 14)

The double use of language, described above, becomes very
problematic here. At one and the same time it is representational
(in the Imaginary register) and it is disruptive and elusive (in the
Symbolic); it is both the source of meanings and their carrier. It is
through 'misrecognition' that development occurs, the Imaginary
belief in oneself as a self; this is akin to 'false consciousness' in
the Marxist sense, and contains the same problems of identifying
the faculty interior to the individual which makes such a consciousness possible.

As well as the concerns discussed above, Lacan's developmental
theory replicates the difficulty mentioned earlier, that a particular
form of social organisation is taken to be identical with 'culture'

in general. In part, this is due to Lacan's reading of culture as a set of linguistically-given rules. As well as being inaccurate (culture is perpetuated in ways other than just through language, however important that mode is), this is an abstract and in the end vacuous idea, taking no note of the concrete patterns of power that operate in any particular social community. Why, for instance, is it the father's 'name' which is incorporated into language – that is, why it is that the 'Law' of culture is patriarchal – is nowhere explained. Instead, 'culture' operates within a very general theory as an absolute entity controlling the construction of every human subject – a 'big Other' which is automatically phallic.

As will be discussed in Chapter 4, this is one source of feminist criticism of Lacan; the main point here is that Lacan's insistence on a view of language as an abstract pattern of rules with a fixed underlying structure is not mixed with any analysis of what the determinants of that structure might be. As an additional consequence of the abstract nature of the theory, little attention is given to the actual psychological mechanisms that might operate to inculcate social divisions into the consciousness of individuals. It also follows from this that despite being a theory of subjectivity, Lacan's approach actually says relatively little about subjective experience; it is couched at too general a level for this.

Despite all these problems, however, Lacan's view of development is challenging in the same way as is his use of linguistic theory. On the whole, it offsets the essentialist tendency of many theories by supplying an account of the way subjectivity itself becomes constructed – of how meanings are structured into the individual subject. It thus extends the psychoanalytic tradition of concern with subjective experience and its development to include an examination of the linguistic and cultural categories in which this subjectivity is embedded. It emphasises the impossibility of any absolute relationship between people that is not mediated in some way by the social structure, and it presents an account of how language might operate not just to convey social values, but also to control and construct the consciousness of individuals. It thus provides a framework in which it becomes possible to theorise the interrelation between social processes and individual experience – that is, to theorise the workings of *ideology* – and to understand the impact of language on experience in a political way. In this respect, it both supplies a critique of conventional, asocial theories of language, and fills out some of the lacunae in other psychoanalytic approaches which, in their concern for microsocial ('Imaginary') interactions between infant and mother, also neglect the power of the wider social structure.

## Conclusion

In this chapter, some of the major psychological and psychoanalytic theories of language development have been described. The psychological theories provide important information on the relationships between language and other cognitive processes, as well as useful observations on the order of acquisition of various linguistic skills and on the conventional patterns of interaction which surround the learning of these skills. On the other hand, they neglect the experiential impact of language learning and (with the possible exception of Chomsky's theory) they fail to consider the extent to which linguistic ability may have a formative impact on consciousness. They also tend to avoid or minimise consideration of social processes, although Vygotsky's work has opened out some possible avenues of investigation here which are being taken up by some contemporary psychologists. Psychoanalytic theories, in contrast, are weak in their description of how the formal properties of language are acquired, but strong in their account of motivation, of the forces (mostly connected with power over separation and loss) that impel a child to symbolise and speak. Lacanian theory adds a particularly important strand to this work by presenting a model for comprehending the links between culture (or social structure), language and subjectivity, even if some elements of the theory are implausible and the approach as a whole is very abstract.

It is clear that the two approaches to language are couched at different levels and are endeavouring to answer rather different questions. This is consistent with the trend noted throughout this book, that psychology focuses on cognitive capacity and functional mental operations, whilst psychoanalysis turns away from these dimensions of the mind and instead explores the subjective ramifications of psychological events and processes. In the area of language development more clearly than in many other areas, each body of theory fills in gaps in the other: for psychology, the motivating power of the experience of language acquisition; for psychoanalysis, the mechanisms through which linguistic ability actually develops.

There is no sense in asking here which are the more important elements of a complete theory of language development; both kinds of approach or, rather, ability to address all the questions listed at the start of this chapter, are necessary. However, there is some interest in considering the implications that arise from the partialities of each method. As ever, psychology's strength lies in its ability to describe the 'how' of linguistic development; its focus is on the child as a complex machine, learning a set of skills which in the abstract appear to be immensely difficult to master. This is congruent with the emphasis identified earlier as psychology's assumption of the pre-determinedness of the human subject – the nature of the 'machine' is never questioned, only its capabilities. The child's inner self is not touched by language, but uses language to express its will.

Psychoanalysis' neglect of skills and competencies is indictable, as it produces implausible, even impossible, models of language development. As with the work described in Chapter 2, however, this runs alongside an intense interrogation of the central consciousness – or unconscious – or the language user. It is not only that psychoanalysts ask the experiential question of what it feels like to 'acquire' language. It is also that they investigate the way language changes meanings, the way it expresses, hides, creates and distorts the intentions of the individual. Thus, psychoanalysis looks both at how language is used, and at what this reveals about the nature of the user, finding that there is a sense in which it can be said that the user is produced by the word. In Lacanian hands, this becomes a theory of the social construction of the individual subject; that is, the study of language development is linked to the creation of a human social being. Amongst psychologists, only Vygotsky has dealt seriously with the mixture of psychological, social and political forces that this simple statement calls into play. In recent psychoanalysis, Lacanian and post-Lacanian in particular, these have become central issues, evident in debates on individuality, on social construction and, as will be seen in the next chapter, on sexual difference.

Through exploration of the meanings of language, several central concerns of a complete human psychological discipline come to the fore: how experience is registered, how meanings are created, how subjectivity and sociality intertwine. It is in this sense that one can argue that experiential, social and constructionist issues are crucial to any complete theory of language development. With all their defects, the richness of psychoanalytic theorising on the subject makes it apparent that it is possible to raise and answer these questions and that psychology's neglect of them threatens to make it impoverished and sterile.

# 4 Gender Differences, Sexual Difference

The theory and politics of gender have been transformed in the past twenty years by the advent of modern feminism.* All recent discussions of sex and gender have to be understood in this context. In psychology, feminism has been a major reason for the interest of female researchers in work in this area. More generally, feminism has problematised descriptions of gender roles and explanations of gender development, making them into value dimensions on which psychologists take up positions. Feminism has had, if anything, an even more profound impact on psychoanalysis. The strength of this impact is due partly to the assault made by feminists on traditional psychoanalytic practice (e.g. Figes, 1970) and, perhaps more importantly, to the use feminists have made of psychoanalytic theories in explaining how femininity and masculinity become constructed (see Frosh, 1987, chapter 7).

This approach links with the most powerful and general impact of feminism, one which has been received more fully by psychoanalysis but which is equally significant for psychology. Developments in feminism have created a more complex and sophisticated analysis of social construction processes, an analysis which can be applied in investigations of gender – for example, by identifying the different discourses that operate to describe women, men and

* The terminology employed in this chapter is that which is now relatively standard in psychological discussions of the area: *sex differences* refers to anatomical distinctions and is associated with the division female/male; *gender identity* refers to a person's consciousness, and *gender role* to the constellation of their attributes, as feminine or masculine. 'Sex differences' is thus a biological notion, 'gender differences' a psychological one. *Sexuality* is in this respect a term more akin to gender: it denotes the organisation of sexual desire into an individual's personality, with *sexual difference* being employed to register a presumed bifurcation between feminine and masculine sexual paths.

159

the relationships between them (Hollway, 1984), or to uncover the way linguistic practices help to produce certain types of knowledge that effectively silence women (Spender, 1980). Feminism's description of how received notions of masculinity and femininity are derivations of specific patriarchal practices and of how, once these are incorporated into common-sense perceptions and received assumptions, they restrict and oppress women, has added urgency to both psychological and psychoanalytic explorations of gender differences. In particular, it has made researchers and theorists look at gender with a vision of change.

The term 'social constructionism' is being used here in two related senses. First, it refers to the argument that concepts such as femininity and masculinity (indeed, all concepts and categories used for understanding the world) have a place in a social space, from which they obtain much of their force and in which they have meaning and consequence (Gergen, 1985). Theories, therefore, whatever their relationship to 'objective' reality, always have social significance and express ideological values. Secondly, social constructionism is a specific approach to individual psychology, holding that personality formation occurs through a process of internalisation of socially-given meanings and experiences; it puts 'emphasis on the person's active role, guided by her or his culture, in structuring reality' (Tiefer, 1987, p. 71), including the perceived reality of the self. Thus, each of us makes sense of our self through concepts and categories which are infiltrated by social values and cultural assumptions; this means that our readings of our own masculinity or femininity are similarly mediated. Moreover, while some approaches restrict themselves to the suggestion that it is *understanding* of the self that is influenced by social assumptions, others suggest that such understanding is an aspect of subjective experience which cannot be divorced from personality; that is, that the self is in its turn a socially constructed phenomenon.

Taken together, these uses of the social constructionist perspective centre the concerns of the psychology of gender on the production of gender identity. This is not to say that research into the ways in which women and men behave (for instance, their communication strategies, work achievements or emotional expression – Aries, 1987; Shields, 1987; Mednick, 1979) is unimportant, but that these areas are all aspects of a wider interrogation of the processes whereby 'masculinity' and 'femininity' come to be experienced as significant – perhaps central – elements in an individual's personality. The issue here is, in a way, simple. If masculinity and femininity, as personality characteristics, gender identities and gender roles, are given automatically by the biological states of male and female (as sociobiologically-oriented psychologists propose – e.g. Kenrick, 1987), then gender differences reduce to 'sex differences' and the task of research is to tease out the relevant biological factors. Feminism, however, clearly opposes this particular reductionist stance, by 'de-constructing' the concepts of masculine and feminine to show how they arise out of sex differences in an ideologically determined rather than a naturally given way. The argument here is that the *meaning* of gender difference takes its particular forms through socially structured readings of the place of women and men; it does not arise automatically from anatomical or hormonal distinctions. That the vast majority of these readings, in psychology and in society, assert the inferiority of women is a message about the patterns of dominance in the world, not about biological necessity. But the question that it does raise for psychologists and psychoanalysts is of how these social readings come to be experienced as 'real' or even 'true' by individuals; that is, of how a person's subjective world as girl or boy, woman or man, becomes central to their self. For central it always seems to be: most people have a strong and stable sense of themselves as female or male, a sense which is formed in early life and which is experienced as a pillar of selfhood (Spence, 1985). Individuals whose gender identity is uncertain or unstable are generally seen as disturbed; trans-sexualism, for example, is viewed as a form of personality (and sometimes sexual) pathology. Despite the common notion that sexual orientation (as heterosexual, homosexual or bisexual) is indicative of gender identity, the experience of oneself as female or male in fact goes much deeper than sexual orientation, with most homosexual women and men feeling clear about, and at ease with, their gender identity (Spence, 1985). In addition, there is an extremely powerful tendency for people to construe others on the basis of their gender, with categorisation as female or male being perhaps the commonest initial judgement and core component of personality perception (Hampson, 1986). All this evidence suggests what most people already know – that gender is a 'superordinate' construct, used by society and by individuals to identify, categorise, explain and divide.

## Constructionist discourse

A central concern of the new psychology of gender, then, is to develop an account of the production of gender identity. This account has to explain the strength of people's experience of themselves as male or female, and the way notions of masculinity and femininity become attached to this experience in deeply personal, but also socially predictable, ways. Traditional psychological research on behavioural sex differences has been wholly inadequate to this task, for reasons that will be set out more fully below. However, there are recent developments in the cognitive social psychology of gender, such as the 'Gender Schema Theory' of Bem (1981), which are characterised by adherence to a view of personality as constructed rather than pre-given, and which are, therefore, potential models for investigations along these lines. This view is part of a wider tendency in psychological, psychoanalytic and cultural theory, in which the human 'subject' is analysed as a complex set of meanings produced through absorption in the social world. Where this view differs from traditional socialisation accounts is that the productive forces are seen not just as direct actions on, or instructions to, the child (as, for instance, is the case in social learning theory), but as subtle and often fragmentary images and 'discourses' through which an individual comes to understand and experience her or his being.

In cognitive social psychology, the constructionist approach is manifested in an interest in how information becomes organised to produce a notion of oneself which is structured in certain ways, for instance according to gender stereotypes. Elsewhere, however, constructionism has been taken further, to include unconscious elements which can be theorised but not directly experienced, because they become part of the structure of the self. This idea has been explored in a number of regions, particularly language and socialisation (Henriques *et al.*, 1984) and mental health (Banton *et al.*, 1985); its most forceful interrogation, however, has been along the divide which is often experienced as fundamental to individual differences – the sexual divide.

What is at stake here is not just the traditional nature–nurture debate, but the whole idea of the composition of social construction. Wetherell (1986) locates the political significance of this debate:

> femininity and masculinity are ideological practices all the more effective because they appear as natural and inevitable results of biology or experience. The appearance of something coherent which could be explained as a property of the individual is precisely the effect of this ideological movement. (p. 77)

The challenge of constructionism is that it disputes all images of the individual as coherent and integrated, with a simple and bounded self which is the origin of meanings and intentions, and which acts in accordance with these intentions. Instead, it 'de-constructs' the individual, hunting out the components of the self, however fragmentary and contradictory they may be. These components, it is argued, are produced from the social practices that surround the individual. In the case of gender, femininity and masculinity are readings of the significance of difference which are internalised from the signs and images in which each child is immersed. The generic term for these signs and images is 'discourses', the ways in which reality is represented by and to people. As described elsewhere (Banton *et al.*, 1985), at the root of this approach is the idea that, being part of the social world, people can never experience it directly, in an unmediated way. Instead, what Althusser (1965) calls an imaginary relationship is formed with the world; that is, experience is produced through representations of possible realities – discourses upon things, which can be contradictory and which compete for dominance, with those that are institutionalised along lines such as class, gender or race generally proving to be most powerful.

Althusserian and discourse theory has been much discussed and criticised in recent years (e.g. Hirst, 1979). Certain aspects of it are highly problematic – for example its lack of clarity on how it is that particular discourses arise and attain dominance, and the relativism that it introduces into discussions of social progress. What has proved robust, however, is the de-constructionist stance that refuses to take apparently 'natural' things as given, and the constructionist analysis that examines the ideological or discursive components out of which the human subject is produced.

An example of how this applies in the area of the psychology of gender can be found in work described by Hollway (1984). She produces a revealing study of heterosexual relations by analysing a number of personal accounts, employing a framework that interprets these accounts in terms of certain discourses – what she calls the 'male sexual drive', 'have/hold' and 'permissive' discourses. The point about these discourses is that they do not derive from the personal accounts of Hollway's interviewees, but from observation of common social representations of heterosexual relations – that men pursue women for sexual reasons, that women do what they can to hold on to their men, or that sexual relations should be free, without implying long-term commitment. These socially-derived discourses are then used to make sense of the experiences of individuals in relationships. What Hollway demonstrates is that the discourses make available certain positions (ways of understanding and behaving in relationships) which are taken up to a greater or lesser extent by real people. Different, even competing, discourses might be adhered to at the same time and to a greater or lesser extent, creating a complex location but one that can still be comprehended in social terms. So, a man describing his sexual history might show allegiance to all three of the discourses listed above, but his most powerful experience might be of his own sexuality as 'driven'.

If the use of this form of analysis were to stop at the point of demonstrating the links between an individual's subjective experience and certain discourses, what would be being proposed is a mechanical and socially reductionist view of individuals as automatically determined by the social representations (discourses) around them. The only differences would be those created by historical alterations in the balance of power between competing ideologies and possibly by the extent of direct exposure of particular individuals to each discourse. In the case of gender, there would be a relatively simple rendering of the link between a person's experience of her or his femininity/masculinity, and the gender-differentiation characteristic of most discourses. What is psychologically interesting here, however, is both the complexity of this project (adherence to multiple discourses being the norm) and the further question of mechanism. In other words, discourse theory does not in itself explain how or why the subjectivity of individuals comes to be fixed along the dimensions given by certain discourses. Still in the context of heterosexual relations, Hollway (1984) presents this point as a question about change:

> Because discourses do not exist independently of their reproduction through the practices and meanings of particular women and men, we must account for changes in the dominance of certain discourses, and the development of new ones (for example, those being articulated by feminists) by taking account of men's and women's subjectivity. Why do men 'choose' to position themselves as subjects of the discourse of male sexual drive? Why do women continue to position themselves as its objects? What meanings might this have for women? . . . By posing such questions, it is possible to avoid an analysis which sees discourses as mechanically repeating themselves – an analysis which cannot account for change. By showing how subjects' investments, as well as the available positions offered by discourses, are socially constituted and constitutive of subjectivity, it is possible to avoid this deterministic analysis of action and change. (pp. 236–7)

This passage suggests that discourses make available certain positions, but that the particular *positioning* of each individual is a product of her or his subjective experience. This experience itself is socially constituted – what Hollway means by 'investment' is the way power operates to bring 'pay-offs' for adhering to particular positions – but it is so through the insertion of particular individuals into specific sets of interaction and representation. These structure subjectivity unconsciously; or, rather, they provide the unconscious structure for subjectivity.

It is here, therefore, that psychoanalysis enters in, and it is for this reason that psychoanalysis has been central to many recent discussions of the construction of the human subject. The constructionist approach to gender suggests that femininity and masculinity are built up from the ideological materials made available by social forces; somehow, these discourses organise subjectivity so that the experience of being female or male becomes a fixed point in consciousness. This form of organisation is unconscious: it is not something which can be reflected upon, but something that determines the direction in which reflection – cognition – goes.

Explaining the organisation of unconscious phenomena and the way subjectivity is structured through experience is the precise province of psychoanalysis. In addition, because of the psychoanalytic proposition that subjectivity and sexuality are intimately combined, the question of gender differences is transformed into the question of the divide between the sexes – of sexual difference.

## Terms of investigation

The material presented above pulls together in a general and applied way many of the ideas which have already been introduced in previous chapters. There is the same stress on the importance of providing explanations of the origins of semantic components of mental life – of, in this case, the content of the difference 'feminine–masculine'. There is also the argument that these origins lie in social practices, which enter unsuspected into the formative procedures laying down the structures of individuality. These social practices are, as feminists never tire of pointing out, connected to power and dominance; that is, they gain their hold over individuals because they are ideologically inscribed as the 'truth' of the material world. How these messages become internalised by individuals and transformed into the apparent certainties of the feminine or masculine self – how, that is, the 'gendered subject' is constructed – is, or should be, the central question for the psychology of gender. This is parallel to the issues raised in studies of socialisation and language: how the parameters of the external, cultural and social environment come to influence or determine the mental contents and behavioural assumptions of each individual child.

In the chapters of this book that deal with those areas, stress was laid on the way sociality is impressed on the child through the intensity of her or his contact with others, who are themselves carriers of the messages of society. Ideology is not taught only in obvious, conscious ways – right and wrong, pink and blue. It is also incorporated in the ways the world is 'naturally' divided: I and you, here and gone, black and white, nature and culture, feeling and thought, mother and father, female and male. The mechanisms of social construction are mechanisms of power and also subtle mechanisms of subjective significance, of finding ways of making sense of the world and of coping with unfulfilled desire. The instruments of investigation here are those which attempt to spell out these mechanisms – identifying the cognitive strategies used to symbolise the gendered self, and the unconscious ones that make it feel real.

In this area of work, psychology and psychoanalysis are once again radically distinct. Feminist theory, as described earlier, has influenced and enriched psychology, but the insistence of the question of the gendered subject always returns us to the psycho-analytic domain. To understand why this should be so, it is necessary to survey critically the direction that psychology's approach to gender has taken, and then to ask the psychoanalytic question: how does sexual difference arise?

**Biological dispositions**

Traditional psychological research into gender differences has not addressed the question of the formation of gender identity, described above as the central issue in this area, but has focused on differences in behaviour and attainments between males and females. This orientation derives from the characteristic stance of empirical psychology, prioritising observable over implicit phenomena. It also, however, expresses psychology's absorption in a set of ideological values which can only be called reactionary, in that they perpetuate conformist and biologistic readings of femininity and masculinity.

At its most explicit, this ideology is present in the continuing concern of many psychologists with biological explanations of supposed differences in the behaviour of males and females, the familiar 'sex differences' research that has dominated the psychology of gender. Arguments for the biological determination of psychological sex differences are made problematic by the inconsistent evidence on the size and durability of these differences, evidence which on balance suggests that males and females do not diverge in their behaviours and abilities to any great extent (Henshall and McGuire, 1986; Deaux, 1984). Nevertheless, there are still substantial claims sometimes made that hormonal and anatomical distinctions produce divergent developmental paths for females and males. The more extreme of these claims come from sociobiologists and need not be described here; they generally offer explanations of contemporary sex typed behaviour (or assumed behaviour) in terms of an evolutionary model based on crude genetic assumptions (see Rose *et al.*, 1984, for a critique of sociobiology). Even relatively sophisticated and interactionist sociobiological accounts (e.g. Kenrick, 1987) are concerned more with establishing a genetic basis for behavioural differences than with elaboration of the mechanisms whereby gender identity becomes constructed.

More moderate biological accounts of gender differentiation take up the fact of hormonal differences between females and males to argue that these influence behaviour in a way that eventually (through transactions with the environment) produces psychological and social role differences. Again, there are difficulties with this position, for example because of the common assumption that early sex differences in behaviour can be construed as a relatively pure culture of these biological influences. Apart from the inconsistency of research findings on perinatal sex differences, there is evidence that adults discriminate between boy and girl children from birth, making it impossible ever to rule out the impact of socialisation processes on behaviour (Archer and Lloyd, 1985). In addition, the kind of behavioural differences claimed at birth may not produce in any simple fashion the differences thought to be present later; for instance, the higher activity level supposed to be characteristic of male infants may or may not be related to later dispositions towards aggression (Henshall and McGuire, 1986). Nevertheless, the hormonal account is an important influence within psychology, so it is worth considering the influential and thoughtful version of it produced by Money, Ehrhardt and their associates (e.g. Money and Ehrhardt, 1972; Ehrhardt, 1985).

The first notable point about this position is that it is not a deterministic biological theory, but a transactional one. The general argument is that hormonal differences create a predisposition towards certain crude directions of behaviour, but it is environmental responses which supply these directions with meaning and either encourage or re-route them. Ehrhardt (1985) thus rejects the 'main effect model' of biological influence in favour of what she terms a 'dynamic interactional model', in which transactions have a formative effect. The hormonal element is provided by the action of the androgens, particularly testosterone, the pre-natal presence of which is the crucial determinant of male sexual differentiation. Various experiments have been carried out with non-human species, involving 'masculinising' and 'defeminising' foetuses and observing the impact on various types of behaviour (aggression, activity maze learning, sensitivity to taste and pain, etc.). In humans, there are a number of 'natural experiments' of this and a related kind, involving hermaphrodites and inadvertent trans-sexuals (Money and Ehrhardt, 1972). This work indicates a link between pre-natal androgen exposure and high levels of physically active outdoor behaviour in childhood; there is also some evidence of effects on aggression, but little that suggests any pre-natal hormonal effect on nurturing. In terms of gender identity, the individual's consciousness of her or himself as feminine or masculine, it seems clear from these marginal cases that assigned gender (i.e. rearing as a boy or girl) is of far greater significance than chromosomal or hormonal constitution (Money and Ehrhardt, 1972). Ehrhardt reiterates the significance of environmental responses to any biological differences and also warns against the kind of over-generalisation from the biological findings that are characteristic of much work in this area. For instance,

if boys show a stronger propensity towards physically active play behaviour than girls show, one should not extrapolate and conclude that girls are more passive and dependent, have less initiative and less leadership behaviour, and generally are less assertive. (1985, p. 46)

The argument here is that whatever predisposing influence biological factors may have on behaviour, the meanings of gender become formulated in a social context which takes the infant child and constructs from it a gendered being.

Ehrhardt's position is exceptional amongst biological work on gender, which is characterised not by its appreciation of the significance of social context, but rather by its adoption of a model of psychological development assuming that gender identity – self-consciousness as a gendered subject – derives in a determined and more-or-less automatic way from behavioural differences, which in turn are derivatives of biological distinctions. Ehrhardt's (1985) argument appears to be that biological differences are too small to carry the whole weight of the gender differentiation programme, and that socialisation influences are necessary for psychological distinctions of any power to be made. However, it is not so much the relative importance of biological and social factors that is of significance, even though this has been the issue that has dominated polemic within psychological research. It is, rather, the underlying perspective that fascination with biology, and, indeed, with 'transactions', reveals. This is the perspective that assumes that behind psychological differences will be found some 'objective' base, some material entity that can make sense of the variations between people in their psychological functioning. Moreover, whatever the persuasion of the researcher, whether it be that biological gender differences are established or not, the significance of this debate is read in political terms, as a debate over whether women and men are fixed in certain positions by their genetic and hormonal heritage. This debate thus becomes an exemplar of the simplest, but not for that reason any less deeply felt, dispute between 'environmentalists' and 'biological determinists', translated into the gender arena as a dispute between liberal feminists and reductionist supporters of the patriarchal status quo.

What is intriguing about the arena for this dispute is the assumption that if biological differences are established, the important aspects of psychological differentiation will have been explained. In part, this attitude is an aspect of the common psychological paradigm of biological reductionism, discussed in Chapter 1, with all its confusions of levels of description and explanation. But here, in the area of gender research, its absorption into an ideology of control is more obvious than in any other sphere of work, with the exception of the psychology of 'racial' differences. The provocativeness of the argument over biology derives from a model of development that genuinely perceives 'anatomy as destiny', and that can, therefore, employ biological variations as explanations of psychosocial ones. Put the other way around, this means that if there are differences in the behaviour and psychology of males and females, they are made immutable by the biological forces determining them. In the political context of an emergent feminism that challenges assumptions about female and male roles, and that presents an explanation of male dominance in terms of social power rather than 'natural' necessity, this debate over biology becomes more pronounced and significant. The adherence of many psychologists to biological models therefore reads as an affiliation with anti-liberationist forces, justifying existing gender inequalities by reference to supposedly determining and immutable underlying forces.

The debate over biology is thus an aspect of a wider political debate; it also reflects a theoretical dispute over how individual and social influences intertwine. The biological approach assumes an internal origin for behavioural differences, which is why it usually appears as a reactionary model. It could, however, be read in a contrary way, as a statement of what would be possible if only the social world allowed the full flowering of 'human nature' to occur. This is the reading of biology which some feminists have used in re-writing the psychoanalysis of femininity, in which the female body is seen as a repressed kernel of naturally explosive sexuality that, if expressed, could overturn the social constraints placed upon it. Femininity is conceived of as opposing the formalities and constraints of masculinity, as an order of being characterised by fluidity, multiplicity, heterogeneity and erotic physicality. This 'true' femininity is held in chains by patriarchy, but possesses the power to flood the dams that masculinity builds, to produce a fertile creativity which has been lost because of alienation from the body.

This jubilant celebration of biology as a subversive entity within an administered and repressive social world is a traditional libertarian one, visible not only in modern feminists such as Irigaray (1977), but also in the work of old-style, non-feminist Freudo-Marxists such as Marcuse (1955). It has its risks: in the libertarian version it becomes a paean to individualism; in the feminist revision it risks absorption in a romantic image of womanhood which characterises some of the crudest sexist discourses. But what this work brings to the fore is a reading of biology as a realm of possibility not just in the sense of constraint (only what is biologically feasible can be achieved), but also in the revolutionary sense of awakening (society makes to seem impossible that which is immanent in all of us). In psychology, however, biology has never been read in this libertarian way; it is always viewed as that which sets limits upon development, that which constrains and orders, and justifies the way things are. Perhaps this reflects a more general contrast in political stance between psychoanalysis and psychology: where the former, at least in some of its manifestations, looks at social reality with a pessimistic but quizzical eye and asks, 'What is being lost here?', the latter seeks mainly to describe how what is must be, to legitimise the organisation of interpersonal relations in terms of some underlying necessity. To summarise: it is a matter of political choice, whether the current arrangement of gender relations is taken as given and the task of psychobiology is to describe it in a legitimising way, or whether it is seen as a distortion of human possibility, and the biological is turned to as a source of inspiration as to what else might be done. Psychology's choice has, more often than not, been the reactionary, legitimising one.

There is a further aspect to the individual–social debate, which is to do with the question of the mechanisms of socialisation. In reality, despite their centrality to polemics of control, discussions of biology provide little insight into the formation of gender identity. This is because of the employment of a model of gender socialisation that makes behaviour primary over cognition; that is, it is implicitly argued that behavioural sex differences, whether determined biologically or not, give rise to particular internal models of gender, rather than the other way around. This, too, is a position with a specific ideological flavour, notably normative in its assumptions about the organisation of the world into which children are socialised. These assumptions can be seen in operation in one of the traditionally dominant psychological models of gender development – social learning theory.

## Social learning theory of gender socialisation

The account of gender differentiation given by social learning theorists treats gender development as a process of learning the behaviours which are appropriate to feminine and masculine social roles. The concepts used are precisely the same as those employed in accounting for any class of behaviours, whether it be phobias, scholasticism or aggressiveness. The only variation is that gender is a high-order category, containing a number of associated behavioural components and expectations: these are passed on to children as correlated sets of attributes. Thus, Mischel (1966), in the seminal statement of the position, proposes that,

the acquisition and performance of sex-typed behaviours can be described by the same learning principles used to analyse any other aspect of an individual's behaviour. . . . In addition to discrimination, generalisation, and observational learning, these principles include the patterning of reward, nonreward and punishment under specific contingencies, and the principles of direct and vicarious conditioning. (pp. 55–7)

Two main stages exist in the development of gendered behaviour. Through observing the actions of adults, children both learn the components of particular actions (e.g. aggressive or nurturing behaviour) and which gender they are associated with. Behavioural expression of this knowledge is then either encouraged or discouraged through reinforcement, both in terms of the contingencies imposed on the model and, more powerfully, the child her or himself. At a 'meta-level', children are rewarded for gender-appropriate behaviour (i.e. for conformity to sex-role expectations), thus making them more attentive and responsive to same-sex models; they are also constantly reinforced or punished for specific acts on a gender-differentiated basis. The most frequently worked example of this is that boys show more aggressive behaviour than girls first because they are more likely to have observed males rather than females being aggressive, and secondly because boys are more likely to be rewarded by adults and peers for their own aggressive behaviour. Girls may also have learnt aggression through observational means, but their behaviour will be inhibited by their awareness that aggression is associated more with males (and they are discouraged from cross-sex allegiances) and also by direct punishments for aggressive acts.

Social learning theory has been extremely influential in psychology, and it is a version of this approach which most people have in mind when they employ the commonsense notion that boys and girls are 'conditioned' into sex-typed role behaviours. It does, indeed, have some empirical support, though this is mostly circumstantial. Although Maccoby and Jacklin (1974) could find little evidence that parents do respond differently to their children on the basis of sex, more recent studies, especially those carried out in family homes rather than in laboratories and through observations rather than interviews, suggest that this does indeed occur, more or less from birth. Archer and Lloyd (1985), for instance, summarise evidence showing that parents react differently to boys and girls in infancy, to some extent being more responsive to boy children. They also typically provide boys and girls with different toys, offer more comfort to girls, impose more negative sanctions on boys, and expect greater conformity to sex typed behaviour from sons as compared to daughters. Boys seem generally to receive more feedback on their behaviour than do girls, and to be encouraged in the development of exploratory, independent types of behaviour (Block, 1981; Singleton, 1986), while girls are encouraged to be more dependent on parental guidance (Henshall and McGuire, 1986). In addition, there is evidence that fathers react differentially to sons and daughters – more so than do mothers (Lewis, 1986); this may be connected with the greater pressures towards gender conformity experienced by boys. Perhaps relatedly, boys from father-absent homes have lower 'achievement motivation' and are more likely to demonstrate disturbed or delinquent behaviour, while girls show more problems in relating to men. However, whether this is to do with absence of role models or simply with the extra stresses imposed by single-parenthood is less obvious; certainly, the evidence from the study by Golombock *et al.* (1984) of children of lesbian mothers suggests that the absence of a father was unimportant when there was a stable, supportive central family relationship. The children of the lesbian mothers in this study showed no signs of any disturbance, in contrast to the children of single-parent mothers.

Social learning theory, then, like all behavioural theories, espouses a model of development that emphasises how children's behaviour is channelled into acceptable moulds by the actions and examples of important people in the immediate environment. On the face of it, this is an approach which is congruent with the concerns of feminists to deconstruct femininity and masculinity, to show how they are not pre-given 'natural' categories, but constructs created through social means. Indeed, this has often been the approximate shape of the debate between biological and social learning theorists, with the former emphasising the fixity of behaviour and the latter its malleability under the influence of social norms. However, there is an ideological position implicit in the social learning account that undermines any claims it might have to gender-liberational status. First, the social learning approach fails to theorise the power of gender to become more dominant over consciousness and self-definition than it is even over behaviour. Indeed, the evidence, mentioned earlier, that behavioural sex differences are rather weak and insignificant calls into question the social learning model with its assumption that socialisation occurs through influence over behaviour first, and cognition only later; it seems that cognitive gender socialisation may be more powerful than its behavioural equivalent. And not just cognitive socialisation: even individuals who make themselves aware of the gendered concepts infiltrating their judgements and attitudes find them extraordinarily hard to change, in all contexts from child rearing to sexual behaviour (e.g. Segal, 1983). That is, gender constructs are so powerful that they infiltrate subjectivity in a way which goes beyond their effect on behaviour, and which is not dependent on the immediate reinforcement history of the child or the direct social contingencies to which she or he is exposed. 'Learning' of gender may by-pass direct behavioural influences and enter the mind through routes not seen by those who look only at surface events.

The effect of social learning theory's prioritising of behaviour is to shift the terms of the debate on gender to an examination of the explicit means by which social influences operate. Its message is that if patterns of socialising behaviour change, particularly patterns of reinforcement for children, then gender behaviour will change also, producing alterations in gender identity and consciousness as a consequence (as behaviour is determinant over subjectivity). The norms of social expectation are assumed to be open to inspection, even if sometimes the contingencies are subtle; gender is not necessarily a divide (although it is researched as such), but a consequence of the quantity of reinforcement that is attached to any particular pattern of action.

What can be disputed here is not just, as described above, the adequacy of this approach as an explanation of the power of gender. It is also the model of social construction that it purveys. For social learning theorists, gender is constituted by a series of behavioural choices producing a relatively coherent repertoire of action and activity. Gender roles are reproduced in the context of a society that has norms which are embodied in the behaviour of individuals and which are passed on through their direct interaction with others. This makes social forces open to immediate inspection: what is powerful is what is overt, and the more overt it is, the more likely it is to be seized upon by a child as a clear marker for

the direction that development should take. What feminists have
often argued, however, is that it is the hidden manifestations of
power that most effectively reproduce the structures of patriarchy;
it is the obscuring of explicit messages that makes them so hard to
contest. In this version of social constructionism, it is because
gender enters as an unseen force into the mind that it succeeds in
organising perceptions and experiences of reality, that it makes
the world appear as if it has to be this, gender-divided, way and
no other. Put baldly, the debate is between a behaviourism that
takes society at face value and suggests that all choices are available
to inspection and change, and a politics arguing that control of
one group over another, of one sex over the other, is perpetuated
because its mode of operation is both obscure and insidious, not
always, or even routinely, open to challenge.

The task for gender researchers, then, is to develop an approach
that explores the way individual subjects become fixed as carriers
of gender positions which are experienced as central, but which
are also aspects of the gender structures of society. This is a
question about ideology, about the power of certain social frames
to determine subjectivity; as noted at the beginning of this chapter,
it concerns the way in which some discourses or readings of gender
become dominant over others. Psychoanalysis lends itself to this
kind of discussion because it deals with unconscious subjective
structures that may have an unacknowledged but powerful influence over conscious beliefs and actions. However, before looking
at the use of psychoanalytic concepts in this way, there is a liberal
feminist tradition within recent social psychology that also has
produced some influential arguments in the gender research field.
The most widespread of these was the work on 'androgyny'
developed in the 1970s, work which can be seen as a paradigm
case of how theories can act as wish fulfilments.

## Androgyny

The concept of 'androgyny' was one of the most powerful influences
on psychological research into gender during the 1970s. In part,
this was a result of disenchantment with the more traditional
behavioural sex difference research, leading to an interest in the
origins and nature of people's perceptions of their own personality

characteristics as 'feminine' or 'masculine'. The androgyny concept, through its view of femininity and masculinity as sets of socially-derived attitudes and self-descriptions, was one manifestation of this tendency. But the attractiveness of the androgyny notion had a source that was less acknowledged just as it was more potent. Bem (1981) attributes it as follows:

> Politically, of course, androgyny was a concept whose time had come, a concept that appeared to provide a liberated and more humane alternative to the traditional, sex-biased standards of mental health. (p. 362)

Deaux (1984) notes,

> Androgyny soon became a code word for an egalitarian, gender-free society, and disciples advocated androgynous therapy, androgynous curricula for school children, and androgynous criteria for professional positions. (p. 109)

What these authors suggest is that at the source of the attractiveness of the androgyny notion to many researchers and polemicists lies a particular kind of politics, the politics of liberal feminism.

There is a wide range of feminist positions that potentially challenge theories and practices of male domination, in psychology as in the rest of the social world. Some of these, locating this domination in deeply embedded structures of power, pose a direct and radical threat to the conventional, patriarchal organisation of society as a whole and to its institutional (for instance, academic) and personal modes of expression. The stance of this kind of feminism within psychology (e.g. Mednick, 1979) is to insist on a re-reading of psychology's principles and practices as ideological in their formulation and oppressive in their implementation. Deconstructing psychology here largely means dismantling it; the methodology is an exposure of its political functions, an analysis and celebration of women's experience and an examination of the way that gender can become so intrinsic to structures of domination that it serves as an organising, apparently natural dichotomy. The individualism of psychology is also challenged by this approach, which constantly reiterates how both the individual gendered subject and the discipline of psychology as a whole are not natural categories, but are socially constructed and socially influential (Henriques *et al.*, 1984).

In the face of this potential onslaught, it is perhaps not surprising that psychology attempted to adapt to feminism by bending rather than breaking, by accepting as its own an approach adopting traditional social psychological questionnaire methods and reformist political principles. The much-honoured originator of androgyny work has herself noted that the androgyny outlook is at the liberal end of the feminist continuum (Bem, 1981). Its assumption is that the differences between women and men derive from social expectations and norms, and are present within individuals as sets of attitudes preventing them from expressing all aspects of their personality. Men are just as constrained as women, in this view; mental health is the ability to escape the rigid social stereotypes of masculinity and femininity, and achieve an integrated state in which the elements of character conventionally ascribed either to one sex or the other, become components of both. Thus, both Bem (1974) and Spence *et al.* (1975) argue that femininity and masculinity should be construed as independent (orthogonal) dimensions which are not necessarily mutually exclusive; that is, it is possible for a person to have both feminine and masculine attributes. This view of androgyny explains why, in opposition to the common idea that women and men have to absorb themselves into their respective gender roles to be 'normal' or healthy, Bem suggests that being sex typed is restrictive, and that it is androgyny which is the mentally healthy state of mind.

> Whereas a narrowly masculine self-concept might inhibit behaviours that are stereotyped as feminine, and a narrowly feminine self-concept might inhibit behaviours that are stereotyped as masculine, a mixed, or androgynous, self concept might allow an individual to freely engage in both 'masculine' and 'feminine' behaviours. (Bem, 1974, p. 155)

Rather than analysing the social processes that fix femininity and masculinity in their respective ideological positions and that construct psychology as a discipline that reiterates these positions, the androgyny work concentrates on the beliefs which individuals have about themselves, and suggests that altering these beliefs will be sufficient to change people's characteristic behaviours and, indeed, their mental health. Morawski (1987) elaborates this point by first noting a related aspect of androgyny's appeal:

> The androgynous image is a mirror of the ideals of contemporary professional life, reflecting a historical moment when women professionals, in particular, required a model that promoted conventionally masculine (instrumental) actions without compromising the feminine self. (p. 53)

Learning new skills to enhance the cognitive and behavioural repertoires of sex-typed individuals is the path to advancement; as the quotation from Morawski suggests, the image is of the new professional woman, able to employ traditional masculine patterns to open up work possibilities whilst maintaining her feminine attributes. It is not deconstruction of masculinity and femininity that this theory proposes, but addition of the two unaltered terms to make one whole, androgynous and idealised being. Androgyny is an attractive concept because it promises to enhance everyone's life, male and female together, at no cost; there is no need to dismantle male power, only to share its spoils and augment masculinity with feminine values. Comparing androgyny research with the more radical feminist position, Morawski draws out its tame attractions and their limitations by arguing that it 'overlooked a crucial component of gender – that of social power. Yet, gender is not simply related to social power, it is constitutive of power relations and is a stable component in social hierarchies of power' (p. 58). But this was no accident, for psychology did not desire a theory of social power; rather, its goal was to defend itself against the effects of exactly such theories. Having to revamp its approach under the pressures of feminism, psychology produced a feminist theory that shared its traditionally individualistic, asocial assumptions. The concept of androgyny cast its spell by allowing psychology to survive; it created a 'new' approach to gender that avoided any fundamental change.

Despite its political attractions, however, androgyny has not survived its own internal contradictions. First, the empirical evidence goes against the claim that androgyny is a good thing in terms of mental health. Taylor and Hall (1982) provide a detailed review of the hypothesis that individuals who have high androgyny scores on the conventional sex role questionnaires (e.g. Bem's

(1974) Sex Role Inventory) will show higher scores on measures of psychological 'well-being' than will sex-typed individuals. Despite lack of clarity and various conceptual problems in the androgyny literature, the results of studies are fairly consistent in showing that it is masculinity, rather than any interaction or additive factor, which is most closely related to positive outcome. Thus, masculinity is not only more strongly associated with psychological health than is femininity, but also gains very little additional predictive power from any form of androgyny. Taylor and Hall conclude from this

> that it is primarily masculinity that pays off for individuals of both sexes . . . it is primarily masculinity, not androgyny, that yields positive outcomes for individuals in American society. (p. 362)

This finding is some confirmation of the idea that adding feminine and masculine characteristics together is not an appropriate strategy for mental health in a society that values them differently; it is still men who hold sway, and the ability to employ the characteristics associated with masculinity – to be in the position of the male – that brings success and psychological health.

There are a number of further attacks on the androgyny work from within psychology which need only be sampled here. The most important of these question the concepts of femininity and masculinity adopted in this literature. For instance, Spence and her associates challenge the assertion that the BSRI and their own Personal Attributes Questionnaire measure femininity and masculinity, even though the original papers by Spence *et al.* (e.g. 1975) adopt precisely this position. Spence (1985) states,

> we have come to reject the proposition that scores on these instruments, which are largely or wholly confined to items describing limited classes of socially desirable gender-differentiating personality traits, can be used to make inferences about individuals' perceptions of their masculinity and femininity or their sex-role orientation. (p. 65)

Specifically, studies of the BSRI and similar instruments indicate that they tap the constellations underpinning many assumptions about feminine–masculine differences: expressiveness and instrumentality. These do indeed appear to be orthogonal dimensions and they also have a bearing on many 'socially important behaviours, some of which are gender related' (Spence and Helmreich, 1981, p. 368). However, Spence and her colleagues claim that they are not closely linked to global self-images of femininity or masculinity. One reason for this is given in another aspect of Bem's work criticised by Spence – its employment of a simplified model of femininity and masculinity as integrated factors which together make up gender identity, alongside a single dimension of sex-typedness which can be used to discriminate between individuals. Spence (1985) argues from the empirical data that femininity and masculinity are multifactorially determined; that is, they are built up from a variety of components with varying degrees of interrelatedness, none of which can be employed as a simple predictor of gender role. The positive expressive and instrumental attributes sampled on the BSRI cannot, therefore, be used as equivalents for femininity and masculinity; there is, instead, great variation in the components of gender, and the meaning that it possesses, for each person.

Few men and women exhibit all or even most of the qualities and behaviours 'typical' of their gender or expected of them by societal stereotypes. Most men and women exhibit a fair number of gender-congruent characteristics, but the particular assortment varies widely from one man or woman to the next. (Spence, 1985, p. 77)

Some more general conclusions arise from this psychological work, to add to the critique presented earlier. The first relates to the ubiquitousness of the expressiveness/instrumentality distinction (also termed communion/agency to bring out the distinction in degree of orientation towards other people) in conceptualisations of gender differences. This appears to be the most strongly held perception of feminine and masculine 'principles' and to be a powerful determinant of the way gender differences are read. The expressiveness/instrumentality dichotomy is also linked to the passive/active one which Freud viewed as synonymous with feminine/masculine: the image is of the male operating on the world while the female nurtures and contains. Presumably the strength of this image arises from assumptions concerning sexual and parenting practices; given the similarities between the actual behavioural attributes of females and males it is clearly an ideological rather than a factual description of gender. This is, indeed, the point: psychologists, even when they have avoided simplistic assumptions about what females and males do, have continued to search for some rather simple distinctions and then to try to uncover the substantive content of these distinctions. Wetherell (1986) expresses this clearly:

> The social psychology of gender identity is thus characterised, first, by the need to find meaning in a feminine/masculine divide, and, second, by the desire to find the definitive content of those categories. These are usually understood in terms of some version of the agency/communion distinction and then fixed as a property of the individual across context and time. (p. 81)

Femininity and masculinity come to be viewed as substances which are inherent inside people, and which are mixed to varying extents to produce particular instances of gender identity – for example as sex-typed or androgynous. There is a slippage in all this work from a description of the way in which gender labels are conventionally used, to an attempt to uncover the essence of gender within individuals – a problem which, in her more recent writings, Bem at least has recognised (e.g. Bem, 1981, p. 363). Not only is this culturally biased, but it misses the point which cognitive social psychologists have themselves emphasised: that gender is a *construction*, in the sense of being a set of perceptions and interpretations that produces certain forms of categorisation and responses to oneself and other people. To repeat once more, gender is best looked at ideologically, as a way of placing, dividing, understanding and controlling phenomena – something which does not have an 'essence' in itself, but which is produced through the absorption of individuals in the social world.

## Gendered ideas

In the introduction to this chapter, it was suggested that one source of the impact of powerful discourses on gender is their influence over the ways in which people symbolise their own personal attributes. The work on androgyny was one attempt to theorise this, taking as its problematic the extent to which individuals conceive of themselves in terms of gender stereotypes. More formally, it is to cognitive psychology that researchers have looked in their attempts to develop a description of people's tendency to construe themselves and others in gender-differentiated ways, using gender as a – perhaps *the* – major categorising principle in everyday life. Psychologists pursuing this route have assumed that people make sense of the social world through cognitive means, speculating and hypothesising about its mode of organisation and governing their own conduct according to the conclusions which they reach. The sources of information at their disposal are primarily the messages conveyed by the behaviour of other people and by the images and social practices to be observed all around. The result is a set of organised gender assumptions which, while in principle open to reflection and inspection, often become the automatic ('unconscious') generators of action and belief. In this way, through observation of others and reasoning about their behaviour, each individual human child imbibes the rules of gender as a map for guidance through the tricky maze of interpersonal relations.

The seminal account couched in these terms is the cognitive-developmental theory of Kohlberg (1966). The general argument is a familiarly Piagetian one. On the basis of unclearly specified events, but presumably their observations of the actions of, and divisions between, the people who constitute their social world, children come to appreciate that social information is gendered. Just as they generate hypotheses concerning the rules governing language and the material world, so children respond to this discovery by developing cognitive schema around gender. It rapidly becomes clear to the child that the division female/male is a crucial one for the organisation of the social world; this also makes it central to self-categorisation, leading to a rather rigid adherence to idiosyncratic rules about gender-appropriate attitudes and behaviours. Attainment of gender identity occurs early (before the age of $2\frac{1}{2}$), but at a time when it is not at all clear to the child that this precious self-categorisation is permanent and safe (Kohlberg places the attainment of 'gender constancy' at nearer seven years of age). Therefore, everything must be done to bolster it. Thus it is that a child may be more sexist than her or his parents, displaying rigid attitudes about the gender appropriateness of particular clothes, games or social roles. Gradually, as the child's cognitive awareness becomes more sophisticated, so the rules she or he employs match more closely those which actually operate in the social world; irrational these may be (although Kohlberg does not say so), but at least they have the irrationality of adulthood.

The attractiveness of the cognitive-developmental view has not depended so much on its own empirical base, which is somewhat uncertain (e.g. Hargreaves, 1986; Henshall and McGuire, 1986), but on its congruence with the general trend in psychology to give primacy to cognitive over behavioural considerations. It is undoubtedly a powerful theory, making sense of a wide range of observations, including many derived from studies employing competing theoretical frameworks (particularly social learning theory). It also meshes well with social psychological approaches emphasising the importance of the self as a cognitive construct organising each individual's personality and imposing demands for consistency. Cognitive-developmental theory explains gender development in terms of this effort towards consistency and integration: one of the central components of a secure sense of self is the construction of a viable gender identity. It is thus a causal theory (behaviour follows from beliefs) which also contains a rationale for the development of the cognitions serving the causal role: they are generated to bolster the self.

It is this last aspect of cognitive-developmental theory which is particularly emphasised in the more recent work of cognitive social psychologists with an interest in the development of gender identity. For example, Spence (1985) argues that,

> Young children's desire to adopt the conspicuous qualities associated with their own sex and age and their tendency to emulate same sex models (. . .) very probably represent their attempt to confirm and define their emerging sense of self-identity in general and their gender identity in particular, as well as an effort to win the approval of others and avoid their disapproval. (p. 82)

This view of gender as a principle according to which the self becomes organised meshes with another topic of immense current interest in personality psychology, the general issue of how the self is cognitively represented (e.g. Khilstrom and Cantor, 1984). A central idea in this work has been of the self as an organised semantic network, a pattern of ideas which nevertheless has an emotional charge. The form taken by the self can be understood in various ways, but the commonest is as a schema, 'a cognitive structure, a network of associations that organises and guides an individual's perception' (Bem, 1981, p. 355). Schemas of various kinds are applied to the information available to the individual, organising it and directing responses. The self is both a body of schemas and object of knowledge in its own right; that is, an individual makes sense of her or himself by employing the rules of interpretation arising from her or his own cognitive schemas. Thus, if gender is one of the major dimensions used to make sense of other people, it will also be an important way of organising knowledge about one's self.

Bem (1981) takes the notion of schematic processing and argues that because gender is such an important way in which information about people is coded, it will also become central to a child's emerging representation of her or his self. As children come to understand the way gender structures the social world, they develop a very strong schema for gender, which is then employed to organise information about their own personality. The gender schema will be more powerful than other possible ways of organising this information simply because it is used more pervasively and extensively in the child's social environment. The world is perceived in a gender-divided frame.

> The child learns to apply this same schematic selectivity to the self, to choose from among the many possible dimensions of human personality only that subset defined as applicable to his or her own sex and thereby eligible for organising the diverse contents of the self-concept. Thus do self-concepts become sex-typed, and thus do the two sexes become, in their own eyes, not only different in degree but different in kind. (Bem, 1981, p. 355)

The immense significance of gender as an organising principle for the self also explains why it becomes so important to children to act in accord with their gender role; 'the gender schema becomes a prescriptive standard or guide, and self-esteem becomes its hostage' (Bem, 1981, p. 355).

Bem's 'Gender Schema Theory' thus proposes that gender schemas develop as a product of the gendered organisation of the social world; that they become a core organising principle for the self, and that this results in the phenomena of sex typing which are observable in the cultural associations to femininity and masculinity. Gender thus becomes a way of understanding and interpreting the world, an ideological dimension filled with the assumptions and practices of sociality but at the same time made personal by the intensity with which the child strives to produce an integrated selfhood. The processes at work here are no different from those operating with regard to other schema which an individual might employ in order to organise information about people (for instance race, class or more specific attributes such as intelligence or attractiveness). But gender is particularly central because it is so critical in society, because it so powerfully dichotomises individuals and because this dichotomisation has such significant practical consequences – even in areas where sex is not of necessity relevant. It is in recognition of this that Bem (1985) argues that feminists need to attend to ways of reducing the 'associative network linked to sex' and proposes ways of raising 'gender aschematic children' (pp. 212, 214); 'The feminist prescription, then, is not that the individual be androgynous, but that the society be aschematic' (Bem, 1981, p. 363).

The cognitive approach to gender construction, particularly as exemplified in Bem's Gender Schema Theory, has a number of attractions. First, it is a theory of how gender categories come to be powerful and to operate at a level of automatic processing which makes them central to the self and difficult to challenge or change. This rectifies the tendency of many psychological approaches to assume that 'attitudes' can be altered through simple persuasive means, a tendency which is strong in the androgyny literature and even stronger in the work on prejudice to be discussed in the next chapter. Secondly, although Bem does not employ a very elaborated model of social processes, she does produce a theory of gender as ideology; that is, as a framework for perceiving the world which is internalised from the assumptions and practices present in the social environment. For instance, Bem (1987) deals specifically with gender categories as products of 'culture', arbitrary lenses for looking at things which are adopted by the child because they have such centrality for social organisation. Thirdly, Bem utilises a notion of *division*: the existence of powerful gender schemas makes the world into a divided place, feminine and masculine. This is true despite the fact that individuals will vary in the strength of their allegiance to gender-differentiated schemas, a variation not fully theorised in Bem's account but presumably produced by variations in socialisation practices.

These elements in the cognitive approach link it with the discourse-based analysis presented earlier, and with the general psychoanalytic project of uncovering the unarticulated principles that govern the experiences of masculinity and femininity. But there the similarities end and a major difference begins, a difference which can be understood as relating to the nature of ideology and, indeed, to the meaning of unconscious perceptions. Cognitive social psychology's notion of 'schema' is as a set of assumptions that orient perception in a specific direction, a set of rules or guidelines for the processing of percepts. One such percept is the self; that is, the self is, for theoretical purposes at least, viewed as a representation and hence as an object of knowledge in the individual's conceptual field rather than, for instance, as the seat of a subjectivity from which perception arises. More importantly, however, it is the theory's emphasis on perceptual ordering and categorising which marks it as an approach linked to a very crude notion of how culture operates. Bem (1987) articulates this by describing the three 'romantic presuppositions' of Gender Schema Theory:

> (a) social reality is sufficiently ambiguous as to afford the imposition on it of many different conceptual schemas; (b) perception and behaviour are shaped in large part by the particular conceptual schemas that are prominent in one's mind; and (c) which conceptual schemas are prominent in one's mind is itself largely determined by which differences between people one's culture emphasises. (p. 265)

Culture operates by emphasising particular rules for making sense of experience; as children seek to understand, so they come to employ those rules which have most power, gender being the prime example. This is a conventional view of how ideology operates: the social world is constructed in a way which is sufficiently ambiguous to allow competing understandings of it to exist; it is the organisation of that social world – social power, to use terms which the cognitivists tend to avoid – that decides which of these understandings will dominate and become 'common sense'. As is argued in the liberal feminism of the androgyny work which preceded Gender Schema Theory, changing these dominating discourses is a matter of seeing through them, of realising that alternative 'lenses' are available and of challenging the emphases of society.

Making society 'aschematic' is, as Bem notes, a political advance on making the individual androgynous, because the emphasis is put at the social level. However, the model of mechanism, of how society and individual operate, remains a simple, 'schematic' one. Each of us has experiences; how we make sense of that experience is dependent on the concepts we have adopted from society; changing means challenging these concepts. So far so good, but what both psychoanalysis and discourse theory propose is that the machinations of ideology go deeper than that. The source of perception may indeed be in experience, but psychoanalysis suggests that experience itself, not just how one understands it, is constructed; that is, the faculty of experiencing within each individual has a history which operates not just at the cognitive level, but at the level of a structured subjectivity. This means that ideology, the internalised values and perceptions of society, should be understood not simply as a way of looking at things, but as a way of *living* them:

> Ideology is indeed a system of representations, but in the majority of cases these representations have nothing to do with 'consciousness': they are usually images and occasionally concepts, but it is above all as *structures* that they impose on the vast majority of men, not via their 'consciousness'. They are perceived-accepted-suffered cultural objects and they act functionally on men via a process that escapes them. (Althusser, 1965, p. 233)

Society, and with it the social structuring of gender relations, enters into each of us not only as a set of cognitive rules, but as an ordering of experience that constitutes our subjectivity as feminine or masculine at its core. It is, in psychoanalytic terms, the 'subject' itself which is gendered, not just the perceptual frame which the subject employs. It is this idea that psychoanalysis edges towards when it replaces the discussion of gender differences with one that emphasises the depth of division – the notion of sexual difference.

## Sexual difference

The claim that psychoanalysis engages more forcefully than psychology with the structure of the gendered subject should not be taken to imply that all psychoanalysts agree on the origins and meaning of sexual difference. Indeed, the contrasting implications of various psychoanalytic theories are nowhere more in evidence than in this area. Debate over the correct interpretation of femininity and the differences between female and male development was heated even during Freud's lifetime. This debate drew together theorists from different perspectives to oppose Freud's formulations on penis envy, but also revealed variations between analysts who took the same side – for example between Jones (1927), who stressed the fear of sexual extinction ('aphanisis') shared by girls and boys, and Horney (1931) who interpreted Freud's theory of femininity as an instance of a more general 'womb envy' evidenced by all men (see Mitchell, 1982, for an account of this debate).

More recently, there has been an upsurge in what may be called 'feminist psychoanalysis'; this has produced a sophisticated body of theory which attempts both to describe female development from a psychoanalytic perspective, and also to show how this development is influenced or determined by the patriarchal nature of the surrounding social world. With the important exception of the Kleinian-derived approach of Dinnerstein (1977), there have been two significant strands to this recent work. One of these has been more characteristic of British and American psychoanalysis, and is derived from the object relations theory of Fairbairn, Winnicott and Guntrip; this focuses on the way the social position of women influences the early mother–daughter relationship.

The argument here is that because of their devalued social position, women internalise images of themselves as powerless and ineffective in areas divorced from childcare or the provision of emotional support to others. This increases the intensity of the early mother–infant relationship and also introduces a gender difference into early life, whereby daughters are identified with by the mother, and sons are perceived as separate and potentially autonomous. Feminine development then follows the line of absorption in the mother, reproduction of a degraded self-image, and difficulty with separations and the formation of a powerful identity outside the arena of mothering. For boys, it is easier to separate; what is more problematic is intimacy and the expression of emotional needs. While the role of fathers is neglected in this theory, there is a consciousness of the context of patriarchy as that which determines the limitations on women's identity and their positioning in the maternal role. In addition, the marginality of the father in children's lives in conventional families encourages even more intensity in the mother–daughter bond whilst modelling to the son the possibilities of separateness and power (Chodorow, 1978; Eichenbaum and Orbach, 1982, 1985; Ernst, 1987).

The second major strand of feminist psychoanalysis has originated primarily in France in response to the work of Lacan. Here, the emphasis is not so much on a developmental account of femininity, but on uncovering the special world of the feminine, particularly as it is expressed through the body and through language. Although there are differences of substance in the arguments of the main protagonists of post-Lacanian feminist positions (see, for example, Moi, 1985), there is also a shared perspective that femininity is distorted because it is always presented from the position of the male – in masculine linguistic usages, for example, or in terms of psychological theories which explicitly envision the feminine as only the 'Other' of the male. In Lacan's theory, women represent otherness to men, an otherness which is in fact illusory, imaginary; the women who contest his theory argue, on the contrary, that femininity is only invisible because it is sought for in masculine representations. In fact, they claim, femininity has its own presence, one which is closer to the body, to ambiguity and poetry, to rhythm and multiple expressions of desire (see Irigaray, 1977; Cixous, 1975; Gallop, 1982). Patriarchy oppresses women by excluding the feminine voice; sexual division is phallic dominance.

This is not the place to provide a full overview of psychoanalytic theories of femininity (see Frosh, 1987, for a description and evaluation of both traditions described above), although it is worth noting that the object relational perspective is congruent with a liberal feminist position seeking more equality in the relations between the sexes, whilst the post-Lacanian literature is closer to a more radical assertion of the positivity of femininity as an alternative to the masculine order. However, what is at issue here is whether psychoanalysis can go further than the psychological approaches described above in supplying an account of the *construction* of sexual difference. In this respect, many of the psychoanalytic theories share with psychology the limiting assumption of the pre-existent gendered subject; that is, they assume that femininity and masculinity are already divided psychologically, with it being only their content which is constructed, either along social or biological lines. For instance, for object relations theorists gender is given automatically by the parent: it is present in the differing patterns of interaction that mothers have with daughters and sons, which lead automatically to the different expectations and emotional structures of girls and boys. Sexual difference is not, therefore, a problematic concept: as in traditional psychological theories, the only question is the exact way in which girls learn what femininity means and boys masculinity, and the precise content of that learning. Feminist object relations theorists differ from psychologists in postulating that much of the process and product of this learning is unconscious; otherwise, the structure of their argument is no different from standard socialisation accounts.

Dinnerstein (1977), following Klein, also constructs a theory which, however interesting it is in its exploration of the consequences of female mothering (particularly the fantasies of women's power that this creates, and the different defences of women and men that are contingent upon these fantasies), renders sexual division and, indeed, sexual identity unproblematic. As Bar (1987) points out, this is a consequence of Klein's focus on innate feelings which are automatically (defensively) directed towards the mother; it is bodily feelings that are innate, and these are different for girls and boys, thus producing a different psychological history. Klein's (1949) version of the Oedipal history of the girl is indicative of this position. Whereas, as will be described below, Freud proposes that the girl's Oedipus complex is structured around a desire to have a penis of her own (that is, it is a response to the castration complex), Klein argues that the girl actually wishes to 'incorporate her father's penis as an object of oral satisfaction' (p. 916). Furthermore, she suggests,

> this desire is not an outcome of her castration complex but the most fundamental expression of her Oedipus trends, and that consequently the female child is brought under the sway of her Oedipus impulses not indirectly, through her masculine tendencies and her penis envy, but directly as a result of her dominant feminine instinctual components. (p. 196)

These 'feminine instinctual components' include a 'wish to rob the mother of the father's penis and incorporate it in herself' (p. 195), a wish that acts together with the girl's resentment of the weaning process to create an intense rivalry, hatred and fear of the mother. In addition, the girl has 'an unconscious knowledge about the vagina' from very early life, and this knowledge is of a particular kind: she 'thinks of it in her unconscious, as many details of her phantasies clearly demonstrate, as a cavity in the genitals which is meant to receive her father's penis' (p. 210). Thus Klein (and, subsequently, Dinnerstein) proposes a history for sexual development which is pre-directed by heterosexual instinctual tendencies, and that automatically differentiates the development of girls from that of boys. In this way, Klein produces a description of development which takes for granted sexual difference (it is instinctually determined) and is therefore restricted to an account of the filling out of different feminine and masculine psychological contents.

The general point here is as follows. Many psychoanalytic theories supply interesting ideas on the differing content of femininity and masculinity. These ideas are distinct from, and an advance upon, those presented in mainstream psychological work because of their focus on emotional and unconscious processes and structures. However, many psychoanalytic theories assume the existence of a division between the sexes which has biological origins and which does not, therefore, need to be explained in terms of the history of the subject. That is, like the psychological approaches, these theories assume the existence of the gendered subject. Yet, the more profound question raised both by discourse

theory and by feminism is of how gender comes to be; that is, the
question of *sexual difference*, of what it is, psychologically, that
produces a division between femininity and masculinity – whatever
the final content of these two states might be.

It is the hope of an answer to this question that has generated
much recent feminist interest in psychoanalysis and, perhaps
surprisingly, it is in the earliest psychoanalytic work that some of
the best leads have been found. Or rather, in the earliest work
and its most radical reconstruction, the two theories that do address
the question of sexual difference more than that of gender
differences are those of Freud and Lacan. For this reason, the
remainder of this chapter is devoted to a brief description of the
elements in these approaches that bear most closely on the origins
of the sexual divide.

## Complex division

Freud's account of the relationship between gender and sexual
development contains a belief in the determining power of anatomical distinctions alongside an apparently contradictory assertion of
the psychosocial genesis of sexual difference. According to Freud,
it is the presence or absence of the penis that determines the
psychological qualities of males and females – the former labouring
under a powerful super-ego as a response to castration anxiety,
while the latter endure penis-envy, a weak and struggling super-
ego, and the famous 'marks of womanhood': masochism, passivity,
vanity, jealousy and a limited sense of justice (Mitchell, 1974). On
the other hand, the influence of anatomy is not something that
operates from birth, nor is it automatic in its effects on the child's
psychology. Instead, Freud proposes, children in the early stages
of development are not psychologically distinct on the basis of
their sexuality; rather, they are 'bisexual' in the sense of containing
and expressing what later will be called feminine and masculine
elements. It is only at the phallic stage, when sexuality centres
around the penis for the boy and the clitoris for the girl, that
sexual division occurs. However, once this sexual division appears
it becomes structuring not only for the rest of development, but
for the meaning that earlier development now has.

The difference between the sexes ultimately cuts back through childhood, dividing up functions and sexual roles . . . But this distribution, after the fact, of the component instincts is not inscribed in the sexual activity of early childhood. (Irigaray, 1977, p. 36)

The power of sexual division is that it re-writes history just as it constructs the future.

There appear to be two aspects to the Freudian notion of bisexuality. On one level, it refers to the sexual neutrality of the early erogenous zones – the mouth and anus. Girls and boys, in Freud's view (contrary to the object relations account), experience the world in the same way during the oral and anal phases, forming their primary attachment to the mother and fantasising in similar ways about the gratification attainable from her body and from their own. The second aspect of bisexuality is concerned with the structure of the drives at this point; in particular, the degree of activity and passivity that they reveal. This is one of the distinctive components of the Freudian vision, although it has an echo in the 'instrumental/expressive' dimension for gender differentiation employed so freely by psychologists. Freud's definition of masculinity and femininity is in terms of active and passive sexual aims.

'Masculinity' and 'femininity' are used sometimes in the sense of *activity* and *passivity*, sometimes in a *biological*, and sometimes, again, in a *sociological* sense. The first of these three meanings is the essential one and the most serviceable in psychoanalysis. (Freud, 1905, p. 141 – footnote added 1915)

It is because of this usage of masculine and feminine that Freud can assert the essential masculinity of libido, 'for an instinct is always active even when it has a passive aim in view' (ibid). During the early developmental phases, active striving for satisfaction is characteristic of children of both sexes; both, in this sense, are masculine in their desires – 'the little girl is a little man' (Freud, 1933, p. 151).

Bisexuality does not suddenly disappear with the entry into the phallic phase. At that point, girls and boys still have identical, masculine aims and use their genital apparatus in the same ways, with the same meanings.

In boys, as we know, this phase is marked by the fact that they have learnt how to derive pleasurable sensations from their small penis and connect its excited state with their ideas of sexual intercourse. Little girls do the same thing with their still smaller clitoris. It seems that with them all their masturbatory acts are carried out on this penis-equivalent and that the truly feminine vagina is still undiscovered in both sexes. (Freud, 1933, p. 151)

This passage typifies the various strands of Freud's theorising: an assumption that it is the masculine sex organ which is primary for the child, that the difference between the sexes remains to be found out (it is not inherently known), but that this difference is along the lines given by anatomy – discovery of the 'truly feminine vagina'. Prior to sexual difference, bisexuality exists in terms of active and passive aims for children of both sexes, as well as the neutrality of the erogenous zones. However, this bisexuality is specious in that it is active, 'masculine' aims which are given the status of libido – genuine sexual energy. It is the *active* desire to achieve gratification that is true sexuality; even in object relational terms, it is masculinity that is dominant in both children. Irigaray (1977) notes: 'In the final analysis, it is as a little man that the little girl loves her mother . . . *[Freud] considers the girl's desire for her mother to be a "masculine", "phallic" desire*' (p. 37).

At this point in Freud's developmental scheme, it is not clear exactly why masculine and feminine should be seen as identical with active and passive. In part, this usage seems to be a reflection of Freud's adherence to the traditional image of masculinity as forceful and thrusting, femininity as receptive; prior to knowledge of the vagina, sexuality for girls and boys is of the former kind and hence, metaphorically, masculine. But the explanation given by Freud for why children might experience themselves as, or wish to be, masculine is rather different: he supposes that children's notions of gendered sexuality derive from their observations of their parents' sexual intercourse in which, Freud assumes, the man is active and the woman apparently passive. Children of both sexes identify with the man in this scenario, presumably because of their experience of their own sexuality as active. Thus, for Freud, in contrast to Klein and others and despite his own references to passive sexual aims, there is only one type of sexuality; this continues to develop for boys, but becomes severely repressed for girls. Parenthetically, the situation is complicated still further by Freud's doubts about the explanatory power of the 'primal scene'. In his important paper, 'Some Psychical Consequences of the Anatomical Distinction between the Sexes' (1925), he suggests:

> It is impossible, however, to suppose that the observations of coitus are of universal occurrence, so that at this point we are faced with the problem of 'primal phantasies'. (p. 334)

This suggests that children are born with, or inherit, some unconscious knowledge of femininity and masculinity – rather more like the Kleinian position than the traditional Freudian one.

What occurs during the phallic phase is that the phallus – anatomically, the penis or clitoris – becomes the central element in sexuality, the tip of a hierarchy of component sexual parts. It is this organisation of sexuality, alongside a more sophisticated object relational awareness, that creates sexual difference. With gratification deriving from the penis/clitoris, it is only a matter of time before children discover that girls and boys are differently endowed. Freud proposes that they react in contrasting manners to this discovery. Boys at first deny the difference: when a boy sees a girl's non-penis, 'he begins by showing irresolution and lack of interest; he sees nothing or disavows what he has seen, he softens it down or looks about for expedients for bringing it into line with his expectations' (Freud, 1925, p. 336). It is only later, under the immense pressure of the threat of castration, that the boy reconsiders his earlier observation and recognises the girl's fate as one that might potentially befall him too. It is in this highly charged emotional context tht the boy comprehends sexual difference; therefore, he not only learns that a difference exists, but he takes up a position with respect to that difference. This position is comprised of two reactions which, Freud suggests, 'may become fixed and which will in that case, whether separately or together or in conjunction with other factors, permanently determine the boy's relation to women: horror of the mutilated creature or triumphant contempt for her' (ibid). Amongst the many criticisms that have been made of Freud's misogynistic attitudes, it is not always recognised that he provides an explanation for masculine derogation of women in terms of primitive and terrifying anxieties.

The girl's response to the discovery of genital difference is much starker and more immediately emotive than that of the boy, because it calls into question all her pre-existing, 'masculine' desire and demands a reconsideration of the active attitude that she has taken up towards her mother. Whereas for the boy anatomical difference only figures when he comes under the threat of castration, girls 'in a flash' realise what they lack and desire.

> They notice the penis of a brother or playmate, strikingly visible and of large proportions, at once recognise it as the superior counterpart of their own small and inconspicuous organ, and from that time forward fall a victim to envy for the penis. (Freud, 1925, p. 335)

This has enormous consequences for the girl. She develops a 'masculinity complex', a hope of someday obtaining a penis and of becoming like a man – a hope which can persist and become a motive for female homosexuality. Alternatively, the narcissistic wound that discovery of genital difference produces can be too much for some girls to bear, leading to disavowal of the lack of a penis and hence to psychosis. But there are also consequences which are general, according to Freud, to all women. Once girls discover that it is not only they as individuals who are 'castrated', but all females, they develop a negative attitude towards women which matches that of males – an attitude of contempt and disgust which can be turned against themselves. They are also more prone to jealousy than are men, because of the continuing impact of penis envy. Additionally, there is 'a loosening of the girl's affectionate relationship with her maternal object' (Freud, 1925, p. 338) which is partly due to her general hatred of all penis-lacking women, but also because she holds her mother responsible for sending her 'into the world so insufficiently equipped' (ibid). Finally, the girl renounces her claim to masculinity by turning away from active masturbation. This is a response to 'her narcissistic sense of humiliation which is bound up with penis-envy, the reminder that, after all, this is a point on which she cannot compete with boys and that it would therefore be best for her to give up the idea of doing so' (Freud, 1925, p. 340). Thus, the result of the girl's crushing discovery that she lacks the equipment to pursue her masculine, libidinous desires to the fullness that is possible for the boy, is that she turns away from masculine activity and searches out a potential feminine heritage of her own. This can only mean replacing the penis with something achievable: a child derived from the incorporation of the father's penis into the vagina and who then – at least when it is a male child – acts as its replacement.

In contrast to the Kleinian position, therefore, Freud suggests that the apparently natural desires of the female are in fact responses to her sexual history. Even though this history is itself infiltrated by the reality of anatomical difference, it is not anatomy itself that is 'destiny', but the subjective registration of the consequences of anatomy – the internalisation of the constraints upon universal desire. Difference is not 'natural' in the sense of predetermined, it is constructed as male and female explore the possibilities for fulfilment of their sexuality. Moreover, this historically produced divergence in the developmental paths of males and females has consequences for all aspects of their lives, for alongside the discovery of anatomical difference and its psychological consequences is the renegotiation of personal relationships which is narrated in the story of the Oedipus complex.

In effect, the trajectory of male and female Oedipus complexes is given by the differing positions of each sex towards the castration complex. For the boy, the phallic stage develops into a desire to express libidinous sexuality through active penetration of the mother; it is the embargo that the incest taboo places upon this, manifested in the perceived threat of the father, that leads to the castration complex. The anxiety generated by this (intensified by the belief that castration has actually happened to girls) causes a deep repression of the desire for the mother and an identification with the father. This in turn leads to the taking up of masculine positions and roles in all areas of development – all premised on the organisation of sexuality which occurs through the operations of the castration complex. In practice there is also a perpetuation of the boy child's passive, 'feminine' aims which are part of his pre-Oedipal bisexuality; alongside the positive Oedipus complex just described is also a negative one, a wish to be the object of the father's desire, to take the mother's place. This is one origin of male homosexuality, but it is also a component of heterosexual development, making the sexual divide less than absolute. Nevertheless, the predominant movement of the boy is a flight from femininity accompanied by repression of incestuous desires, the formation of a strong super-ego, and identification with the father.

The girl's interpersonal history is clearly different. For her, it is the castration complex that produces the Oedipus complex: it is revulsion and hatred of the mother that propels her towards her father in the hope of obtaining from him the lacked and desired penis and of escaping her female heritage. The failure of this to translate into reality forces her to make the penis–baby symbolic substitution; in this way, she eventually represses the unbearably poignant wish to be male and begins to recover her pre-Oedipal identification with the mother, albeit accompanied by powerfully ambivalent feelings.

> [The] girl's libido slips into a new position along the line – there is no other way of putting it – of the equation 'penis–child'. She gives up her wish for a penis and puts in place of it a wish for a child and *with that purpose in view* she takes her father as a love object. Her mother becomes the object of her jealousy. The girl has turned into a little woman. (Freud, 1925, p. 340)

Although the Oedipal history of boy and girl go in opposite directions – in the former case from desire to castration, in the latter from castration to desire – at a meta-level Freud uncovers a structural isometry: 'the castration complex always operates in the sense implied in the subject-matter: it inhibits and limits masculinity and encourages femininity' (Freud, 1925, p. 341). The response to castration in children of both sexes is to repress its reality and turn away from it; that is, to repudiate femininity. But, as Mitchell (1974) asks, 'why should it be femininity that is repudiated?' (p. 306).

Freud's account of sexual difference thus has several components, some of them contradictory. It is a biological theory in the sense of being based on anatomical difference and arguing that this difference necessarily produces different feminine and masculine characteristics. Even though he allows that real women and men are made up of both feminine and masculine attributes, he is unwilling to allow an equality either of structure or of value between the sexes.

We must not allow ourselves to be deflected from such conclusions by the denials of the feminists, who are anxious to force us to regard the two sexes as completely equal in position and worth . . . (Freud, 1925, p. 342)

Apart from arguments derived from the technicalities of super-ego formation, the attitude that females are inherently inferior follows automatically from Freud's espousal of the view that there is only one type of libido, and that this should be termed masculine. Irigaray (1977) articulates the kind of sexual difference which this produces:

> The 'feminine' is always described in terms of deficiency or atrophy, as the other side of the sex that alone holds a monopoly on value: the male sex . . . All Freud's statements describing feminine sexuality overlook the fact that the female sex might have its own 'specificity'. (p. 69)

Cixous (1975) sees this model of sexual difference as motivated by the aim of denying the force of femininity, and characteristically reverses its terms.

> *The 'Dark Continent' is neither dark nor unexplorable.* It is still unexplored only because we have been made to believe that it was too dark to be explored. Because they want to make us believe that what interests us is the white continent, with its monuments to lack. (p. 68)

As will be described below, this is also the language of the feminist critique of Lacan, who makes the impossibility of a feminine psychology a major component of his description of the Symbolic.

In summary, Freud provides a model of development that does not assume a pre-given organisation of gender, but instead interprets sexual difference as something constructed through the processes of maturation and experience. Once this difference occurs, it is deeply subjective, structuring the unconscious of girls and boys in different directions and, despite the bisexual components of each, creating an unbridgeable divide. However, Freud's absorption in patriarchal attitudes and biologistic assumptions actually produces an account of sexual difference that recognises only one form of sexuality, which he regards as masculine. Many feminists and others have criticised this and note that Freud does not examine the social forces that contribute to the devaluing of women and the ideological links between masculinity and activity, femininity and passivity. More subtly, recent critics have argued that Freud does not recognise the degree to which femininity and masculinity can be understood as discourses, as representations of sets of meanings which are historically constructed. Cixous (1975) combines these points:

> There is 'destiny' no more than there is 'nature' or 'essence' as such. Rather, there are living structures that are caught and sometimes rigidly set within historico-cultural limits so mixed up with the scene of History that for a long time it has been impossible (and it is still very difficult) to think or even imagine an 'elsewhere'. (p. 83)

In producing a theory of sexual difference that does not assume its pre-given nature, but that traces its history in the life of each individual, Freud challenges all preconceived notions of the nature of sexuality and of gender. The trajectory of this argument is to suggest that sexual difference is a constructed phenomenon; not arbitrary, indeed, as it follows the structures of social relations, but also not determined by some biological 'necessity'. In addition, Freud's assertion that sexual difference structures subjectivity through its unconscious effects, opens the way for a non-cognitivist reading of gender as ideology. It is in the lived relationship between child and parents, between the individual 'subject' and the social reality to which she or he is subjected, that sexual difference originates and has its immense material effects. But it is as if the recognition of the precariousness of masculinity is too daunting for full articulation in Freudian theory: femininity is continually derogated and the power of social construction repeatedly circumscribed by a biologism that seeks to sustain an image of male superiority, of masculine 'activity' and power. In this way, Freud's biologism continually undermines his own constructionist insights.

## Symbol and sexuality

The re-reading of Freud's work produced by Jacques Lacan

has been much debated in recent years, with widely differing interpretations placed upon it – from those who see Lacan as simply replicating biologistic assumptions about male superiority, to those who view his work as an elaborate deconstruction of the patriarchal order. Lacan has certainly been provocative of an entirely new vision of 'femininity' and of the most enterprising (anti-Lacanian) feminist psychoanalysis (see Frosh, 1987, for a description of these trends). Yet, his own views are difficult to pin down, not just because of the obscure nature of their presentation, but because of a constant slippage between different registers of reference, a seemingly deliberate parody of conventional theories interlaced with complex and sometimes confused linguistic and philosophical leaps. When Lacan states 'We know that the unconscious castration complex has the function of a knot' (1958, p. 75), he could also be describing his own knotted/ropy theory. Nevertheless, it is worth pursuing some of his central ideas or, rather, readings of Freud, because his is the origin of a body of work that does recognise the status of femininity/masculinity as discourse, as a divide created in representation rather than tied to anatomical 'reality'.

Lacan, following Freud, places the origin of sexual difference in the Oedipal and castration complexes. What is new in his approach, however, is that these are read as aspects of the entry of the child into the order of language, the Symbolic (see Chapter 3). Prior to this, the infant has been absorbed in the Imaginary order, fantasising wholeness as a real state, in which the ego is integrated and the subject is at one with the other. The Symbolic introduces a split into the subject, creating desire through its enforcement of a prohibition and hence of the recognition of loss. The signifier of this state, the prime signifier of subjecthood, is the phallus: the power of the phallus to constrain sexuality is structured into the order of language, cutting the subject off from any possibility of the fulfilment of desire and making the Other an impossible aim. Because language is organised around the phallus, because it is *castration* which is the knot that ties the subject down, the divide is a sexual one, creating the separate worlds of female and male. The subject is split by language, split by culture, split by sexuality.

If the phallus is a signifier then it is in the place of the Other that the subject gains access to it. But in that the signifier is only there veiled and as the ratio of the Other's desire, so it is this desire of the Other as such which the subject has to recognise, meaning, the Other as itself a subject divided by the signifying Spaltung (split). (Lacan, 1958, p. 83)

The organisation of desire that occurs through the Symbolic is one characterised by splitting and loss. Because the split is sexual in nature, the loss is experienced as sexual, and individuals of each gender fantasise individuals of the other gender as able to complete them. However, the masculine registration of the discourse around castration and sexuality means that all subjects are split in the same way, with the phallus coming to be represented by the masculine penis, and with femininity symbolising lack – the absence that is the consequence of castration. Thus, there is no essential masculinity or femininity moving along their predetermined paths; rather, as in Freud's theory, there is a sexuality which is split along a single divide, on either side of which lie masculinity and femininity.

In splitting, the subjectivity of the subject disappears. The horror is about the loss of oneself into one's own unconscious – into the gap. But because human subjectivity cannot ultimately exist outside a division into one of two sexes, then it is castration that finally comes to symbolise this split. The feminine comes to stand over the point of disappearance, the loss. (Mitchell, 1984, p. 307)

Femininity is constructed outside the system of the Symbolic – the feminine has no voice of its own because it is excluded from discourse, because language is patriarchal and phallocentric and orders subjectivity along these lines. Lacan (1958) refers to femininity as 'masquerade', because of this: 'It is for what she is not that she expects to be desired as well as loved' (p. 84). Lacan assumes that it is only the masculine voice that can speak; femininity, being only a lack, has no language.

There is woman only as excluded by the nature of things which is the nature of words, and it has to be said that if there is one thing they themselves are complaining about enough at the moment it is well and truly that – only they don't know what they are saying, which is all the difference between them and me. (Lacan, 1972–3, p. 144)

Not surprisingly, there have been many heated disputes over the nature of femininity in the Lacanian system, involving expulsions and abuse as well as argument and poetry (see Gallop, 1982). Lacan's principal opponents such as Irigaray and Cixous assert that femininity does have content and that it is Lacan's loss (lack?) if male discourse is unable to deal with it.

The production of ejaculations of all sorts, often prematurely emitted, makes him miss, in the desire for identification with the lady, what her own pleasure might be all about.
And . . . his? (Irigaray, 1977, p. 91)

Lacan's defenders emphasise the non-identity of phallus and penis, and interpret his work as an assault on the arrogance with which masculinity is made dominant under patriarchy. Rose (1982), for instance, reads Lacan's account of the phallus as an exposure of the fantasy upon which the apparently substantial entities 'female' and 'male' are built: sexuality is an unstable entity, drifting through demand and desire, each sex mythically representing to the other the satisfaction of a continuing emptiness. Lacan is only phallocentric because he is intent on exposing the fictitiousness of the phallic claim to dominance; anatomical difference is set up as if it truly signified sexual difference, when the latter in fact eludes its grasp.

It thus covers over the complexity of the child's early sexual life with a crude opposition in which that very complexity is refused or repressed. The phallus thus indicates the reduction of difference to an instance of visible perception, a *seeming* value. (Rose, 1982, p. 42)

Each side accuses the other of biologism; each claims to be describing the construction of representations of sexual difference in discourse. Lacan stresses the impossibility of 'The Woman'; Cixous in particular celebrates her overflowing content.

She has never 'held still'; explosion, diffusion, effervescence, abundance, she takes pleasure in being boundless, outside self, outside same, far from a 'centre', from any capital of her 'dark continent', very far from the 'hearth' to which man brings her so that she will tend his fire, which always threatens to go out. (Cixous, 1975, p. 91)

Femininity here is seen as a separate and more vibrant order, with its own history and challenge. As noted earlier, the radical feminism of this idea lies in its assertion of an opposition to patriarchy, a subjectivity and a politics which exist in different terms from the conventional organisation of things. Whether this is a fantasy, possibly strategic, possibly reductionist, or whether it is a revolutionary approach to the reconstruction of gender – these are the terms of the post-Lacanian debate.

It is not necessary here to decide between these positions. What the work of Lacan and the writers and psychoanalysts he has influenced continually reasserts is that sexual difference occurs within ideology – it is not a simple reading of anatomical distinction, but the assignment of certain meanings that in turn organise subjectivity. This work recognises the productivity of representation, that is, the way systems of representation produce sexual difference in a form which is not given automatically by biology, but which is mediated by unpredictable, but systematic, social forces. There are distinct problems of various kinds with the theory: not just those already mentioned, but also the confusing essentialism which marks its appeal to experience, to a vision of the penis as phallus. This essentialism undermines the otherwise dominant emphasis on symbolic representation and the theory's studied avoidance of simple readings of the body (Williamson, 1987). But Lacanian and post-Lacanian work has succeeded in producing a reading of Freud that asserts the significance of sexual division and gives it a history linked to sociality and cultural construction. Whether it takes this process far enough is a moot point. In the end, it may be that psychological processes can only be fully de-constructed when they are located in their historical context, something that neither psychologists nor psychoanalysts routinely do. A final quotation from Irigaray makes this point strongly in relation to Lacanian psychoanalysis, but the same or similar could be said of the psychological theories outlined in the first part of this chapter.

Psychoanalytic theory thus utters the truth about the status of female sexuality and about the sexual relation. But it stops there. Refusing to interpret the historical determinants of its discourse . . . and in particular what is implied by the up-to-now exclusively masculine sexualisation of the application of its laws, it remains caught up in phallocentrism, which it claims to make into a universal and eternal value. (Irigaray, 1977, pp. 102–3)

# 5 The Racist Subject

## Reductionism and social explanation

One of the issues raised by any consideration of psychological and psychoanalytic theories is the extent to which their locus of applicability is restricted to the understanding of individuals. Clearly, the focus of both approaches is on individuals – their psychological processes, developmental history or differences from one another. Where social events are considered it is usually either to fill out the picture of individuality (e.g. the effects of socialisation on the development of the individual child), or it is in small-scale contexts where the interaction of individuals can be examined (e.g. studies of small groups or families). Attempts to employ psychological and psychoanalytic approaches to throw light on fully social phenomena have been relatively few, although, at least in the case of psychoanalysis, some of these attempts have been quite influential – notably Freud's (1930) account of the relationship between individual repression and cultural development and the 'Freudo-Marxist' analyses of such writers as Reich, Fromm and Marcuse (see Frosh, 1987).

The major problem faced by psychologists and psychoanalysts wishing to use the insights derived from their disciplines to augment understanding of the workings of society, is how to integrate social and individual levels without reducing the former to the latter. This can be seen in the difficulties which have faced researchers investigating gender differences; specifically, the heated argument between those who regard biological processes as determinant and those who explain differences in terms of socialisation events, is also a dispute about the appropriate level of autonomy to allow social and individual levels of explanation. Sometimes, as mentioned in Chapter 1, the results of psychological and psychoanalytic accounts are explicitly reactionary in a political sense. Thus, sociobiology, which attempts to explain social behaviour in evolutionary terms, provides a direct rationalisation of current patterns of social organisation in terms of genetic necessity. This leads to legitimation of competitiveness, gender inequality, and ethnocentrism in terms of the biological propensity to protect the genes of one's own family group (Wilson, 1975; see Rose *et al.*, 1984, for a critique of sociobiological and similar approaches).

Sociobiology is one relatively extreme example of reductionism. It was suggested in Chapter 1 that the reductionist procedure, which attempts to provide explanations of phenomena in terms of forces acting at a more 'molecular' level, has resulted in some major advances in neuropsychology and psychophysiology. However, it is an inappropriate general philosophy for psychology because the level at which reductionist explanations are couched are not those that are informative about *psychological* processes. This is particularly the case when neurological or physiological information is offered as an account of the causal mechanisms that produce events with intentional or interactional components. In social psychology, however, the problem is not so much reduction of phenomena to the biological level (except in the case of sociobiology), but the use of reductionist explanatory modes in place of an appreciation of the impact of forces acting at the level of social structures. In the field of social theory, it is specifically *individualism*, rather than the biologism with which it is associated, which is the more relevant accusation against psychology and psychoanalysis.

When social phenomena are explained solely in terms of individual psychology, reductionism slips into an ideological stance that takes society as 'given' and places the weight of all change on individuals. It is, for example, as a product of this stance that the socially common state of depression is explained as the result of biochemical disturbances in individuals and is treated through the mass prescription of tranquillisers and anti-depressants, rather than by action on the conditions of isolation and urban alienation which are clearly implicated in its causation (Brown and Harris, 1978; Peele, 1981). The use of enormous quantities of psychotropic drugs in British prisons (Rose *et al.*, 1984) and the abuses of psychiatry in the Soviet Union (e.g. Lader, 1976) stand as evidence that no one political system has a monopoly on this kind of thinking. In a context relevant to the main concerns of this chapter, the suggestion that the inner-city riots in Britain in the early 1980s may have been partially caused by damage to rioters' brains through lead poisoning is only one of the more bizarre manifestations of a philosophy of individualism.

The argument here is not that a social theory should avoid concepts operating at the level of individuals. Indeed, it is important to include such concepts in any complete account of social events: whatever first influences what, it is clear that social events have implications and effects upon individuals, and that psychological factors contribute to the way people read the social world, and hence to its reproduction. This argument simply states that questions concerning the final cause of events are less important than explorations of the interlocking levels of phenomena which are incorporated in any manifestation of sociality; that accounting for events in terms of economic and political processes does not preclude a parallel account of the subjective ramifications of those same events. The kind of explanation which is appropriate depends on the question being asked: if this question concerns the origins, structure or social functions of a social phenomenon, the account should be couched in economic and political terms. If, on the other hand, the question at issue is the way in which this social phenomenon is experienced and lived out by actual people, then the explanation may be in sociological terms, but is equally likely to be helpfully informed by psychological considerations. It is a failure to appreciate the logic of these interlocking levels that has contributed to the viciousness of much of the debate surrounding the use of psychology for social explanations. Psychological accounts are only imperialistic when they seek to do away with social ones; for a complete understanding of the structure and impact of any social force – for a complete account, that is, of the ideological structure of sociality – psychological explanations are necessary.

The subject of this chapter is one that has consistently polarised theorists and political activists along the lines sketched above – that of the psychology of racism. Racism is indubitably a social phenomenon: it has roots in economic oppression and imperialism, it is institutionalised in the structures of Western society, it is widespread across gender and class divisions, and it serves the specific political and economic interests of dominant social groups. These characteristics make the development of a socio-political theory of racism essential; indeed, any history of racism can only be written from such a point of view. However, whilst racism is a social phenomenon, it operates at more than just the macro-social level. Just as sexism is something which is institutionalised but is also manifested in the power laden interactions between individuals, so racism is something which is acted out both at the level of social organisation and in encounters between individuals. Furthermore, just as sexist beliefs, attitudes and emotions are present within individuals, so racism is something which is deeply embedded in the psychology of each individual racist. A psychological account of racism is not a substitute for a socio-political account, but it is necessary for any complete description of how racism is reproduced within society.

The general point here is that social forces do not operate on a solely structural plane, but they become inextricably bound up with the subjective experiences of individuals, which in turn contribute to their perpetuation (see Frosh, 1987; Banton *et al.*, 1985). The specific point is that racism, which is the most vicious and dangerous form of social oppression, achieves part of its power through being inscribed deeply in individual psychology. A theory of what this means and how it happens is therefore necessary if racism is to be fully understood and combated. This chapter examines some of the major efforts on the part of psychologists and psychoanalysts to provide such a theory. The starting point is the position that racism cannot be written off as some form of aberrant irrationality located solely within the life history of individuals, but rather that a theory of racist psychology must take cognisance of the social determinants of racism and hence must show how psychology and sociality interact. In terms of practice, there is no more important area of research in sociology and psychology than that of racism; in terms of theory, investigations of racism reveal the limitations and potential of psychological and psychoanalytic theories of individuals, society and the possibilities for change.

## The racist heritage

The objection of many people to psychological and psychoanalytic accounts of racism has one historical context which it is important to acknowledge: this is that both disciplines have a racist heritage of their own. Billig (1978) points out that psychology's first Nobel laureate, Konrad Lorenz, carried out most of his major research and obtained his professorship in Nazi Germany; the content of his work also had a potentially fascist subtext in that 'chauvinism for ingroups, aggression towards outgroups, hierarchy and respect for a dominant leader were all claimed to be instinctual in man' (Billig, 1978, p. 15). The eugenic interests of many of the originators of psychological 'science' have been well documented (e.g. Rose *et al.*, 1984); take, for example, the claim by Terman (1916) that the low IQ scores of black and other American minority groups had racial origins, leading to the suggestion that 'Children of this group should be segregated in special classes . . . They cannot master abstractions, but they can often be made efficient workers . . . from a eugenic point of view they constitute a grave problem because of their unusually prolific breeding' (pp. 91–2; quoted in Rose *et al.*, 1984).

The 'racial' determination of IQ has been a consistent theme in the history of psychology, with the most famous modern example being Jensen's (1969) *Harvard Educational Review* article, in which he echoed Terman's sentiments by ascribing the largest source of variation between blacks and whites in IQ test performance to genetic differences. The political consequences of this view are evident in Jensen's proposal for different kinds of schooling for blacks and whites; where this leads can also be seen in the way the case for the genetic inferiority of the intelligence of blacks was presented by a British sympathiser of Jensen's position, H. J. Eysenck, in the pages of a magazine published by the fascist National Party (Billig, 1978). The sorry history of racism of this kind has been extensively described by Kamin (1974) and Rose *et al.* (1984) and, fortunately, need not be dwelt upon here.

The history of psychoanalysis' involvement with racist modes of thought and investigation is also not a particularly attractive one. In some instances, overtly racist sentiments have been expressed in the name of variants of psychoanalysis; for example, Jung suggested that the Negro 'has probably a whole historical layer less' mind than the Caucasian, and warned white Americans that 'living with barbaric races exerts a suggestive effect on the laboriously tamed instinct of the white race and tends to pull it down' (Dalal, 1988, pp. 271, 276). Jung can also be found employing analytic concepts to bolster the racist philosophy underpinning Nazism. Take, for example, the following differentiation of Aryan from Jewish science, made in 1934:

> The Jew, as relatively a nomad, never has and presumably never will produce a culture of his own . . . Therefore the Jewish race as a whole has, according to my experience, an unconscious which can only conditionally be compared to the Aryan . . . the Aryan unconscious has a higher potential than the Jewish . . . In my opinion, it has been a great mistake of all previous medical psychology to apply Jewish categories, which are not even binding for all Jews, indiscriminately to Christian Germans or Slavs. (Jung, 1934, in Poliakov, 1974, p. 374)

Although Jung's is the best known example of collaboration with Nazi racism, Billig (1978) makes it clear that it was by no means the only one, amongst psychologists and psychoanalysts alike. The emphasis on instinct and biological inheritance in Jung's theory made his work particularly susceptible to such uses, but the Nazi mythology of the will and of the power of the heroic personality to triumph over social constraints was one into which the individualistic focus of psychoanalysis could be made to blend. As usual, it is not the whole of psychoanalysis that is in the dock here, but those elements within it that neglect or refute the role of social and political realities in the production of individual qualities.

In addition to explicitly racist formulations, there is also a more subtly racist trend in psychoanalysis which has been manifest in its anthropological branch. McCulloch (1983) points out that most researchers exploring the psychology of colonial people have been motivated by a desire to understand the assumed origins of *Western* culture. Using an evolutionary framework of highly doubtful validity, this involves an assumption that the current patterns of culture to be found in non-industrialised peoples can be regarded as a fossilised version of the actual pre-history of Western culture; studies of such 'primitive' cultures therefore have a value equivalent to that of studies of children for explanations of adult functioning. Indeed, the strongest ideological determinant of this work is an assumed equivalence between so-called 'primitive' people, children and the insane. Alongside this has been a psychologistic approach which commonly fails to appreciate the structural characteristics of non-Western cultures, instead seeing them as more-or-less straightforward representations of internal mental states.

In addition, a related tendency common to many psychoanalytic studies and evident even in Benedict's (1935) seminal text, *Patterns of Culture*, is to view Western culture as the pinnacle of development, with non-industrialised societies representing either or both of fixation at childhood points of development, or pathological regressions. The result of all these assumptions is work that reduces both the culture and the political conditions of the people being studied to the expression of 'primitive' psychological urges. Even progressive theorists can employ psychoanalytic notions to such retrogressive ends. Mannoni (1950), for instance, suggests that the Malagasy people were tied to dependent personality structures by their worship of the dead and belief in magic and witchcraft. 'Wherever Europeans have founded colonies of the type we are considering,' he argues, 'it can safely be said that their coming was unconsciously expected – even desired – by the future subject peoples' (1950, p. 86).

A question raised by the list of troubles given above, is the extent to which racist theorising follows automatically from the structure of psychological and psychoanalytic thought. To some extent, racism resides as a possibility in any approach that takes the individual as the unquestioned subject of its discourse, especially if that discourse incorporates value-laden notions of ideal versus deviant development. Failure to recognise the power of the social world to fix the positions of individuals and groups within it leads inexorably to explanations of the different status of people in terms of individual difference and thence of biology. In addition, the same neglect of sociality makes a discipline permeable to ideological positions claiming scientificity and neutral 'objectivity', when in fact they are full of value positions and assumptions derived from the patterns of dominance that characterise the social world. On the other hand, awareness of the role of social forces has made it possible for some psychologists and psychoanalysts to take up positions opposing the racist tendencies already described. There are several famous examples of such investigators, including the group around Adorno (whose work is described later in this chapter), Reich and Fromm, but also a host of social psychologists employed in more mundane attempts to spell out the forces operating to perpetuate prejudice and discrimination. Not all this work is of the same quality, but much if it is motivated by genuinely anti-racist aims. In addition, while both psychologists (especially behaviour therapists) and psychoanalysts have been criticised for imposing ethnocentric controls and attitudes upon their patients under the guise of value-free advice and interpretations, there appears to be an increasing awareness on the part of practitioners of the need to ground their work in the culture and true subjectivity of those with whom they deal (see Littlewood and Lipsedge, 1982).

The argument here is that the implicit biologism and reductionist individualism present both in psychology and in psychoanalysis makes these disciplines particularly likely to reproduce racist ideology. In some ways, this is only to be expected: in a society in which racism is deeply embedded, it is not surprising if intellectual disciplines dramatise racist ideas. However, this may not be a *necessary* consequence. As various theorists and researchers have demonstrated, psychological and psychoanalytic concepts can be employed to oppose racism – either in practice or in the sphere of 'ideological struggle', the provision of concepts and insights which can oppose the ideological givens that structure the racist world.

Development of such oppositional concepts requires a clear view of the operation of social (economic and political) forces as well as a sophisticated account of how these forces are internalised and reproduced in the psychology of individuals. Particular questions worthy of attention here include the impact of racism on the psychological development of members of oppressed groups and the possible uses of psychological and psychoanalytic therapy as elements in anti-racist actions. However, it is in the provision of an account of the psychology of racism itself that psychological and psychoanalytic theorists have their most urgent task to fulfil. In the remainder of this chapter, some classic accounts of racism derived from the two disciplines will be examined in order to derive some principles upon which such work can be based. In particular, it will be argued that, although psychologists investigating prejudice and small group processes have provided important descriptions of some of the factors that contribute to racist mental functioning, psychoanalysis has portrayed more fully the possible connections between subjective events and social realities. In this way, the use of psychoanalysis to offer a critique of psychology is extended into the crucial area of anti-racist practice.

## Racism and prejudice

The dominance of psychology by cognitive theories has been as
apparent in social psychology as in other areas. In part, this may
be a product of the split between psychology and psychoanalysis,
with psychologists attempting to establish the autonomy and
scientificity of their discipline by concentration not just on rational
modes of exploration, but on the potentially rational aspects of
mental life. This cognitive emphasis may also have been produced
through the tendencies described in the earlier chapters of this
book. Psychology has systematically devalued the significance of
human subjectivity, concentrating instead on the processes and
principles that make certain attainments and behaviours – actions –
possible. These actions include apparently irrational phenomena
such as visual illusions or distorted judgements, but they do not
include the affective experiences which accompany them; instead,
irrationality is explained in terms of the breakdown or imperfection
of rational systems. In social psychology, the picture is complicated
further by the uneasy relationship between psychology's general
focus on the individual and the sub-discipline's concern with social
material. Although many researchers have shown a willingness to
address this relationship and to attempt to develop explanatory
concepts of a genuinely social (or at least micro-social) kind (see,
for example, Tajfel, 1978), the dominant tendency in social
psychology has been to investigate the impact of socialisation
experiences and social events on *individual* processes.

It is in this light that the specific contribution of social psychology
to studies of racism should be understood. Notwithstanding the
openness of some important researchers, notably Allport (1954),
to insights from psychodynamic theory, psychologists have made
little headway on the affective components of racism – the way in
which racism becomes an integral part of the emotional life of the
racist individual. Similarly, despite some elegant descriptions of
the responsiveness of groups to social manipulations, making them
more or less competitive and either enhancing or ameliorating
the rigidity of ingroup/outgroup distinctions (e.g. Sherif, 1966),
psychologists have offered few guidelines for understanding either
the social structure and functions of racism, or the reasons for the
emotional and ideological intensity with which group identity is
constructed. In this area, sociological theories able to articulate

the economic and political functions of racism are far more helpful (see Jones, 1972, for a psychological account along these lines).

Where psychologists have supplied important insights, however, has been in describing the cognitive processes that underpin *prejudice*, that aspect of racism which translates into conscious belief and which forms the basis of systems by means of which oppression becomes rationalised. This contribution is rather double-edged: whilst it provides a significant component of any general theory of racism, it has also led many theorists to reduce racism to prejudice, that is, to view racism as nothing more than a collection of irrational beliefs and stereotypes arising from faulty judgemental processes. As will be argued at various points in this chapter, this reduction of racism to prejudice is part of a wider tendency to interpret racism as an irrational product of ignorance – an ideology of the 'false perception' kind – with the objective balance of liberalism being its opposing philosophy.

Allport's (1954) definition of prejudice has been adopted by later theorists under various guises.

> Ethnic prejudice is an antipathy based upon a faulty and inflexible generalisation. It may be felt or expressed. It may be directed toward a group as a whole, or toward an individual because he is a member of that group. (p. 9)

A similar definition is provided by Jones (1972), who sees prejudice as:

> the prior negative judgement of the members of a race or religion or the occupants of any other significant social role, held in disregard of facts that contradict it. (p. 61)

Levin and Levin (1982) specify the 'components' of prejudice in their definition:

> From a psychological perspective, prejudice can be regarded as a negative attitude toward the members of a minority group . . . As such, prejudice is a learned disposition consisting of the following components or dimensions: (1) negative beliefs or sterotypes (cognitive component), (2) negative feelings or emotions (affective component). (p. 66)

These definitions have a number of noteworthy attributes, many of them described in Allport's original account, which differentiate them from dictionary approaches. Allport points out, for example, that whereas the strict meaning of 'prejudice' allows unfavourable or favourable pre-judgements (biases) to operate, 'ethnic prejudice' is 'mostly negative' (1954, p. 6). The relevant aspect of prejudice for theories of racism is certainly the idea of negative valuing of the despised group; this already removes the necessary account from being a simple description of how judgement processes operate to one which must include an explanation of the systematic negativity of those judgements.

Secondly, there is the notion of prejudice as a judgement which is a 'faulty and inflexible generalisation', 'held in disregard of facts that contradict it'. There are two related ideas here which are worth noting. The suggestion of a 'generalisation' and the reference to 'facts' introduce the notion of truth-testing, that what is wrong with prejudiced perceptions is that they are at variance with the actuality of the pre-judged group. Again, this variance is seen as unamenable to change: it is 'inflexible' because it does not respond to experience. It is this feature of prejudices which distinguishes them from simple misconceptions: '*Prejudgements become prejudices only if they are not reversible when exposed to new knowledge*' (Allport, 1954, p. 9). This is both a feature of the irrationality of prejudices and a defining attribute; reasonable people can have misconceptions, but prejudice is unreason in action.

One characteristic of prejudice with which the definitions quoted above fail to engage, is the intensity of its negative value charge. In the psychological literature, this is usually conceived of in terms of *hostility*: a cognitive attitude of negative direction which is affectively intense. The reason why the definitions often fail to register this fully is perhaps also the reason why much of the active research into prejudice by psychologists has failed to deal with the intensity of the racist imagination: that the affective dimension is omitted in favour of accounts of the irrational structure of prejudiced cognitions. Stereotyping, ethnocentrism and disparagement of outgroups are the favoured attitudes for study; these are clearly central elements in racist thinking, but they attain their centrality partly through their affective loading. Whilst psychologists have been aware of this in the abstract, their studies have not dealt with the emotional context of racism. Instead, they have focused on the distortions of judgement that can be revealed by examination of the relationship between racial prejudice and ordinary cognitive categorisation processes. These processes are assumed to be natural within the human mind – necessary means by which information is organised and stored. Hence the title of chapter 2 in Allport (1954), 'The Normality of Prejudgement', which argues that:

> man has a propensity to prejudice. This propensity lies in his normal and natural tendency to form generalisations, concepts, categories, whose content represents an over-simplification of his world of experience. His rational categories keep close to first-hand experience, but he is able to form irrational categories just as readily. In these even a kernel of truth may be lacking, for they can be composed wholly of hearsay evidence, emotional projections, and fantasy. (p. 27)

More recent accounts of prejudice (e.g. Ehrlich, 1973) have provided a far more sophisticated analysis of the cognitive processes that are involved in social and personality judgements, but the general approach evident in Allport's analysis can still be found throughout the literature. This reduces to the idea that racial prejudice is an irrational mode of judgement, derived from the inappropriate use of social categories and from limited cognitive resources. Thus, Allport proposes what he terms 'the most momentous discovery of psychological research in the field of prejudice': that 'the cognitive processes of prejudiced people are *in general* different from the cognitive processes of tolerant people' (pp. 174–5). Specifically, prejudiced individuals are more likely to make dichotomised ('black and white') judgements and prefer 'monopolistic' categories, reflecting a pervasive intolerance of ambiguity – an idea also present in Adorno *et al.* (1950). What these tendencies represent, however, is a distortion of normal categorisation processes; categorisation itself remains a necessary aspect of social (and cognitive) functioning.

The cognitive distortion view of prejudice suggests that the aim of anti-racist programmes should be to make social categorisations more realistic – that is, to reduce the amount of stereotyping of, and increase the detailed knowledge concerning, other ethnic groups. Programmes aimed at increasing social contact between members of different ethnic groups follow the logic of this reasoning, as do 'multicultural' educational practices that introduce children to the customs, beliefs and history of the various 'cultural' (a euphemism for 'ethnic', itself a euphemism for racial) groups present in society. The hope which lies behind these programmes is that as people come to experience one another directly they will discover the truth about each other – that everyone shares a basic humanity, that the racial prejudices which people hold are indeed prejudices and not based on reality, and that it is possible to like, and share with, people of all ethnic groups. In this model, racial prejudice is viewed as a kind of mistake, a false perception of the world which can be cleared up by a good dose of reality. There is, however, recognition that such reality has to be fairly carefully laundered if it is not to prove counter-productive. From Allport onwards, promoters of multiculturalism have known that contact between groups can *increase* prejudice and racism if it is organised wrongly; for example, to be productive such contact has to be validated by high-status authority figures or institutions, and has to promote cooperation rather than competition.

Even under such conditions, the results of racial contact pro-grammes have been less than might have been hoped: in the United States, for instance, racial mixing seems to have generally increased mutual acceptance at work whilst having no impact on wider social relations (Jones, 1972). The more intimate the relationship being considered, the more difficult it seems to be for prejudices to be rooted out simply by the provision of more 'accurate' information, perhaps because what is at stake is more personally central. Jones (1972), reviewing the literature on interpersonal attraction, suggests that although similarity of beliefs, attitudes and interests is usually the most powerful determinant of attraction, 'one difference – race – may negate a whole range of similar attributes' (p. 83). This is particularly true for clearly prejudiced individuals, who may make inferences about belief dissimilarity solely on the basis of race (ibid., p. 84), but the general point is that race is often far too powerful a discriminating characteristic for prejudice to be overcome by simple exposure to members of the scapegoated group.

One common cognitive strategy observed by social psychologists amongst their subjects is the creation of a distinction between 'ingroups' and 'outgroups' which can become invested with immense emotional and practical significance. These ingroups and outgroups are not necessarily objective distinctions (although they will usually refer to some real boundary); rather, they are creations of identification and antagonism – psychological rather than sociological entities. As such, they are both basic (for instance, in the patterns of identification and shared ideology that characterise family and other 'kin' groups, with the notion of 'blood' links being an important expression of ingroup status) and malleable through social means. Sherif's (1966) experiments demonstrate the latter tendency, with the strength of group antagonism in a boy's camp being highly responsive to changes in the pattern of competitiveness and cooperation demanded of the groups. Conversely, Tajfel's studies of 'minimal groups' (e.g. Tajfel *et al.* 1971; Tajfel, 1979) used arbitrarily structured groups in laboratory settings to eliminate any 'real' differences between the groups. Despite this, when given tasks which involved the distribution of points to others, subjects systematically discriminated in favour of ingroup members and against outgroup members. This finding held even when all other subjects, whether ingroup or outgroup, were unknown. Tajfel's conclusion is that there are basic cognitive categorisation processes within people, operating to produce ingroup/outgroup distinctions even in the absence of any rational basis for such distinctions – a sort of fundamental need to differentiate oneself from others shifted into the social domain.

There are several methodological problems with this research, particularly concerning the untheorised role of the experimenter and of the subjects' readings of the purpose of the discriminations being required of them (see Henriques, 1984), but it is revealing of the rationalist logic behind cognitively-based social psychology. The argument, which parallels that concerning individual prejudices described above, is that ingroup/outgroup differentiations are produced under all circumstances by the operation of basic cognitive processes; in the case of racist discriminations, these processes become exaggeratedly intense or illogical, with their irrationality being the defining characteristic of their pathology. Variants of this idea have been applied to 'ethnocentrism', seen as 'based on a pervasive and rigid ingroup–outgroup distinction' involving 'stereotyped negative imagery and hostile attitudes regarding ingroups, and a hierarchical, authoritarian view of group interaction in which ingroups are rightly dominant, outgroups subordinate' (Adorno *et al.*, 1950, p. 150). The use of conspiracy theories by racists has also been explained in terms of attempts to simplify the complexities of the world and to provide cognitively acceptable explanations of events in terms of ingroup/outgroup dynamics (e.g. Billig, 1978). Once again, although the intensity and direction of the cognitive strategies employed here may be wayward, the strategies themselves are seen as products of normal cognitive operations.

The problem posed to cognitive researchers is of how to explain the distortions of cognition present in racial prejudice. Two main strategies are employed here. The first is to recognise the activities of affective processes, an approach which, perhaps ironically, leads to the adoption of psychodynamic concepts as a way of repairing the lacunae in cognitive theories. The most popular idea is one which asserts that prejudice fulfils a defensive function for the individual concerned, either simplifying the terrifying complexity of the world in a manageable way, or bolstering self-esteem through the denigration of an outgroup, or allowing for the projection of unwanted impulses  this being also the most common psychoanalytic explanation of racism (see below). Thus, Levin and Levin (1982) propose that 'discrimination and prejudice can be employed to displace aggression, protect self-esteem, and reduce uncertainties' (p. 156) and see in prejudice,

> a method of defending self-image, whereby a minority group becomes a *negative reference group* for the majority group member. By using a minority group as a negative reference group, an individual need not acknowledge truths about him or herself or about threatening aspects of his or her environment. (p. 156)

For prejudiced individuals, who are intolerant of ambiguity and often 'incapable of estimating qualities of others from the cues given in interactional settings' (p. 157), culturally supported prejudices provide ready-made expectations allowing simple person-perception categories to be used. More psychodynamically, prejudice produces a scapegoat on to whom unacceptable or frightening aspects of the self may be projected, thereby benefiting both the individual ego (by giving feelings such as aggression an aim and thereby making them tolerable) and the social status quo.

On a collective level, scapegoating may serve as a *safety valve* whereby feelings of hostility are diverted to substitute objects, thereby protecting the leaders of a group from becoming the recipients of aggression. (Levin and Levin, 1982, p. 186)

Hostility emerges as a major underlying theme – according to Allport (1954), 'erroneous generalisation and hostility' are 'natural and common capacities of the human mind' (p. 17) – providing the emotional impetus for prejudice; this hostility may have internal roots within the individual, but is directed outwards at available scapegoats in order to make it manageable. Internal hostility translates into interpersonal hostility, which is manifested as racial prejudice.

The second strategy employed by social psychologists to explain the occurrence of prejudice is to emphasise the role of social events in perpetuating racist beliefs, particularly through the medium of socialisation. On the whole, a simple method of cultural transmission is proposed, whereby the norms of a racist society are acted out within the family and hence imitated by the growing child. Jones (1972) provides a classification of possible socialisation outcomes:

The most important determinant of whether and/or how an individual becomes a racist is the environmental norm to which he is socialised. If there is a norm of hating blacks, then a child is likely to grow up doing so. If there is a norm of feeling blacks are inferior but a counsel of polite avoidance, a child is likely to become an aversive racist [i.e. one characterised by passive, avoidance tendencies towards blacks]. Most subtle is the ethnocentric norm which is not avowedly racist but which, when applied to blacks, produces unchallenged feelings of white superiority. This child is neither aversive nor dominative, but bases his judgements of black people solely on norms which greatly restrict the range of black people with whom any association at all is desirable. (p. 128)

The relationship between social norms and individual belief is seen as a determinant one, with many theorists proposing a more or less linear connection between them. According to Jones, racism is 'inherited as a natural consequence of being socialised into a culture that from the beginning has been based on the assumption of white superiority over black' (p. 121). For Milner (1983),

> When racism has taken root in the majority culture, has pervaded its institutions, language, its social intercourse and its cultural productions, has entered the very fabric of the culture, then the simple process by which a culture is transmitted from generation to generation – the socialisation process – becomes the most important 'determinant' of prejudice. (In Brittan and Maynard, 1984, p. 99)

Racism is inherent in the way society is organised; most social psychologists recognise that on the whole it is not at the level of psychology that this is to be explained. But if it enters into the head of the individual, it is as the emotionally-driven use of specific defences which are activated according to the categories made available by sociality. Prejudice serves functions for the individual, but it takes its form from the inherited structure of the social world.

There are a number of points to raise concerning the conventional approach to understanding racism as prejudice. The strength of the approach lies in its description of attitudinal components of racism, its account of the way these are built upon common cognitive strategies which are not necessarily 'pathological' in themselves, and its identification of socialisation practices serving to perpetuate racist beliefs. In addition, the work on groups has drawn attention to the way manipulations of the immediate environment can have substantial effects on ingroup/outgroup attitudes, even though other research suggests that making such ingroup/outgroup distinctions may be a basic and universal tendency. In terms of practice, the psychological research on prejudice has been one motivator for multicultural approaches that attempt to combat racism by breaking down ignorance and hence subverting prejudice. This has produced some imaginative and useful educational programmes and some important alterations to work practices. On its own, however, it is clearly a very limited response to the intensity and self-sufficiency of racist activity.

It may already be clear where the inadequacies of the prejudice literature reside. First, there is a problem with all approaches which prioritise attitudes: this is that the link with actions is anything but clear. In the field of racism, studies have not shown any strong predictive links between prejudice and discriminatory behaviour (Ehrlich, 1973). On occasions, it even appears that prejudices may develop in order to justify discriminatory practices which are already in operation (Levin and Levin, 1982), a form of cognitive functioning ('cognitive dissonance') familiar from other areas of social psychology. Thus, approaches which emphasise prejudicial attitudes may have only limited relevance for the explanation of racist behaviours.

There is a more significant criticism of the psychology of prejudice, which relates more closely to its philosophical underpinnings. The explicit consideration that social psychologists give to socialisation processes and to the place of racism in the social world, is an important contribution to the research literature. However, it is also belied by the adoption of a model which in its cognitivism is highly individualistic. In the approach described above, prejudice is a manifestation of distorted cognitive processes which have their origin in the immediate experience and psychology of the individual. Alterations in prejudiced outlooks come about through exposing individuals to alternative experiences which will supply new and more accurate information on which a more realistic set of judgements can be premised.

There are numerous things wrong with this formulation. Despite its acknowledgement of the importance of socialisation, it omits social phenomena from its conceptualisation of how racism operates. More precisely, the social world is reduced to a collection of attitudes which are passed on to the individual child. There is no recognition of the *materiality* of racism, the way it is embedded in society as a set of practices, represented both in the activities of institutions and the social positioning of oppressed groups. In other words, racism is not just a matter of the absorption of prevalent ideas about ethnic groups, but of the internalisation of the power relationships that are structured into the social world.

> When we say that racism is transmitted through socialisation, we have to assume that racism is not simply a set of beliefs which people reproduce and internalise – but rather that the reproduction of these beliefs is tied into the reproduction of power relations. (Brittan and Maynard, 1984, p. 99)

This is why it is insufficient to theorise prejudice as a manifestation of distorted thinking: the discriminatory practices that are part of racism have real social effects and real social benefits for some people; under these circumstances, prejudicial thinking is not some distortion or cognitive inadequacy, but a reflection of material reality. It is not, therefore, 'irrational' in a dysfunctional sense, but a part of a wider rationality which benefits from oppression. Thus, the focus on prejudice not only neglects consideration of institutional and cultural racism (which would be acceptable if it were made clear that only one aspect of racism was being studied), but it also obscures the position that racism has in the social world, and thereby misplaces its political and its psychological dynamics. Prejudicial thinking is not some erroneous use of cognitive strategies which can be made good by a dose of the real world; it is, rather, a more accurate reflection of how the world is actually structured – of how racism is built into white society – than is the false liberalism that asserts egalitarianism where in fact there is domination and oppression.

There is a final point concerning the 'irrationality' argument. As noted above, in attempting to explain the motivation for prejudicial thinking, many social psychological theorists have fallen back on the use of psychodynamic concepts, particularly those of defence mechanisms and projection. Apart from the notion that it is important for people to make sense of the world and that the cognitively simple categories of racial prejudice make this possible for individuals who find it hard to tolerate ambiguity, the underlying impulses which create the need for these defences are theorised as emotional. In particular, the inability of the individual to withstand her or his own (unexplained) hostile and aggressive feelings is made the origin of antagonism towards convenient outgroups. As Billig (1978) points out, this reading of racism in terms of prejudice which in turn is a product of interpersonal hostility neglects the organised, ideological elements in racism, apparent most clearly in racist conspiracy theories. This point will be dealt with in more detail in connection with psychoanalytic approaches, but it does call into question any simple reduction of racism to emotional disturbance. There is also a more compelling problem with social psychology's use of the emotional irrationality argument. Because of the paucity of concepts of affect with which social psychology is faced, it employs psychodynamic notions in a loose and untheorised way, to fill in the gaps in its own discourse.

The result on the whole is that a descriptive theory of prejudicial cognitions is left without a properly theorised motor; there is only cognitive error and a vague reference to emotional disturbance in order to explain it. Henriques (1984) expresses the problem thus:

> The idea of error continues to crop up in social psychology's attempts to explain racial prejudice without addressing either the socio-historical production of racism or the psychic mechanism through which it is reproduced in white people's feelings and their relations to black people. (p. 78)

As before, it is the lack of any theory of subjectivity that impoverishes psychological approaches, making it impossible for them to produce a satisfactory account of the way racism, which is generated in the social sphere, becomes embedded in the psychology of the individual.

The reference to subjectivity is, once again, the cue for an investigation of some psychoanalytic approaches to the psychology of racists. In this instance, rather than review a generally fragmentary and inadequate literature, the approach will be to provide a reading of racism as a response to social forces, through the use of some particularly provocative texts that deal especially with the anxieties created by the experience of modernity. Much of the work to be described deals with anti-semitism, although some deals explicitly with anti-black racism. The argument is that, directly and indirectly, psychoanalysis presents a vision of racism as a series of violent and desperate defensive manoeuvres. This vision has some severe limits; for example, it does not adequately acknowledge the economic and political benefits of racism for dominant groups and it does not deal with the specificity of racism amongst and between different groups (e.g. the differences between middle-class and working-class racism, or between anti-semitism and anti-black racism). But when read alongside socio-political accounts that do describe the structural aspects of racism, these psychoanalytic views provide a model for theorisation of the interplay between the structure of society and the subjectivity of the individual racist. It is here more than in any other area covered in this book, that the political significance of such a theory comes to the fore.

**Modernity and fragmentation**

One of the major contributions of contemporary psychoanalysis to conceptualisations of the modern psyche lies in its vision of the ego as something fragile and uncertain, with its integrity constantly threatened by internal and external forces. Lacanians, for instance, portray the ego as a fortress against fragmentation, but one which is inherently unstable, built upon an imaginary identification with something outside itself. In the mirror phase, it is the apparent wholeness of the visual image that impresses the infant; Lacan (1949) describes what happens as a 'jubilant assumption of his specular image by the child' (p. 2), creating the notion and experience of 'I' as something unified. The child's 'jubilation' at perceiving the external image of wholeness derives from the freedom this wholeness promises from the chaotic state of non-integration and conflicting desire which is the actual experience of infancy. The mirror-image 'I' is the originator of the ego, creating a fiction of personal coherence to which the subject clings.

> [This] form situates the agency of the ego, before its social determination, in a fictional direction, which will always remain irreducible for the individual alone, or rather, which will only rejoin the coming-into-being of the subject asymptotically, whatever the success of the dialectical syntheses by which he must resolve as 'I' his discordance with his own reality. (Lacan, 1949, p. 2)

The condition of existence which this 'I' defends the subject against is the threatening condition of absorption in multiplicity and chaotic desire – what Lacan designates as the desire of the fragmented body, unintegrated and uncontrollable.

> This fragmented body . . . usually manifests itself in dreams when the movement of the analysis encounters a certain level of aggressive disintegration in the individual. (Lacan, 1949, p. 4)

Its form is of 'disjointed limbs', organs which grow wings and take up arms for 'intestinal persecutions', the figures of Hieronymous Bosch (pp. 4–5). It is against this that the ego strives: the ego is an imaginary representation of personal integrity when underneath is contradiction; it is formed in the mirror phase as an attempt to paper over the dissolution that unconscious desire produces.

This image of fragmentation, of a psyche which at best is tenuously integrated and at permanent risk of collapse into warring pieces, is the strongest image in the contemporary psychoanalytic heritage. For Lacan, as well as being present in the notion of the speciousness of the ego, it is also contained in the symbolism of the phallus. The phallus, which through the operations of the Oedipus complex represents the inauguration of the Symbolic order under which the individual becomes a cultural subject, also has an imaginary status, promising a realm of wholeness and oneness, with no differences and with infinite power of definition and designation. In its full form, this is a fascist order, a patriarchal structure that attempts to impose a single will on the multiple phenomena of the real world. Many non-Lacanians, too, have as their problematic the experience of multiplicity, contradiction and dissolution. Kleinians view infants as riven with hatred and love, envy and guilt; the first developmental experience is of split and dangerous desires, with pressures towards fragmentation persisting throughout life in the form of recurrent paranoid-schizoid processes. At best, people learn to tolerate the ambivalence of their feelings, recognising their complexity and inconsistency, seeing in them the conflicts which are dialectically reproduced in the social world. But this personal integrity is never guaranteed: Kleinians such as Bion (1961) have shown how in groups, in crowds and in dreams experiences of the loss of self, which parallel the experience of psychotic disintegration, reappear. The anti-Lacanian originators of 'schizoanalysis', Deleuze and Guattari (1977), also promote an image of the personality as constituted by desiring fragments: their notion of the unconscious as a machine is saved from being a fascistic image by their celebration of the multiple connections between body parts and part objects. Integration of these parts is, according to Deleuze and Guattari, fictitious; what exists is the productive desire of the unconscious, pumping away.

This is not the place to evaluate these various versions of the image of fragmentation. It should be noted, however, that they do not stand in isolation from images to be found elsewhere. Whether their theoretical framework is that of post-modernism (Jameson, 1984) or of modernity (Berman, 1982), the humanities are currently celebrating the multiplicity of things, their contradictions, realignments and flows. The representation of modernity presented in these images is of a world full of multiple events which at one and the same time present each individual with stunning possibilities and terrifying prospects. In Berman's words, 'To be modern is to find ourselves in an environment that promises us adventure, power, joy, growth, transformation of ourselves and the world – and, at the same time, that threatens to destroy everything we have, everything we know, everything we are' (Berman, 1982, p. 15). What is so unsettling about the contemporary arena of the arts is also what is so disturbing about the modern psyche: to borrow Berman's title, itself borrowed from Marx, 'All that is solid melts into air'.

What has this to do with racism? Balancing the two faces of the experience of modernity, are two types of response. Multiplicity, contradiction, flow, celebration of heterogeneity – this is only one side of the modern world. The other is rigidity, domination, totalitarianism, a rejection of the possibilities generated by the modern environment in favour of a tight control over events, crushing all spontaneity but making life apparently manageable. This side of things has a specific political manifestation as fascism, and a general psycho-political expression in racism. It is a much-criticised strategy of psychoanalysis to interpret extreme forms of politics as the result of psychological disturbance or emotional defence, but here there is some justification. What is present in the racist psyche, psychoanalysis suggests, is repudiation of multiplicity and heterogeneity, the most challenging aspect of modernity. Racist ideology serves as a fortress against the dangers of the world and racist actions as an army to go with it – to defend, frequently through assault, the integrity of the disintegrated self. When all apparently solid things melt away or spiral kaleido-scopically, when the seemingly absolute truths on which society rests become uncertain and relative, the weak ego searches for something rigid to bolster it, to explain the disintegration surrounding it, and to oppose that disintegration through absorption in a powerful totality. It is here that psychoanalysis intervenes, exploring the machinations of the racist defence as it attempts to repulse the threat posed by the heterogeneity of the surrounding environment, to remain stable through the employment of meagre but extreme resources. Psychoanalytic theorists of racism, whether explicitly or implicitly, have expressed this idea in a number of productive ways, some of which have been expressly political, others more tangentially so. In the remaining sections of this chapter, some examples of the psychoanalytic account of the racist imagination will be examined in the light of the psychoanalytic image of the fragmented psyche.

## The authoritarian personality

The classic text linking the psychoanalytic and social psychological traditions of research on racial prejudice is *The Authoritarian Personality* (Adorno *et al.*, 1950). This work, which comprises a theoretical account of 'fascist' personality attributes built around a series of investigations of attitudes amongst a large sample of Americans, has suffered from a systematic misreading in which it is reduced to a collection of questionnaire studies, with the easiest-to-use of these questionnaires (the 'F' scale) being widely employed in a range of general studies that take no account of its original context. The result of this history has been that the sophistication of the arguments in *The Authoritarian Personality* has been lost, and it has been made to appear simple-minded and crudely superficial.

There are, indeed, limitations to the approach adopted by Adorno *et al.* For instance, methodologically, one problem of which the authors were well aware was that the sample of individuals upon whom their study was based was a narrow one (though no more narrow than in most social psychological research): they note that 'the findings of the study may be expected to hold fairly well for non-Jewish, white, native-born, middle-class Americans' (p. 23). As Billig (1978) stresses, none of these subjects was actually fascist in terms of membership of political groups or parties, which may have limited the authors' ability to study different forms of racism in depth. This is part of a wider problem, that authoritarianism is treated as a character-trait with a variety of sources, but without consideration of the extent to which it actually is the structure that underpins all racist psychology. In other words, there is no consideration of the possible *specificity* of different forms of racism – a problem shared with most other psychoanalytic and psychological accounts.

On the theory side, there are difficulties with the use of a traditionally psychodynamic concept of 'personality' as a relatively stable organisation of needs that determine attitudes and actions – a concept also used in Fromm's (1942) study of authoritarianism and the power of the leader in fascism. More recent psychological research has persuasively demonstrated that the cognitive and situational influences on actions are more significant than was recognised in theories of this kind. However, as will be described below, Adorno *et al.* do appreciate the important disjunction between attitudes and behaviour, seeing the personality attributes of the individual as requiring the stimulus of certain social configurations before they become manifest in action.

One major limitation of *The Authoritarian Personality*, which it shares with the psychological research on 'prejudice' described above, resides in its adoption of the assumption that prejudice is best understood as an irrational phenomenon, its opposite being clear-thinking liberalism. It is this assumption that provides the frame for the book. In their introduction, Adorno *et al.* argue that an understanding of fascism and anti-semitism cannot be derived solely from 'objective' economic determinants, but additionally requires an appreciation of 'irrational' aspects of the personality – emotional needs which are often 'the most primitive and irrational wishes and fears' (p. 10). Using the model of psychological health provided by ego psychology, Adorno *et al.* propose that advances in mental stability occur as the ego gains control over these wishes and fears – that is, as rational appreciation of reality becomes dominant within the personality. Hence, their own project in *The Authoritarian Personality* is one which is both academic and political: revealing the patterns of irrationality which give fascism a hold also enables the ego to become more powerful. 'It is the ego that becomes aware of and takes responsibility for nonrational forces operating within the personality. This is the basis for our belief that the object of knowing what are the psychological determinants of ideology is that men can become more reasonable' (p. 11). In their conclusion, too, Adorno *et al.* spell out the links between fascism and irrationality.

It is safe to assume . . . that fascism is imposed on the people, that it actually goes against their basic interests, and that when they can be made fully aware of themselves and their situation they are capable of behaving realistically. That people too often cannot see the workings of society or their own role within it is due not only to a social control that does not tell the truth but to a 'blindness' that is rooted in their own psychology. (p. 480)

The implications of this statement, as drawn out by the authors, are actually very interesting, pointing to the possibility of using psychoanalytic expertise in the area of identifying and unravelling defences to overcome the resistance that people have to seeing things as they really are. But the model of ideology on which this argument is based is the familiar and unsatisfactory 'distorted perception' one, suggesting that once fascist ideology is seen through, a more correct, rational and liberal view of the world will automatically prevail.

In historical as well as psychological terms, such a view seems unduly optimistic. It is based on the assumption that there is a qualitative distinction between the mode of perception which results in an irrational, distorted ideology and that which enables a person to see clearly how reality is structured. This links with another statement of Adorno *et al.*, that the production of 'nonethnocentric personalities' requires only that 'children be genuinely loved and treated as individual humans' (p. 479), a state of affairs which they acknowledge would require a total change in society. The implication is that the state of rationality is the natural state of the individual, responsive to a non-intrusive and nurturing upbringing, whilst irrationality is a distortion brought about by the exploitative operations of the present social world.

This humanistic viewpoint is a traditionally liberal one; its shortcoming is its non-recognition of the socially constructive processes which operate in the structuring of every individual. Put simply, if every individual is part of a social totality, then it is never possible to perceive that totality in some absolute and 'undistorted' way. Instead, each of us takes up a position with respect to sociality which is generated by our experiences, many of which operate to lay down unconscious structures of feeling and desire. Any attitude to the world is 'irrational' in the sense that it is influenced by unconscious factors; this does not mean that some of these views are not more humane or more accurate than others, but it does prevent any simple identification of reason and reality.

This last point actually leads on to the great strength of *The Authoritarian Personality*. This is not so much in the documentation of the attitudes and personality characteristics of prejudiced and 'authoritarian' individuals which makes up a large part of the book and which has been the main element in social psychological readings. This documentation is, in many ways, very interesting, but it is vitiated by the authors' own mistrust of the relatively superficial results of questionnaire studies (Henriques, 1984). Rather, the strength of the book lies in the qualitative analysis of the forces underlying anti-semitism and ethnocentrism, an analysis for which Adorno himself seems to have been largely responsible. The general model here is a sophisticated one linking individual and social factors: whilst it is argued that it is personality that generates racist (specifically anti-semitic) attitudes, social conditions enter in in two ways. First, *The Authoritarian Personality* is concerned with individuals who have the potential to become authoritarian and fascist under certain conditions ('the forces of personality are not responses but *readiness for response*' (p. 5)); these conditions are socially given. Throughout the book, the authors emphasise that their concern is with the individual differences that make some people more prone than others to the lures of fascism and racism; the more general conditions making these ideologies powerful are seen as requiring explanation on a sociological rather than a social-psychological level. The second way in which sociality operates in *The Authoritarian Personality* is, however, of central psychological concern: this is the theory that it is through processes of social development that the irrational and proto-fascist elements of the personality are formed. The claim is that the individual's personality structure is socially constructed during development, becoming the template from which all later attitudes and perceptions – including authoritarian ones – emerge.

The interviews which Adorno *et al.* carried out with individuals who had scored highly on their tests of authoritarianism and prejudice revealed a systematic pattern of childhood relationships. These were characterised by:

> a tendency toward rigid discipline on the part of the parents, with affection that is conditional rather than unconditional . . . Related to this is a tendency apparent in families of prejudiced subjects to base interrelationships on rather clearly defined roles of dominance and submission, in contradistinction to

equalitarian policies. Faithful execution of prescribed roles and the exchange of duties and obligations is, in the families of the prejudiced, often given preference over the exchange of free-flowing affection. (p. 276)

This family pattern produces personalities which are extremely conformist and uncertain, unable to form genuinely reciprocal relationships based on true object-love. It is also the breeding ground for projection of angry and hateful emotions. The authoritarianism of the father and the absence of affection interferes with a full resolution of the Oedipus complex and a gradual acceptance of ambivalence. Instead, a sado-masochistic structure develops in which the individual finds comfort in submission to authority whilst projecting (displacing) much of her or his aggressiveness on to an outgroup. This scapegoated outgroup must have certain characteristics:

It must be tangible enough; and yet not too tangible, lest it be exploded by its own realism. It must have a sufficient historical backing and appear as an indisputable element of tradition. It must be defined in rigid and well-known stereotypes. Finally, the object must possess features, or at least be capable of being perceived and interpreted in terms of features, which harmonise with the destructive tendencies of the prejudiced subject. (p. 300)

Given this, the thwarted hostility of the repressed individual will be projected on to such a substitute object. This projection is a *necessary* process: without it, the individual's aggressiveness will undermine the personality and destroy rationality to such an extent that psychosis will ensue. The prejudiced person needs her or his hated object in order to survive.

The postulation by Adorno *et al.* of a relatively straightforward link between certain family configurations and authoritarian personality structures follows in a tradition which has its most famous manifestation in Reich's (1946) *Mass Psychology of Fascism*. Like Reich, Adorno *et al.* also assume that these family configurations are themselves produced by social factors; Reich is actually more precise in his description of what these might be (the patriarchal–authoritarian and sexually repressive structures of capitalism).

Where the projection model described in *The Authoritarian Person-ality* is more sophisticated than many, however, is in its recognition of the power of the threat that makes projection necessary. It is in order to protect the personality against psychotic dissolution that the extreme violence of the racist mentality operates. Adorno provides an account of the processes occurring here which remains unsurpassed in its linkage of the social order with the desperation of the individual personality. First, the social link: the potential fascist has no comprehension of social processes operating beyond her or his immediate experience; instead, the world appears as a buzzing and threatening confusion, offering no anchor points and no possibility of control.

> The objectification of social processes, their obedience to intrin-sic supra-individual laws, seems to result in an intellectual alienation of the individual from society. This alienation is experienced by the individual as disorientation, with concomitant fear and uncertainty . . . the [Jew's] alienness seems to provide the handiest formula for dealing with the alienation of society. (pp. 310–11)

Anti-semitic stereotypes are 'interpreted as means for pseudo-orientation in an estranged world, and at the same time as devices for "mastering" this world by being able completely to pigeonhole its negative aspects' (pp. 314–15). But this procedure requires that the pigeon-holing be absolute, that nothing creeps out that could destroy the precariously balanced ideology that makes the racist personality tenable. In this way,

> the extremely prejudiced person tends towards 'psychological totalitarianism'; something which seems to be almost a microcos-mic image of the totalitarian state at which he aims. Nothing can be left untouched, as it were; everything must be made 'equal' to the ego-ideal of a rigidly conceived and hypostatized ingroup. The outgroup, the chosen foe, represents an eternal challenge. As long as anything different survives, the fascist character feels threatened, no matter how weak the other being may be. (pp. 324–5)

Eventually, the desperation of the racist's retreat from personality fragmentation leads to a process of internal rationalisation in which the super-ego becomes filled with racist stereotypes to justify the attitudes and behaviours espoused by the rest of the psyche. This means that there are no longer any internal checks to destructiveness: while the personality does hold together, it is at the price of becoming a spiralling, out-of-control, mechanism of hate.

> Hatred is reproduced and enhanced in an almost automatised, compulsive manner which is both utterly detached from the reality of the object and completely alien to the ego . . . The extreme antisemite silences the remnants of his own conscience by the extremeness of his attitude. He seems to terrorise himself even while he terrorises others. (p. 325)

No wonder, then, that simple anti-racist measures such as educating people about cultural differences or introducing racists to individuals of the despised group, have such little effect. As Adorno *et al.* note,

> closer association with members of minority groups can hardly be expected to influence people who are largely characterised by the inability to have experience, and liking for particular groups or individuals is very difficult to establish in people whose structure is such that they cannot really like anybody. (p. 477)

*The Authoritarian Personality* remains one of the most substantial attempts to unravel the psychology of racism. Although its questionnaire findings now seem temporally and culturally overspecific, its general understanding of the interaction between social and individual variables is still a powerful one. Most of all, the description that Adorno *et al.* provide of the underlying psychodynamics of racist experience is a compelling one, linking with a more modern understanding of the impact of fragmentation fantasies and the terror of psychosis imbued in people by the modern world. What *The Authoritarian Personality* achieves in an unsurpassed way, is to convey the intimacy of the link between those social processes that make modernity such an unnerving experience, and the viciously defensive enclosure that is the racist response.

## Projection, identity and conspiracy

*The Authoritarian Personality* adopts as its main explanatory model the familiar psychoanalytic concept of projection: that racism is generated by the expulsion of disturbing or painful feelings from inside the individual on to a socially legitimised other – a scapegoat theory, in conventional parlance. Sherwood (1980), whose book *The Psychodynamics of Race* is a detailed study of three families living in a racially mixed area, presents a more recent example of this tradition in a progressive form, which also reveals some of the limitations of a too-simple employment of concepts of psychodynamic defence. The essence of her argument is contained in the following quotation:

> Throughout development, but especially under stress, we all at times use social groups as repositories for our projections, providing a way out for the individual from experiencing inner conflicts that we would otherwise consider too disturbing or painful to face . . . The groups chosen as repositories are felt to be 'safe' in the sense that they are unconsciously regarded as fitting receptacles to 'hold' the anxiety and contain it. Since racial groups outwardly differ in appearance, the choice of a racial group as a repository for unwanted and denied aspects of the self is particularly seductive, because it gives the added advantage of putting a wider visible social distance between the person acting to offload denied aspects of his identity and the racial group chosen as a receptacle. (p. 493)

The conflicts which provoke projections of this kind (called 'racial misuse' by the author) are, according to Sherwood, best grouped under the heading 'identity conflicts', derived for example from clashes between positive and negative identity elements, sexual conflicts, feelings of inadequacy, encroachments on personal space or pressures to change. The wider social setting contains forces which function as 'activators' or 'constraints' on the tendency for identity conflicts to become racialised, including family factors, the accessibility of racial groups as targets, ideology and the 'stress of change' as opposed to 'continuity'.

Sherwood suggests that the 'social magnetism' of racial groups as 'repositories' of unwanted feelings derives from their visibility,

238 *Psychoanalysis and Psychology*

their real cultural differences (falsely interpreted by the racist as aspects of race), and by the climate created by institutionalised racism 'due to historic, economic and political forces' (p. 494). In addition, there is a symbolic function to racial prejudice which apparently transcends specific cultures, and which has to do with associations of brown and black with 'death, dirt and danger', on the one hand, and white with 'purity, goodness, chastity, innocence and cleanliness', on the other (ibid.). It is perhaps this latter, symbolic process that makes racism such a widespread solution to the problem of identity maintenance. Indeed, for Sherwood, it is clearly the case that identity maintenance is a universal psychological problem which is commonly countered in this way.

> Racial prejudice occurs so universally and is so widespread in different societies that it clearly serves a psychological need . . . What it seems to do for the individual is to protect and preserve his identity and bolster a psychological equilibrium which is felt to be precarious. (p. 503)

On the face of it, Sherwood's argument is close to the idea that racism is an expression of the anxiety of a disintegrating personality, bolstered and channelled by the political strategies of the social world. Although the concept of 'identity conflict' is vague and lacking in the intensity which Adorno *et al.* show to be significant in generating racism, it hints at that demolition of ego identity which is at issue in modernity. Sherwood shows how such identity conflicts might be expressed racially. However, she obscures the potential of her own phenomenological approach by articulating conventional perceptions of the 'equality' of racism which are not simply apolitical, but ideological. For instance, the concept of 'racial misuse' is a drastic watering-down of that of racism: it trivialises the latter by removing its power components and, crucially, by accepting the language of 'race' which actually underpins racist thought. This is perhaps how Sherwood moves to the idea of reciprocal racial misuse between different racial communities, stratified only by the power of each respective group. There is no *history* here, no vision of the structural factors that produce racism as an opponent of modernity; instead, racism is reduced to a convenient channel for universal psychological problems. Finally, Sherwood does not elaborate her thesis to account for the level of threat which the racist experiences to the ego, and hence cannot convey the viciousness of the response that is provoked.

The example of Sherwood (1980) has been given to suggest the need for a more powerful explanatory mechanism than the simple idea that 'identity conflicts' require the use of a scapegoat, thus producing racist ideology. It is only through a deep analysis of the intensity of the threat experienced by the racist that the apparent 'irrationality' of racism can be explicated. This 'irrationality' is, as discussed earlier, not completely straightforward, for racism does serve certain rational purposes and also is a representation of an ideology and a political reality that has a material existence in the world. When the 'irrationality' of racism is faced head-on, it tends to slip away, to be replaced by terms such as intensity or violence. Thus, despite the formulations given by Adorno *et al.* (1950), it is not so much the irrationality of the racist that is in the forefront of their account, but the desperation that produces these destructive patterns of hate. Nevertheless, there is a certain kind of irrationality too, and the direction which this takes is equally revealing: it is the age-old ideological rationalisation of racism found in the conspiracy theory.

When the world is crumbling all around, when all that defines reality seems to swirl away, the search for explanations is not just a cognitive strategy, but a deep emotional need. It is here that conspiracy theories appear: always they have been present in anti-semitism; at particular historical junctures (the defeat of Germany in the First World War, the challenge to the British imperialist ethos by colonial independence and the influx of black immigrants in the 1950s) they are generalised to other communities. One of the many striking results described by Adorno *et al.* (1950) is of the centrality of the idea possessed by anti-semites that Jews are *threatening*. This threat is of two kinds. First, Jews present a moral threat to the anti-semite, appearing as 'violators of important standards and values' (p. 95), as immoral, sensuous and prying, and liable to contaminate the purity of the gentile. Adorno *et al.* perceive this sense of moral threat as so powerful that they propose that it must be generated by a projective mechanism: 'It is possible . . . that antisemites are struggling to inhibit in themselves the same tendencies that they find so unbearable in Jews. Jews may be a convenient object on which they can project their unconscious desires and fears' (p. 96).

As well as being a moral threat, anti-semites see Jews as a social threat, having immense power which links with their clannishness to present an organised challenge to the autonomy of the non-Jewish world. It is this element, the 'Jewish conspiracy', that has the most visible place in the history of anti-semitism. Billig's (1978) study of the National Front in Britain demonstrates how powerful a hold such conspiracy theories continue to have over fascists and racists. In the case of the National Front, it is still belief in a worldwide Zionist conspiracy that is the foundation for racist ideology, with black people often seen as pawns of the Zionists, used to encourage the 'mongrelisation' of the white race (p. 194).

But the general features of conspiracy theorising can be seen in many ordinary racists' attitudes, whichever group their hostility is directed towards. Billig mentions possible cognitive explanations of the power of conspiracy theories, for example that they provide causal schema which can be used to make sense of personal and national 'failure', particularly if the surrounding culture is one in which causal attributions tend to be personal rather than situational, and if there are readily available and victimisable outgroups. There is also room here for explanations in terms of projection, in particular if the cognitive 'simplicity' and intolerance of ambiguity claimed by Adorno *et al.* (1950) to be aspects of the authoritarian personality are indeed associated with racism. As described above, in the rendering of this theory given in *The Authoritarian Personality*, the threat posed by the child's authoritarian father makes it impossible for her or him to express or integrate hostile elements of the personality. These then threaten to plunge the individual into a state of psychotic disorganisation unless a scapegoat can be found; the splitting of an idealised ingroup versus a denigrated outgroup is one solution.

These explanations are helpful as far as they go, identifying mechanisms which are commonly at work in producing specific racist attitudes or acts. But, as Billig points out, they assume a consciously non-ambivalent attitude towards the despised group, one in which it is the negative features of that group which are highlighted. In fact, while racist propaganda stereotypes and derogates the objects of its hatred, racist thinking is often infused with admiration. It is the *power* of the hated group which is emphasised: the cleverness of the Jew, the physicality of the black. The conspirators are brilliant schemers, worthy enemies: to the fascist they are opponents who must be crushed because they are dangerous. Indeed, they are often fascinating: the obsession of anti-semites with Jews is extraordinarily out of line with the actual experience of most of these anti-semites; Jews represent for them the deepest principle of destruction and degeneration, and of a subversive, unnerving power. This mixture of hatred and admiration has often been noted in the psychoanalytic literature; for instance, Freud's (1939) account of anti-semitism in *Moses and Monotheism* mentions, amongst other things, the possibility that 'jealousy of the people which declared itself the first-born, favourite child of God the Father, has not yet been surmounted among other peoples even today' (p. 336). Kleinians, too, will recognise what is happening here. Faced with the violence of internal desires and external failure, with the threat of being torn apart by hostility and destroyed by the confusion of forces in the world, projections from the ego are swamped with envy – a spoiling hatred that is directed at one and the same time against the admired and the despised. It is, therefore, not just rejected aspects of the racist's identity which are projected outwards, but a bitter hatred that idealises that which it strives to crush.

Billig proposes that the force behind the projection cannot be that of denied impulses, but is rather an admiration for the super-ego qualities of the enemy. Discussing the racist's belief in the existence of the conspiracy, he argues that,

> Sexual fantasy cannot be claimed to be the dominant motivating force behind this particular belief. The image of the conspirators themselves often depicts an enemy who is dangerous because he is without the frailties of human passion. (p. 337)

However, it seems possible that this image of the emotionally hyper-controlled enemy may itself be a defensive one. The admiration of the racist for the conspirators is that they are secret, organised, impermeable, unfeeling and without passion. These are precisely the attributes desired by the threatened ego; they are all, of course, imaginary attributes and all part of the world that rejects modernity. If the racist's deep fear is of disorder – disorder within as well as without – then the admired enemy is the one who has overcome disorder and created an efficient and ruthless world. Racist violence under these circumstances can then be an outpouring of the racist's own disorder, directed against the boundary of the other rather than against the self. Projection and projective identification: these are indeed the mechanisms at work here. But what of the desire that underpins them? Although Billig may be right to reject a simple formula that explains racism as projection of unwanted sexual feelings, he has perhaps underestimated the power of sex to express the elements of boundary loss and ego-destruction which the racist so fears. To approach this idea, it is useful to look at a psychology of anti-black racism that regards biological and sexual images of the black person – or, rather, the black man – as the core components of racism's emotionality.

## Sex and the Other

One of the many problems inherent in reading the works of Franz Fanon is the uneasy imbalance between psychological and political explanations of colonialism and its effects (see McCulloch, 1983, for a discussion of the development of Fanon's thought). Certainly, there is a difference in level between the account of colonial psychology presented in *Black Skin, White Masks* (1952) and the more political and existential views of *The Wretched of the Earth* (1961), which calls into question many of the earlier work's perceptions. Nevertheless, it is in *Black Skin, White Masks* that Fanon deals most fully with the psychology of the racist, so it is this work which is relevant for the current discussion.

Much of *Black Skin, White Masks* is concerned with the impact of racism on the psychology of the oppressed. Fanon adopts a version of Adlerian psychology to explain the impact of racist ideology and practice on black people; his argument is that the colonial situation of racist oppression produces psychological disturbances and that these can be fully understood in social terms as a result of racism and imperialism. This account has been very influential in promoting positive evaluations of black identity and explorations of the response of oppressed groups to racist structures. However, Fanon's analysis of the psychology of racists is no less important, as it represents one of the few major attempts to theorise the subjectivity of racism without neglecting its social determination.

Fanon is in no doubt that what he calls 'Negrophobia' has sexual origins.

> For the majority of white men the Negro represents the sexual instinct (in its raw state). The Negro is the incarnation of a genital potency beyond all moralities and prohibitions. (p. 177)

In part, this is a matter of projection. Fanon uses the Freudian idea that civilisation is built at the expense of sexual urges:

> Every intellectual gain requires a loss in sexual potential. The civilised white man retains an irrational longing for unusual eras of sexual licence . . . Projecting his own desires onto the Negro, the white man behaves 'as if' the Negro really had them . . . The Negro symbolises the biological danger, the Jew the intellectual danger. (p. 165)

Negro and Jew are both phobic objects for white society and, like all phobic objects, are sources of attraction as well as repulsion. They represent the underside of society, the hidden aspect of human nature, containing all the projected impulses that, if released, hinder the progress of civilisation. The Negro is the scapegoat for social failings, but more than that he (for in Fanon it is always *he*) is a reminder of the instinctual basis of all energy, once again the 'dark side of the soul' (p. 190). This is where Jew and Negro differ: it is the abstract idea of the Jewish race that disturbs the anti-semite (the conspiring Jews who will rob white Christians of the world), but it is the physicality of the Negro that threatens. The white man projects his repressed sexuality on to the black, constructing him in fantasy as a sexual paragon and an object for his homosexual desire. The white's relationship to the black is then mediated by this sexuality; the existence of the black man is a constant threat to the potency of the white man, a stimulus to the desire of the white woman. Racist persecution of the black is, therefore, *sexual* revenge.

For Fanon, then, anti-black racism takes as its form a vicious sexual hatred which arises as the white man projects his sexual fantasies on to the body of the black. The black then comes to represent biology – to be the incarnation of sexual power. To explain the systematic way in which it is black people who become the repositories of these fantasies. Fanon makes use of the Jungian notion of the collective unconscious, albeit with a social rather than a biological underpinning. At the heart of European civilisation, he proposes, there is a shared fantasy of the black man which is founded around a deep, unconsciously structured image of baseness and vileness, associated with the sexual imagery described above. Fanon makes explicit reference to Jung here:

> European civilisation is characterised by the presence, at the heart of what Jung calls the collective unconscious, of an archetype: an expression of the bad instincts, of the darkness inherent in every ego, of the uncivilised savage, the Negro who slumbers in every white man. (p. 187)

Where Fanon differs from Jung is in his explanation of how this collective unconscious, this shared channel for projection, is formed and perpetuated. In Jung's theory, the mode of transmission is biological, a process inherent in the accumulated matter of the human cerebrum. The archetypes within the collective unconscious are found throughout a race, perhaps throughout the world; if blackness as evil is a real and shared phenomenon, it is generated biologically. Fanon, however, converts the notion of the collective unconscious into a theory of ideology by arguing that the archetypes he is dealing with are produced through historically specific cultural processes, notably those of colonialism and the linked sexual repressions of Europe. The perpetuation of racist archetypes then derives from a form of social reinforcement. As McCulloch (1983) shows, this argument leads Fanon into some difficult areas – for instance, he rejects a biological base for the archetype but asserts the universality of the sexual fantasies promoted by the repressions of civilisation. Nevertheless, what makes Fanon's theory possible as a socio-political explanation of racism is its awareness of the way social practices can be translated into ideological givens which can reproduce particular sets of feelings – complexes – that are vitally racist.

To this point, the focus has been upon Fanon's description of the sexual fetishising of the black man by the white, as it expresses the intensity of racist fear and the construction of the black as a phobic, biological other. It is this way of reading Fanon that has made his work amenable to Lacanians, who have their own method of describing the disintegration of the contemporary personality. Fanon provides an explicit starting point here in his references to the way the black is constructed as the 'other' for the white. At one level, Fanon describes simply the inability of the white racist to tolerate difference:

> The white man is convinced that the Negro is a beast; if it is not the length of the penis, then it is the sexual potency that impresses him. Face to face with this man who is 'different from himself', he needs to defend himself. In other words, to personify The Other. The Other will become the mainstay of his preoccupation and his desires. (p. 170)

This concept of The Other is linked both to psychoanalysis and to existentialism, representing the way history and oppression produce a divide between people, creating The Other as an alienated image of the self. However, as Bhabha (1986) discusses, Fanon's treatment of otherness is an ambivalent one, mixing a form of existential humanism (overcome the barriers between people through true recognition) with a more psychoanalytic awareness that it is in the context of otherness that subjectivity is formed – that The Other contains the divisions which desire produces within each psyche. Fanon expresses this side of the argument in a footnote on Lacan's mirror phase:

> When one has grasped the mechanism described by Lacan, one can have no further doubt that the real Other for the white man is and will continue to be the black man. And conversely. Only for the white man The Other is perceived on the level of the body image, absolutely as the not-self – that is, the unidentifiable, the unassimilable. For the black man, . . . historical and economic realities come into the picture. (pp. 161–4)

In other places, Fanon discusses the absorption of the racist image of otherness to the image of the Master, particularly in the consciousness of the oppressed black. But in this quotation, he is concerned to differentiate between black and white psychology, arguing that the black man represents to the white all his own otherness – the threat which arises from the mystery of his own body and its desires. As in Lacan's mirror phase, it is the visual image of The Other that makes it possible for it to become a container for the racist's internal otherness, for the fragmentation that is central to the experience of infancy and, indeed, to the experience of modernity itself. The immense terror which is at the centre of the racist's psychology derives, in this account, from the aggression to the precarious sense of ego-integrity that proceeds from an encounter with the black other: the *visibility* of difference undermines the abstract sense of homogeneity which so shakily supports the ego. Into this is poured the sexual distress of the white; supported by the economic and political pay-offs of oppression, racism becomes a fortress for the fragments of the self.

**Sexual terror and the masculine order**

One of the troubling doubts that a reading of Fanon produces is his neglect of femininity or – more strongly – his adoption of misogynistic positions. Fanon, too, has an aversion to fluidity and multiplicity; his assault on racism is through an ironic and bitter attack on the way specific sexual impulses are projected on to the black man from the white. Of the woman of colour he says, with more than a slight echo of Freud, 'I know nothing about her' (1952, p. 180). His language is fragmentary, poetic and strong – fluid, in its way – but it is a masculine language. Yet, it is worth considering again the nature of the threat to the ego that produces the benighted defences considered here. The threat is of disintegration in the face of a fragmentary world, one that offers no firm ground for the construction of a strong self, one in which the potential joy of multiplicity is obscured by the terror of disappearance in the heterogeneous. What is this threatening world if not that of the fantasised feminine principle, that image of the feminine which sees in it anti-phallicism, fluidity and heterogeneity? To a considerable extent, this is a male romanticisation of femininity, but it is also an image adopted by feminists seeking to destroy masculine 'mastery'. Cixous' (1975) image of womanhood, for example:

Heterogeneous, yes, to her joyful benefit, she is erogenous; she is what is erotogenous in the heterogenous; she is not attached to herself, the airborne swimmer, the thieving flier. Stunning, extravagant, one who is dispersible, desiring and capable of other, of the other woman she will be, of the other woman she is not, of him, of you. (p. 89)

This is the radical feminist other to the rigid phallocentrism of masculine ideology, but it is also the other to the controlling boot of fascism. The two, it seems, go together. Masculinity as an ideology, as a fantasy of how the world can and should be, like fascism and racism, idolises mastery, ordering reality into firmly held blocks, kept down, kept predictable, kept subordinate. In this way, 'both racism and sexism belong to the same discursive universe' (Brittan and Maynard, 1984). This is the phallic mastery which Lacan so clearly describes, the ideal of oneness, of clarity and of single, intended meanings. The opposite of metaphor, of the unconscious, in fact. Blackness, femininity and the unconscious go together in representing the subversion of mastery; for the Nazis, it will be remembered, psychoanalysis itself held a radical, Jewish threat. When psychoanalysts explicitly examine blackness, it is subversion of the established order that they uncover.

Darkness, *night-time knowledge* as revealed in myths and dreams, passions and desires, madness, mass phenomena and war, has been relegated to another realm, which is regarded as unworthy. It is precisely *this realm, which Aryan European ideology has localised in blackness and the unconscious.* (Da Conceicao Dias and De Lyra Chebabi, 1987, p. 198)

It is terror of this 'night-time knowledge' that is revealed most clearly in Theweleit's (1977) analysis of the writings of the men of the fascist Freikorps of Weimar Germany. First, he identifies the deadness of the language of these men and their fetishising of the Fatherland and of the all-male soldier world – and of violence. Then there is their rejection of womanhood in all its sexual forms, shown not only in the conventional splitting of women into good and bad, mothers and whores, but also in a desperate and vicious fantasy of total annihilation of the 'red woman'. This woman is partly phallic, armed and violent. But she is also part of the 'red flood' (compare the image of 'floods' of immigrants), the tumult that breaks down the dams which protect both the nation and the self. As with all things modern, the flood produces ambivalent feelings: excitement at the sweeping away of things which are frozen and dead, but terror at the dissolution of identity that this brings in its wake. In the end, it is all of unbridled life that poses the threat to fascism.

> The monumentalism of fascism would seem to be a safety mechanism against the bewildering multiplicity of the living. The more lifeless, regimented and monumental reality appears to be, the more secure the men feel. The danger is being-alive itself. (Theweleit, 1977, p. 218)

Later, dealing with the energy displayed in the mass rallies of fascism and Nazism. Theweleit comments,

> Men themselves were now split into a (female) interior and a (male) exterior – the body-armour . . . What we see being portrayed in the rituals are the armour's separation from, and superiority over, the interior: the interior was allowed to flow, but only within the masculine boundaries of the mass formations. (p. 434)

As with the external forms of mass fascism, so with the internal forms of racism. The hater of flow and multiplicity also hates women, hates the whole image of the feminine other, hates the dangers and unpredictability of contemporary life. In the modern world, this type of masculine order is part of the hatred of all that modernity brings – of its terrors and disconnections, of its promise and its fertile creativity. Racism is not just anti-semitic or anti-black; it is anti-world, anti-desire, anti-modernity itself.

## Conclusion

This chapter has explored the contributions of social psychology and psychoanalysis to the project of understanding the psychology of racism. Such an enterprise is not meant to replace historical, sociological, economic and political analyses; on the contrary, it is only in conjunction with these other approaches that the psychology of racism can have any meaning. Racism is a real phenomenon in the social world, serving particular purposes and acting in the interests of some groups over others. It is also a variable phenomenon in the sense that it has historical specificity, taking different forms at different times and in different contexts. None of the theories discussed here takes full account of this specificity. However, some major contributions have been made. Social psychologists have documented the operations of prejudice and the manner in which group phenomena can influence the manifest form that racist beliefs and practices take. What social psychologists have not been able to do, however, is provide a picture of the subjectivity of the racist, and of how this relates to the social structures of the outside world.

Psychoanalysts, on the relatively rare occasions when they have addressed the issue of racism, have described mechanisms through which racist psychology expresses its emotional charge. They have also developed a portrait of the racist psyche that links it with an intense and violent fear of the structures of the modern environment, and hence positions it socially rather than marginalising it as irrationality. This social positioning is a complex matter, raising complicated questions concerning the modes of action necessary to bring about changes that will reduce the presence of racism amongst individuals and in society. But, however indirectly it has come about, those radical theorists who employ psychoanalytic means to explore racism have opened out the possibility of a full understanding of racist psychology, one which can account both for its subjective intractability and its social force.

# Conclusion: The Different Subject

This book has been concerned with the psychological 'subject' in a number of ways: as the 'subjects' (in the sense of disciplines) of psychology and psychoanalysis, as the objective focus of investigation of these disciplines (that which is subjected to their enquiry), as the experiental core ('subjectivity') of each individual, and as the forces to which this core is 'subjected'. All these issues have been compressed into a discussion of the question of the most appropriate formulation of the task of psychology – whether it should focus on empirical phenomena which can be modelled cognitively and experimentally, or whether the subject of psychological investigations should include the more intangible and yet experientially central phenomenon of subjectivity. Conventionally, academic psychology has explored mental processes, mapping their relationships and the transformations that they impose on behavioural and cognitive 'information'. Psychoanalysis, in contrast, focuses on the conscious and unconscious subjective structure of each individual – the patterns of intention and desire which provide putative explanations of the direction which mental processes may take. Psychology takes as the object of its discourse the already-constructed individual 'subject' and asks, 'How do her or his psychological parts work?' Psychoanalysis looks at the fragmented neonate and questions, 'How does this one become a "subject" at all?'

The organising metaphor in this book is a linguistic one: put simply, the argument is that academic psychology articulates a syntactic account of human functioning, whereas psychoanalysis attempts to provide a semantic one. This means that psychology presents descriptions of the 'grammar' of mental life, the processes whereby, for example, a child learns to code experience linguistically, or to act in accordance with gendered instructions. Psychoanalysis, on the other hand, searches for the content and personal significance of the 'information' itself, the meaning which both generates and is generated by the 'syntactic' transformations. It is clear that these are both respectable endeavours: as with language, semantics can only be expressed if it can find an appropriate syntactic form; conversely, syntax is useless if it contains a meaningless message. This need not imply, however, that the relations between the two disciplines, psychoanalysis and psychology, are simply additive, that incorporating a psychoanalytic understanding of desire into psychological accounts of mental processes will in any straightforward way provide a 'complete' view of human psychology. It could be, for instance, that psychology provides the wrong kind of syntax for psychoanalysis, or that psychoanalysis produces incoherent contents of which psychology can make no use.

In the discussions of the previous chapters, there have been regular criticisms of psychoanalytic theories and approaches. Some of these have been conceptual, for instance with regard to the Lacanian view of language or the lack of an overt social perspective in the theories of racism. In particular, the failure of psychoanalysts to recognise adequately the importance of cognitive processes has limited their insights into many aspects of ordinary psychological functioning. In addition, the psychoanalytic enterprise is plagued by severe methodological problems, due mostly to the special conditions under which analytic 'data' are collected, and to the lack of direct access to the hypothesised internal states which are the central objects of psychoanalytic theory.

However, what this book strives to demonstrate is the potential ability of psychoanalysis to offer a critique of academic psychology, particularly in those areas where individual subjectivity and social relations intersect to produce the social 'subject'. Psychology has generated a variety of descriptions of mental processes, some of them extremely elegant (for instance, in artificial intelligence and Piagetian work), some of them confused and weak (as in the more 'social' areas of gender differences and 'prejudice'). What even the most elegant psychology of this form cannot do, however, is to develop an understanding of the resonances of subjective experience. It might be, and often has been, argued that a scientific psychology should properly stand apart from attempting this,

because 'explanations' of subjectivity have no possibility of achievement except as speculations linked to a mythology of consciousness.
Notwithstanding its methodological deficiencies, psychoanalysis
demonstrates that this view is too narrow, that without addressing
the questions of subject-formation posed automatically by
psychoanalysis, psychology is relegated to speechlessness on central
aspects of human functioning. Indeed, as the previous chapters
have been concerned to demonstrate, the provision of a psychoanalytic discourse on subjectivity automatically acts as a critique
of psychology, because it shows the shallowness of many of the
questions addressed by psychology and the consequent inadequacy
of its theoretical stance.

Of the many issues that arise from psychoanalysis' critique of
academic psychology, only a few general ones will be drawn out
here. The first concerns its implications for the conceptualisation
of individuality. Psychology's concentration on the provision of
syntactic descriptions of mental processes produces a theoretical
perspective which is not at the level of the individual human
subject, but is at the more peripheral level of the already-formed
subject's actions. Thus, it tacitly assumes the existence of that
subject, taking for granted the internal registering of experience
as components of subjectivity. The important questions become
those of how this experience is registered, represented and communicated to others – of perception, cognition and speech.

The image of individuality drawn upon and reproduced here is
thus of a central state of 'self' which is always existent (even if it
may become more cognitively elaborate over time), and which has
a faculty of experience which does not have to be created, but
which is part of the individual's inherited structure. By saying
nothing about how the subject comes to be constructed, psychology
produces an image of pre-existent, essential subjecthood which
can be taken for granted as the origin of personal meanings and
the recipient of social messages. This will always result in a view
of the individual as self-contained; social forces may impact upon
her or him, but from the outside, causing distress or joy, promoting
or inhibiting development, but never touching the central core of
self that defines each person's inherent individuality.

Psychology fails to question at the level of the subject; this
failure has its consequences for its account of social relations. For
instance, psychology's concern with cognitive processes when

describing the principles of mental functioning becomes, in its 'applied' form, a vision of gender differences as alternative cognitive strategies. Racism, too, is theorised as a set of beliefs, cognitive distortions which are produced by certain personal needs and socialisation pressures, but which represent an irrationality of processing rather than a central element in subjecthood. Perhaps most revealingly, language is theorised as a structure for the naming of experience; experience, being pre-existent, is not mediated by social patterns, but arises directly from a faculty inherent in the individual.

It is certainly not the case that all psychoanalytic theories effectively oppose this form of essentialism. But there is an important subversive element in the general psychoanalytic project which always raises the question of the nature of the subject – of what it is that constructs subjecthood. This subversiveness lies in psychoanalysis' constant interrogation of the basis of experience, its refusal to take consciousness and self-reflection at face value and its insistence that behind the apparent intention reflected in action lies a deeper wish and a more complex meaning. Even those approaches that do theorise a pre-existent subject (for example, object relations theory), have to do so explicitly: their acceptance of the task of mapping the structure of consciousness and the unconscious, presents the issue of the origins of subjecthood as an immediate concern. The psychoanalytic exploration of meanings automatically problematises the notion of an essential self by unravelling the components of subjectivity; it thus operates at a 'deeper' level than psychology, questioning the foundations of that individuality which, in the latter discipline, is taken for granted.

The conceptual significance of this psychoanalytic stance is immense. Not only does it place personal experience at the centre of its investigative concerns, but it also adopts a critical stance that announces the need for analysis and explanation of experience itself. Unlike phenomenology, which accepts the account that each self gives of itself, psychoanalysis forces the observer (whether self or other) away from simple acceptance and towards critical dissolution. There is no fixed entity, the individual, only a subject which becomes fixed through the activities of sociality and of desire – a subject which is open to construction, which is no more the starting point of all meanings than it is the end point of all social action. Whether one accepts or rejects the details of the various psychoanalytic theories, psychoanalysis makes it impossible to leave unquestioned any ascription of inviolable individuality.

It is in part this alternative vision of the subject that differentiates the psychoanalytic understanding of personal change from the psychological one. First, it should be noted that it is not an empirical question that is at issue here, in the sense of determining the degree to which a particular 'treatment' is effective in reducing distress. Such a practical question, concerning the conditions under which particular forms of therapy should be made available, is important (albeit difficult to answer) and has been a traditional focus for debate between psychologists and psychoanalysts (e.g. Sloane *et al.*, 1975). However, the point raised by the discussion of the formation of the subject concerns the image of personal potential which is promoted by the different approaches. Through its neglect of subjectivity, psychology fails to theorise change as more than the adoption of different strategies for coping with experience by a central, unchanging self.

The limited nature of this vision of change can be seen in the conventional therapeutic methods adopted by psychologists. Behaviour therapy, for instance, teaches patients new skills for dealing with disturbing situations, whether skills of relaxation when anxious, of social interaction, or of bolstering one's confidence when facing adversity. Cognitive therapy (e.g. Beck *et al.*, 1979) likewise asks the individual to rationally restructure her or his thoughts so that they are more appropriate and helpful, interfering less with transactions with the environment. Both these approaches, and other, similar ones, are of value in many circumstances in which a person requests help from another in the managing of her or his psychological affairs. But as a *theory of change*, as a vision of personal possibility, they offer little; they make, indeed, no real attempt at subjective change, only at the provision of a little more confidence, a little less fear. Hence the use by researchers and clinicians of behavioural outcome measures of problem resolution: it is the attainment of more effective encounters with reality that is sought, rather than the more intangible goals of personality development. The utopian vision of behaviourism and its cognitive derivatives centre on efficiency and rationality, just as the overall vision of psychology is of a smoothly functioning and well-managed machine. Perhaps inherent in this is one source of psychology's tendency to political conformism: the foundations of conventional images of the self are taken as given, while psychological research concentrates on identification of the routes of expression of this self, rather than on questioning its reality.

The psychoanalytic vision of change is different. Although there is a strong therapeutic tradition of ego support, which has its origins in Freud's work and in that of his daughter (A. Freud, 1936), the psychoanalytic enterprise as a whole, and especially in some of its manifestations (e.g. Kleinian therapy), holds out hope for changes in the structure of subjectivity as well as in the manoeuvrings of ego functions. This is because psychoanalysis operates *at the level of the subject*, rather than with the subject's strategies for coping. Psychoanalysis explores the structures that give experience its form; these structures are not pre-given, but are themselves constructed through the trajectories taken during development. In the psychoanalytic encounter, through the medium of the transference and the long process of uncovering unconscious material, the relationships, experiences and desires which constitute the atoms of the personality are, ideally at least, expressed, renegotiated, and reintegrated in a transformed way. Nothing can be taken for granted, because it is the basic building-blocks of the self that are being examined. Change, in principle, can mean the production of a completely new reading of reality, a reading which is deeply felt, encroaching on the analysand as an alteration of the entire structure of subjectivity. Although some approaches presume that the drives impose a biological limit to the possibilities of transformation, the 'analytic attitude' of psychoanalysis is always in large part open-ended, as everything is called in question, every presumed solution and cherished certainty is analysed for its underlying cause.

Again, the challenge to psychology inherent in this stance does not concern the matter of what can be achieved most easily and productively as part of a psychiatric service – this is an important issue, but a different one. The issue here is of the image of human nature, of what is pre-given and what is open to interrogation and analysis. What is suggested by psychoanalysis is that, as every element of the subject is constructed through history, it is possible to go further than psychology might suggest, and envisage a subject which is not just altered in its method of action, but is transformed in its very core.

What of the transformation of psychology itself? The juxtaposition of psychoanalysis and psychology throughout this book has been based on the premise that, while psychoanalysis has much to learn methodologically and empirically from psychology, it also presents a challenge which, if taken seriously, requires a reconsideration of the premises of psychology rather than a simple addition of some extra concepts. Perhaps through fear of the 'unscientific' consequences of moving too far away from what is observable or easily modelled, psychologists have neglected the problematic issues at the centre of the *human* science of psychology, the status of subjectivity and, alongside it, the meaning and origin of the human 'subject'. This has impoverished the discipline in numerous ways: it has restricted the range of its concepts, it has created false emphases and experimental trivialities, it has become affiliated with an ideological image of the individual which systematically underplays the power of social forces. Most of all, academic psychology has abrogated its responsibility to explore the development and significance of meanings – of the intentions, wishes, fears and desires which should be a central object of enquiry for any psychological science. It is not so much that psychoanalysis fills this gap, although there are many elements in psychoanalytic theories which do offer useful guidance. It is, rather, that psychoanalysis demonstrates the range of questions which need to be asked, and the possible forms of the theories which may be produced to encompass them. In so doing, it presents this challenge to psychology: what is it that makes psychology lower its sights, renounce its intellectual aspirations, descend to the journeyman level of tabulator of small gains and losses, part functions and miniature processes? What fear is it, that prevents psychologists taking stock of the questions raised by their own personal lives, and asking: what has our science to say to this?

# References

Adorno, T., Frenkel-Brunswik, E., Levinson, D., and Sanford, R. (1950) *The Authoritarian Personality* (New York: Norton, 1982).

Allport, G. (1954) *The Nature of Prejudice* (Reading, Mass.: Addison-Wesley, 1979).

Althusser, L. (1965) *For Marx* (London: Verso, 1979).

Archard, D. (1984) *Consciousness and the Unconscious* (London: Hutchinson).

Archer, J. and Lloyd, B. (1985) *Sex and Gender* (London: Cambridge University Press).

Aries, E. (1987) 'Gender and Communication', in P. Shaver and C. Hendrick (eds) *Sex and Gender* (London: Sage Review of Personality and Social Psychology, vol. 7).

Banton, R., Clifford, P., Frosh, S., Lousada, J. and Rosenthall, J. (1985) *The Politics of Mental Health* (London: Macmillan).

Bar, V. (1987) 'Change in Women', in S. Ernst and M. Maguire (eds) *Living with the Sphinx* (London: Women's Press).

Beck, A., Rush, A., Shaw, B. and Emery, G. (1979) *Cognitive Therapy of Depression* (London: Wiley).

Bem, S. (1974) 'The Measurement of Psychological Androgyny', in *Journal of Consulting and Clinical Psychology*, 42, pp. 155–62.

Bem, S. (1981) 'Gender Schema Theory: A Cognitive Account of Sex Typing', in *Psychological Review*, 88, pp. 354–64.

Bem, S. (1985) 'Androgyny and Gender Schema Theory: A Conceptual and Empirical Integration', in *Nebraska Symposium on Motivation, 1984*, pp. 179–226.

Bem, S. (1987) 'Gender Schema Theory and the Romantic Tradition', in P. Shaver and C. Hendrick (eds) *Sex and Gender* (London: Sage Review of Personality and Social Psychology, vol. 7).

Benedict, R. (1936) *Patterns of Culture* (London: Routledge and Kegan Paul).

Benvenuto, B. and Kennedy, R. (1986) *Introduction to the Work of Jacques Lacan* (London: Free Association Books).

Berman, M. (1982) *All that is Solid Melts into Air* (London: Verso).

Bhaba, H. (1986) 'Remembering Fanon', Foreword to F. Fanon, *Black Skin, White Masks* (London: Pluto).

Billig, M. (1978) *Fascists: A Social Psychological View of the National Front* (London: Harcourt Brace Jovanovich).

Bion, W. (1961) *Experiences in Groups* (London: Hogarth).

Bion, W. (1963) *Elements of Psychoanalysis* (London: Karnac, 1984).

258     *References*

Block, J. (1981) 'Gender Differences in the Nature of Orientations Developed about the World', in E. Shapiro and E. Weber (eds) *Cognitive and Affective Growth: Developmental Interactions* (Hillsdale, N.J.: Lawrence Erlbaum).

Boden, M. (1979) *Piaget* (London: Fontana).

Boden, M. (1987) *Artificial Intelligence and Natural Man* (London: MIT Press).

Bowlby, J. (1969) *Attachment* (Harmondsworth: Penguin).

Brittan, A. and Maynard, M. (1984) *Sexism, Racism and Oppression* (Oxford: Basil Blackwell).

Brown, G. and Harris, T. (1978) *Social Origins of Depression* (London: Tavistock).

Brown, N. (1959) *Life against Death; The Psychoanalytical Meaning of History* (Middletown: Wesleyan University Press).

Bruner, J. (1983) *Child's Talk* (Oxford: Oxford University Press).

Bruner, J. and Haste, H. (1987) 'Introduction', in J. Bruner and H. Haste (eds) *Making Sense: The Child's Construction of the World* (London: Methuen).

Bryant, P. (1982) *Piaget: Issues and Experiments* (Leicester: British Psychological Society).

Butterworth, G. (1984) 'The Relation between Language and Thought in Young Children', in J. Nicholson and H. Beloff (eds) *Psychology Survey 5* (Leicester: British Psychological Society).

Chamberlain, D. (1987) 'The Cognitive Newborn: A Scientific Update', in *British Journal of Psychotherapy*, 4, pp. 30–71.

Chodorow, N. (1978) *The Reproduction of Mothering* (Berkeley: University of California Press).

Chomsky, N. (1959) Review of *Verbal Behaviour* by B. F. Skinner in *Language 35*, pp. 26–58.

Chomsky, N. (1965) *Aspects of the Theory of Syntax* (Cambridge, Mass.: MIT Press).

Chomsky, N. (1980) *Rules and Representations* (Oxford: Basil Blackwell).

Cioffi, F. (1970) 'Freud and the Idea of a Pseudo-Science', in R. Borger and F. Cioffi (eds) *Explanation in the Behavioural Sciences* (Cambridge: Cambridge University Press).

Cixous, H. (1975) 'Sorties', in H. Cixous and C. Clement, *The Newly Born Woman* (Manchester: Manchester University Press, 1986).

Cixous, H. (1976) 'The Laugh of the Medusa', in E. Marks and I. de Courtivon (eds) *New French Feminisms* (Sussex: Harvester Press).

Clifford, P. and Frosh, S. (1982) 'Towards a Non-Essentialist Psychology: A Linguistic Framework', in *Bulletin of the British Psychological Society*, 35, pp. 267–70.

Clinical Commentary VI (1986) 'Infant Observation', in *British Journal of Psychotherapy*, 3, pp. 72–87.

Coltheart, M. (1985) 'Cognitive Neuropsychology and the Study of Reading', in M. Posner and O. Marin (eds) *Attention and Performance XI* (Hillsdale, N.J.: Lawrence Erlbaum).

Cromer, R. (1974) 'The Development of Language and Cognition: The

Cognitive Hypothesis', in B. Foss (ed.) *New Perspectives in Child Development* (Harmondsworth: Penguin).

Cromer, R. (1979) 'The Strengths of the Weak Form of the Cognitive Hypothesis for Language Acquisition', in V. Lee (ed.) *Language Development* (London: Croom Helm).

Da Conceicao Dias, C. and De Lyra Chebabi, W. (1987) 'Psychoanalysis and the Role of Black Life and Culture in Brazil', in *International Review of Psychoanalysis*, 14, pp. 185–202.

Dalal, F. (1988) 'Jung: A Racist', in *British Journal of Psychotherapy*, 4, pp. 263–79.

Deaux, K. (1984) 'From Individual Differences to Social Categories', in *American Psychologist*, 39, pp. 105–16.

DeCasper, A. and Fifer, W. (1980) 'Of Human Bonding: Newborns Prefer their Mothers' Voices', in *Science*, 208, pp. 1174–6.

Deleuze, G. and Guattari, F. (1977) *Anti-Oedipus* (New York: Viking).

Dennett, D. (1979) 'Artificial Intelligence as Philosophy and as Psychology', in M. Ringle (ed.) *Philosophical Perspectives in Artificial Intelligence* (Sussex: Harvester Press).

Dennett, D. (1980) 'The Milk of Human Intentionality', in *The Behavioral and Brain Sciences*, 3, pp. 428–30.

Dinnerstein, D. (1977) *The Mermaid and the Minotaur* (New York: Harper and Row).

Dunn, J. (1986) 'Growing Up in the Family World: Issues in the Study of Social Development in Young Children', in M. Richards and P. Light (eds) *Children of Social Worlds* (Cambridge: Polity Press).

Ehrhardt, A. (1985) 'Gender Differences: A Biosocial Perspective', in *Nebraska Symposium on Motivation, 1984*, pp. 37–57.

Ehrlich, H. (1973) *The Social Psychology of Prejudice* (New York: Wiley).

Eichenbaum, L. and Orbach, S. (1982) *Outside In, Inside Out* (Harmondsworth: Penguin).

Eichenbaum, L. and Orbach, S. (1985) *Understanding Women* (Harmondsworth: Penguin).

Elkind, D. (1964) 'Editors Introduction', in J. Piaget, *Six Psychological Studies* (London: Harvester Press, 1980).

Erdelyi, M. (1985) *Psychoanalysis: Freud's Cognitive Psychology* (New York: Freeman).

Ernst, S. (1987) 'Can a Daughter be a Woman? Women's Identity and Psychological Separation', in S. Ernst and M. Maguire (eds) *Living with the Sphinx* (London: Women's Press).

Eysenck, H. (1985) *Decline and Fall of the Freudian Empire* (Harmondsworth: Viking).

Fanon, F. (1952) *Black Skin, White Masks* (London: Pluto, 1986).

Fanon, F. (1961) *The Wretched of the Earth* (Harmondsworth: Penguin, 1967).

Fantz, R. (1967) 'Visual Perception and Expression in Early Infancy', in H. Stevenson, E. Hess and H. Rheingold (eds) *Early Behaviour: Comparative and Developmental Approaches* (New York: Wiley).

Farr, R. (1987) 'The Science of Mental Life: A Social Psychological

Perspective', in *Bulletin of the British Psychological Society*, 40, pp. 2–18.

Farrell, B. (1981) *The Standing of Psychoanalysis* (Oxford: Oxford University Press).

Figes, E. (1970) *Patriarchal Attitudes* (London: Faber).

Fodor, J. (1980) 'Searle on What Only Brains Can Do', in *The Behavioral and Brain Sciences*, 3, pp. 431–2.

Forrester, J. (1980) *Language and the Origins of Psychoanalysis* (London: Macmillan).

Forrester, J. (1987) 'The Seminars of Jacques Lacan: In Place of an Introduction. Book 1: Freud's Papers on Technique, 1953–1954', *Free Associations*, pp. 10, 63–93.

Freud, A. (1936) *The Ego and the Mechanisms of Defence* (London: Hogarth Press, 1948).

Freud, A. (1966) *Normality and Pathology in Childhood* (Harmondsworth: Penguin, 1973).

Freud, S. (1905) *Three Essays on the Theory of Sexuality* (Harmondsworth: Penguin, 1977, Pelican Freud Library, vol. 7).

Freud, S. (1908) *On the Sexual Theories of Children* (Harmondsworth: Penguin, 1977, Pelican Freud Library, vol. 7).

Freud, S. (1915) *Papers on Metapsychology* (Harmondsworth: Penguin, 1984, Pelican Freud Library, vol. 11).

Freud, S. (1917) *Introductory Lectures on Psychoanalysis* (Harmondsworth: Penguin, 1974, Pelican Freud Library, vol. 1).

Freud, S. (1920) *Beyond the Pleasure Principle* (Harmondsworth: Penguin, 1984, Pelican Freud Library, vol. 11).

Freud, S. (1923) *The Ego and the Id* (Harmondsworth: Penguin, 1984, Pelican Freud Library, vol. 11).

Freud, S. (1925) *Some Psychical Consequences of the Anatomical Distinction between the Sexes* (Harmondsworth: Penguin, 1977, Pelican Freud Library, vol. 7).

Freud, S. (1926) *Inhibitions, Symptoms, Anxiety* (Harmondsworth: Penguin, 1979, Pelican Freud Library, vol. 10).

Freud, S. (1930) *Civilisation and its Discontents* (Harmondsworth: Penguin, 1985, Pelican Freud Library, vol. 12).

Freud, S. (1933) *New Introductory Lectures on Psychoanalysis* (Harmondsworth: Penguin, 1973, Pelican Freud Library, vol. 2).

Freud, S. (1939) 'Moses and Monotheism', in S. Freud, *The Origins of Religion* (Harmondsworth: Penguin, 1985, Pelican Freud Library, vol. 13).

Fromm, E. (1942) *The Fear of Freedom* (London: Routledge and Kegan Paul).

Frosh, S. (1987) *The Politics of Psychoanalysis* (London: Macmillan).

Gallop, J. (1982) *Feminism and Psychoanalysis* (London: Macmillan).

Gallop, J. (1985) *Reading Lacan* (Ithaca: Cornell University Press).

Gergen, K. (1985) 'The Social Constructionist Movement in Modern Psychology', in *American Psychologist*, 40, pp. 266–75.

Gleitman, L. and Wanner, E. (1982) 'Language Acquisition: The State of the State of the Art', in E. Wanner and L. Gleitman (eds) *Language*

*Acquisition: The State of the Art* (Cambridge: Cambridge University Press).

Golinkoff, R. and Gordon, L. (1983) 'In the Beginning was the Word: A History of the Study of Language Acquisition', in R. Golinkoff (ed.) *The Transition from Prelinguistic to Linguistic Communication* (Hillsdale, N.J.: Lawrence Erlbaum).

Golombock, S., Spencer, A. and Rutter, M. (1984) 'Children in Lesbian and Single Parent Households: Psychosexual and Psychiatric Appraisal', in *Journal of Child Psychology and Psychiatry*, 24, pp. 551–72.

Goodwin, R. (1980) 'Two Decades of Research into Early Language Acquisition', in J. Sants (ed.) *Developmental Psychology and Society* (London: Macmillan).

Goren, C., Sarty, M. and Wu, P. (1975) 'Visual Following and Pattern Discrimination of Face-Like Stimuli by New-Born Infants', in *Pediatrics*, 56, pp. 544–9.

Greenberg, J. and Mitchell, S. (1983) *Object Relations in Psychoanalytic Theory* (Cambridge, Mass.: Harvard University Press).

Guntrip, H. (1973) *Psychoanalytic Theory, Therapy and the Self* (New York: Basic Books).

Halliday, M. (1979) 'One Child's Protolanguage', in M. Bullowa (ed.) *Before Speech* (Cambridge: Cambridge University Press).

Hamilton, V. (1984) *Narcissus and Oedipus: The Children of Psychoanalysis* (London: Routledge and Kegan Paul).

Hamlyn, D. (1971) 'Unconscious Intentions', in D. Hamlyn, *Perception, Learning and the Self* (London: Routledge and Kegan Paul, 1983).

Hamlyn, D. (1978) *Experience and the Growth of Understanding* (London: Routledge and Kegan Paul).

Hampson, S. (1986) 'Sex Roles and Personality', in D. Hargreaves and A. Colley (eds) *The Psychology of Sex Roles* (London: Harper and Row).

Hargreaves, D. (1986) 'Psychological Theories of Sex Role Stereotyping', in D. Hargreaves and A. Colley (eds) *The Psychology of Sex Roles* (London: Harper and Row).

Harré, R. (1979) *Social Being* (Oxford: Basil Blackwell).

Harris, M. and Coltheart, M. (1986) *Language Processing in Children and Adults* (London: Routledge and Kegan Paul).

Harris, P. (1982) 'Cognitive Prerequisites to Language?', in *British Journal of Psychology*, 73, pp. 187–95.

Hartmann, H. (1959) *Ego Psychology and the Problem of Adaptation* (London: Hogarth Press).

Henriques, J. (1984) 'Social Psychology and the Politics of Racism', in J. Henriques, W. Hollway, C. Urwin, C. Venn and V. Walkerdine, *Changing the Subject* (London: Methuen).

Henriques, J., Hollway, W., Urwin, C., Venn, C. and Walkerdine, V. (1984) *Changing the Subject* (London: Methuen).

Henshall, C. and McGuire, J. (1986) 'Gender Development', in M. Richards and P. Light (eds) *Children of Social Worlds* (Cambridge: Polity Press).

Hirst, P. (1979) *On Law and Ideology* (London: Macmillan).

Hollway, W. (1984) 'Gender Difference and the Production of Subjectivity', in J. Henriques, W. Hollway, C. Urwin, C. Venn and V. Walkerdine, *Changing the Subject* (London: Metheun).

Horney, K. (1931) 'The Distrust between the Sexes', in K. Horney, *Feminine Psychology* (New York: Norton, 1967).

Hughes, M. and Donaldson, M. (1979) 'The Use of Hiding Games for Studying the Coordination of Viewpoints', in *Educational Review*, 31, pp. 133–40.

Humphreys, G. and Riddoch, J. (1987) *To See but Not to See* (London: Erlbaum).

Irigaray, L. (1977) *This Sex which is not One* (Ithaca: Cornell University Press, 1985).

Jackson, S. (1982) *Childhood and Sexuality* (Oxford: Basil Blackwell).

Jakobson, R. (1962) *Selected Writings* (The Hague: Mouton).

James, W. (1890) *The Principles of Psychology* (New York: Holt, Rinehart and Winston).

Jameson, F. (1984) 'Postmodernism, or the Cultural Logic of Late Capitalism', in *New Left Review*, 146, pp. 53–92.

Jensen, A. (1969) 'How Much Can We Boost IQ and Scholastic Achievement?', in *Harvard Educational Review*, 39, pp. 1–123.

Johnson-Laird, P. (1983) *Mental Models* (Cambridge: Cambridge University Press).

Jones, E. (1927) 'The Early Development of Female Sexuality', in *International Journal of Psychoanalysis*, 8, pp. 459–72.

Jones, J. (1972) *Prejudice and Racism* (Reading, Mass.: Addison-Wesley).

Kamin, L. (1974) *The Science and Politics of IQ* (Potomac: Erlbaum).

Kenrick, D. (1987) 'Gender, Genes and the Social Environment: A Biosocial Interactionist Perspective', in P. Shaver and C. Hendrick (eds) *Sex and Gender* (London: Sage Review of Personality and Social Psychology, vol. 7).

Khilstrom, J. and Cantor, N. (1984) 'Mental Representations of the Self', in L. Berkowitz (ed.) *Advances in Experimental Social Psychology*, vol. 16 (New York: Academic Press).

Klein, M. (1928) 'Early Stages of the Oedipus Complex', in J. Mitchell (ed.) *The Selected Melanie Klein* (Harmondsworth: Penguin, 1986).

Klein, M. (1930) 'The Importance of Symbol Formation in the Development of the Ego', in J. Mitchell (ed.) *The Selected Melanie Klein* (Harmondsworth: Penguin, 1986).

Klein, M. (1949) *The Psychoanalysis of Children* (New York: Delta, 1975).

Klein, M. (1955) 'The Psychoanalytic Play Technique: Its History and Significance', in J. Mitchell (ed.) *The Selected Melanie Klein* (Harmondsworth: Penguin, 1986).

Klein, M. (1957) 'Envy and Gratitude', in M. Klein, *Envy and Gratitude and Other Works* (New York: Delta, 1975).

Kohlberg, L. (1966) 'A Cognitive-Developmental Analysis of Children's Sex-Role Concepts and Attitudes', in E. Maccoby (ed.) *The Develop-*

*ment of Sex Differences* (Stanford: Stanford University Press).

Kohut, H. (1977) *The Restoration of the Self* (New York: International Universities Press).

Kuhn, T. (1970) *The Structure of Scientific Revolutions* (Chicago: Chicago University Press).

Lacan, J. (1949) 'The Mirror Stage as Formative of the Function of the I as Revealed in Psychoanalytic Experience', in J. Lacan, *Ecrits: A Selection* (London: Tavistock, 1977).

Lacan, J. (1953) 'The Function and Field of Speech and Language in Psychoanalysis', in J. Lacan, *Ecrits: A Selection* (London: Tavistock, 1977).

Lacan, J. (1957) 'The Agency of the Letter in the Unconscious of Reason since Freud', in J. Lacan, *Ecrits: A Selection* (London: Tavistock, 1977).

Lacan, J. (1958) 'The Meaning of the Phallus', in J. Mitchell and J. Rose (eds) *Feminine Sexuality* (London: Macmillan, 1982).

Lacan, J. (1972–3) 'Seminar XX: Encore', in J. Mitchell and J. Rose (eds) *Feminine Sexuality* (London: Macmillan).

Lader, M. (1976) *Psychiatry on Trial* (Harmondsworth: Penguin).

Langs, R. (1976) *The Therapeutic Interaction* (New York: Jason Aronson).

Laplanche, J. and Leclaire, S. (1966) 'The Unconscious', in *Yale French Studies*, 48, pp. 118–75 (1972).

Lenneberg, E. (1967) *Biological Foundations of Language* (New York: Wiley).

Levin, J. and Levin, W. (1982) *The Functions of Discrimination and Prejudice* (New York: Harper and Row).

Lewis, C. (1986) 'Early Sex-Role Socialisation', in D. Hargreaves and A. Colley (eds) *The Psychology of Sex Roles* (London: Harper and Row).

Lichtenberg, J. (1983) *Psychoanalysis and Infant Research* (Hillsdale, N.J.: Lawrence Erlbaum).

Light, P. (1986) 'Context, Conservation and Conversation', in M. Richards and P. Light (eds) *Children of Social Worlds* (Cambridge: Polity Press).

Littlewood, R. and Lipsedge, M. (1982) *Aliens and Alienists: Ethnic Minorities and Psychiatry* (Harmondsworth: Penguin).

Luria, A. (1969) *The Mind of a Mnemonist* (Harmondsworth: Penguin).

Luria, A. (1973) *The Working Brain* (Harmondsworth: Penguin).

MacCabe, C. (1981) (ed.) *The Talking Cure* (London: Macmillan).

Maccoby, E. and Jacklin, C. (1974) *The Psychology of Sex Differences* (Oxford: Oxford University Press).

Mahler, M., Pine, F. and Bergman, A. (1975) *The Psychological Birth of the Human Infant: Symbiosis and Individuation* (New York: Basic Books).

Mannoni, M. (1970) *The Child, His 'Illness', and the Others* (London: Tavistock).

Mannoni, O. (1950) *Prospero and Caliban: The Psychology of Colonisation* (New York: Praeger, 1964).

Mannoni, O. (1971) *Freud: The Theory of the Unconscious* (London: New Left Books).

Marcuse, H. (1955) *Eros and Civilisation* (Boston: Beacon Press, 1966).

Marr, D. (1982) *Vision* (San Francisco: Freeman).

McCulloch, J. (1983) *Black Soul, White Artifact* (Cambridge: Cambridge University Press).

Mednick, M. (1979) 'The New Psychology of Women: A Feminist Analysis', in J. Gullahorn (ed.) *Psychology and Women: In Transition* (New York: Wiley).

Mehler, J., Morton, J. and Jusczyk, P. (1984) 'On Reducing Language to Biology', in *Cognitive Neuropsychology*, 1, pp. 83–116.

Miller, G., Galanter, E. and Pribram, K. (1960) *Plans and the Structure of Behaviour* (New York: Holt, Rinehart and Winston).

Mischel, W. (1966) 'A Social-Learning View of Sex Differences in Behaviour', in E. Maccoby (ed.) *The Development of Sex Differences* (Stanford: Stanford University Press).

Mitchell, J. (1974) *Psychoanalysis and Feminism* (Harmondsworth: Penguin).

Mitchell, J. (1982) 'Introduction', in J. Mitchell and J. Rose (eds) *Feminine Sexuality* (London: Macmillan).

Mitchell, J. and Rose, J. (1982) (eds) *Feminine Sexuality* (London: Macmillan).

Mitchell, J. (1984) 'The Question of Femininity and the Theory of Psychoanalysis', in J. Mitchell, *Women: The Longest Revolution* (London: Women's Press).

Moi, T. (1985) *Sexual/Textual Politics* (London: Methuen).

Money, J. and Ehrhardt, A. (1972) *Man and Woman, Boy and Girl* (London: Johns Hopkins University Press).

Morawski, J. (1987) 'The Troubled Quest for Masculinity, Femininity and Androgyny', in P. Shaver and C. Hendrick (eds) *Sex and Gender* (London: Sage Review of Personality and Social Psychology, vol. 7).

Neisser, U. (1967) *Cognitive Psychology* (New York: Appleton Century Crofts).

Nisbett, R. and Wilson T. (1977) 'Telling More Than We Can Know', in *Psychological Review*, 84, pp. 231–59.

Peele, S. (1981) 'Reductionism in the Psychology of the Eighties', in *American Psychologist*, 36, pp. 807–18.

Peterfreund, E. (1978) 'Some Clinical Comments on Psychoanalytic Conceptualisations of Infancy', in *International Journal of Psychoanalysis*, 59, pp. 427–41.

Piaget, J. (1951) *The Child's Conception of the World* (London: Routledge and Kegan Paul).

Piaget, J. (1971) *Biology and Knowledge* (Edinburgh: Edinburgh University Press).

Piaget, J. and Inhelder, B. (1969) *The Psychology of the Child* (London: Routledge and Kegan Paul).

Poliakov, L. (1974) *The Aryan Myth* (London: Heinemann).

Putnam, H. (1973) 'Reductionism and the Nature of Psychology', in *Cognition*, 2, pp. 131–46.

Pylyshyn, Z. (1980) 'The "Causal Power" of Machines', in *The Behavioral and Brain Sciences*, 3, pp. 442–4.

Reich, W. (1946) *The Mass Psychology of Fascism* (Harmondsworth: Penguin).

Rey, G. (1986) 'What's Really Going On in Searle's "Chinese Room"', in *Philosophical Studies*, 50, pp. 169–85.

Riley, D. (1983) *War in the Nursery: Theories of the Child and Mother* (London: Virago).

Rose, J. (1982) 'Introduction', in J. Mitchell and J. Rose (eds) *Feminine Sexuality* (London: Macmillan).

Rose, S., Kamin, L. and Lewontin, R. (1984) *Not in Our Genes* (Harmondsworth: Penguin).

Rustin, M. (1987) 'Psychoanalysis, Philosophical Realism, and the New Sociology of Science', in *Free Associations*, 9, pp. 102–36.

Rutter, M. (1982) *Maternal Deprivation Reassessed* (Harmondsworth: Penguin).

Sacks, O. (1985) *The Man who Mistook His Wife for a Hat* (London: Picador).

Sandler, J., Dare, C. and Holder, A. (1973) *The Patient and the Analyst* (London: Maresfield Reprints, 1979).

Sayers, J. (1986) *Sexual Contradictions* (London: Routledge and Kegan Paul).

Sayers, J. (1986) 'Sexual Identity and Difference', in S. Wilkinson (ed.) *Feminist Social Psychology* (Milton Keynes: Open University Press).

Scarr, S. and Dunn, J. (1987) *Mother Care/Other Care* (Harmondsworth: Penguin).

Schaffer, H. (1977) *Studies in Mother–Infant Interaction* (London: Academic Press).

Schaffer, H. R. (1984) *The Child's Entry into a Social World* (London: Academic Press).

Searle, J. (1980) 'Minds, Brains and Programs', in *Behavioural and Brain Sciences*, 3, pp. 417–57.

Searle, J. (1984) 'Intentionality and its Place in Nature', in *Dialectica*, 38, pp. 87–99.

Segal, H. (1957) 'Notes on Symbol Formation', in H. Segal, *The Work of Hanna Segal* (London: Free Association Books, 1986).

Segal, H. (1964) 'Phantasy and Other Mental Processes', in H. Segal, *The Work of Hanna Segal* (London: Free Association Books, 1986).

Segal, H. (1973) *Introduction to the Work of Melanie Klein* (London: Hogarth Press).

Segal, H. (1979) 'Postscript 1979: Notes on Symbol Formation', in H. Segal, *The Work of Hanna Segal* (London: Free Association Books, 1986).

Segal, L. (1983) 'Sensual Uncertainty, or Why the Clitoris is not Enough', in S. Cartledge and J. Ryan (eds) *Sex and Love* (London: Women's Press).

Sherif, M. (1966) *In Common Predicament* (Boston: Houghton-Mifflin).

Sherwood, R. (1980) *The Psychodynamics of Race: Vicious and Benign Spirals* (Sussex: Harvester Press).

Shields, S. (1987) 'Women, Men and the Dilemma of Emotion', in P. Shaver and C. Hendrick (eds) *Sex and Gender* (London: Sage Review of Personality and Social Psychology, vol. 7).

Singleton, C. (1986) 'Sex Roles in Cognition', in D. Hargreaves and A. Colley (eds) *The Psychology of Sex Roles* (London: Harper and Row).

Skinner, B. (1957) *Verbal Behavior* (New York: Appleton Century Crofts).

Skinner, B. (1971) *Beyond Freedom and Dignity* (Harmondsworth: Penguin).

Skuse, D. (1984) 'Extreme Deprivation in Early Childhood', in *Journal of Child Psychology and Psychiatry*, 25, pp. 523–72.

Sloane, R., Staples, F., Cristol, A., Yorkston, N. and Whipple, K. (1975) *Psychotherapy versus Behavior Therapy* (Cambridge, Mass.: Harvard University Press).

Spence, J. (1985) 'Gender Identity and its Implications for the Concepts of Masculinity and Femininity', in *Nebraska Symposium on Motivation, 1984*, pp. 59–95.

Spence, J. and Helmreich, R. (1981) 'Androgyny versus Gender Schema: A Comment on Bem's Gender Schema Theory', in *Psychological Review*, 88, pp. 365–8.

Spence, J., Helmreich, R. and Stapp, J. (1975) 'Ratings of Self and Peers on Sex Role Attributes and their Relation to Self-Esteem and Conceptions of Masculinity and Femininity', in *Journal of Personality and Social Psychology*, 32, pp. 29–39.

Spender, D. (1980) *Man Made Language* (London: Routledge and Kegan Paul).

Stern, D. (1985) *The Interpersonal World of the Infant* (New York: Basic Books).

Stern, D., Hofer, L., Haft, W. and Dore, J. (1985) 'Affect Attunement: The Sharing of Feeling States between Mother and Infant by Means of Inter-Modal Fluency', in T. Field and N. Fox (eds) *Social Perception in Infants* (Norwood, N.J.: Ablex).

Tajfel, H. (1978) 'Intergroup Behaviour', in H. Tajfel and C. Fraser (eds) *Introducing Social Psychology* (Harmondsworth: Penguin).

Tajfel, H. (1979) 'Individuals and Groups in Social Psychology', in *British Journal of Social and Clinical Psychology*, 18, pp. 183–90.

Tajfel, H., Flament, C., Billig, M. and Bundy, R. (1971) 'Social Categorisation and Intergroup Behaviour', in *European Journal of Social Psychology*, 1, pp. 149–78.

Taylor, M. and Hall, J. (1982) 'Psychological Androgyny: Theories, Methods and Conclusions', *Psychological Bulletin*, 92, pp. 347–66.

Terman, L. (1916) *The Measurement of Intelligence* (Boston: Houghton Mifflin).

Theweleit, K. (1977) *Male Fantasies* (Cambridge: Polity, 1987).

Thom, M. (1981) 'The Unconscious Structured as a Language', in C. MacCabe (ed.) *The Talking Cure* (London: Macmillan).

Tiefer, L. (1987) 'Social Constructionism and the Study of Human Sexuality', in P. Shaver and C. Hendrick (eds) *Sex and Gender* (London: Sage Review of Personality and Social Psychology, vol. 7).

Timpanaro, S. (1976) *The Freudian Slip* (London: New Left Books).

Turing, A. (1950) 'Computing Machinery and Intelligence', in D. Hofstadter and D. Dennett (eds) *The Mind's I* (Harmondsworth: Penguin, 1982).

Urwin, C. (1984) 'Power Relations and the Emergence of Language', in J. Henriques, W. Hollway, C. Urwin, C. Venn and V. Walkerdine, *Changing the Subject* (London: Methuen).

Urwin, C. (1986) 'Developmental Psychology and Psychoanalysis: Splitting the Difference', in M. Richards and P. Light (eds) *Children of Social Worlds* (Cambridge: Polity Press).

Venn, C. and Walkerdine, V. (1978) 'The Acquisition and Production of Knowledge: Piaget's Theory Reconsidered', in *Ideology and Consciousness*, 3, pp. 67–94.

Vygotsky, L. (1934) *Thought and Language* (Cambridge, Mass.: MIT Press, 1962).

Waddell, M. (1988) 'Infantile Development: Kleinian and Post-Kleinian Theory, Infant Observational Practice', in *British Journal of Psychotherapy*, 4, pp. 313–28.

Walker, S. (1984) *Animal Thought* (London: Routledge and Kegan Paul).

Walkerdine, V. (1984) 'Developmental Psychology and the Child-Centred Pedagogy: The Insertion of Piaget into Early Education', in J. Henriques, W. Hollway, C. Urwin, C. Venn and V. Walkerdine, *Changing the Subject* (London: Methuen).

Wetherell, M. (1986) 'Linguistic Repertoires and Literary Criticism: New Directions for a Social Psychology of Gender', in S. Wilkinson (ed.) *Feminist Social Psychology* (Milton Keynes: Open University Press).

Will, D. (1986) 'Psychoanalysis and the New Philosophy of Science', in *International Review of Psychoanalysis*, 13, pp. 163–73.

Williamson, D. (1987) 'Language and Sexual Difference', in *Screen*, 28, pp. 10–25.

Wilson, E. (1975) *Sociobiology: The New Synthesis* (Cambridge, Mass.: Harvard University Press).

Wilson, G. (1979) 'The Sociobiology of Sex Differences', in *Bulletin of the British Psychological Society*, 32, pp. 350–3.

Wolkind, S. and Rutter, M. (1985) 'Separation, Loss and Family Relationships', in M. Rutter and L. Hersov (eds) *Child and Adolescent Psychiatry* (Oxford: Basil Blackwell).

# Index